REVELATION RIDDLE:
GLORY OF EDEN

Benjamin Thomas

gloria media

REVELATION RIDDLE: GLORY OF EDEN
Copyright © 2024 by Gloriam Media LLC

Scripture quotations marked KJV are taken from the King James Version of the Holy Bible (Public Domain). Scripture quotations marked YLT are taken from the 1898 YOUNG'S LITERAL TRANSLATION OF THE HOLY BIBLE by J.N. Young, (Author of the Young's Analytical Concordance), public domain. Quotations from 1 and 2 Enoch are adaptations from translator R.H. Charles, 1911, public domain. Quotations from Baruch (marked "Bar.") are from translator R.H. Charles, 1896, public domain.

Scripture quotations marked ASV are taken from the (NASB®) New American Standard Bible®, Copyright © 1960, 1971, 1977, 1995, 2020 by The Lockman Foundation. Used by permission. All rights reserved. lockman.org

Scripture quotations marked by ESV are taken from The ESV® Bible (The Holy Bible, English Standard Version®), © 2001 by Crossway, a publishing ministry of Good News Publishers. Used by permission. All rights reserved.

Scripture quotations marked TPT are from The Passion Translation®. Copyright © 2017, 2018, 2020 by Passion & Fire Ministries, Inc. Used by permission. All rights reserved. ThePassionTranslation.com.

Scripture quotations marked NRSV are taken from the New Revised Standard Version of the Bible, copyright © 1989 Division of Christian Education of the National Council of the Churches of Christ in the USA. Used by permission. All rights reserved.

Scripture quotations marked CEV are from the Contemporary English Version Copyright © 1991, 1992, 1995 by American Bible Society. Used by Permission. All rights reserved.

Scripture quotations marked AMPC are taken from the Amplified® Bible, Copyright © 1954, 1958, 1962, 1964, 1965, 1987 by The Lockman Foundation. Used by permission. lockman.org.

Scripture quotations marked NLT are taken from the Holy Bible, New Living Translation, Copyright ©1996, 2004, 2015 by Tyndale House Foundation. Used by permission of Tyndale House Publishers, Carol Stream, Illinois 60188. All rights reserved.

Scripture quotations marked MSG are taken from The Message, Copyright © 1993, 2002, 2018 by Eugene H. Peterson. Used by permission of NavPress. All rights reserved. Represented by Tyndale House Publishers.

Scripture quotations marked NCV are taken from the NEW CENTURY VERSION®. Copyright© 2005 by Thomas Nelson, Inc. Used by permission. All rights reserved.

All emphasis in Scripture quotations is added by the author.

ISBN: 979-8-9909434-0-7 (eBook)
ISBN: 979-8-9909434-1-4 (Paperback)
ISBN: 979-8-9909434-2-1 (Hardcover)
ISBN: 979-8-9909434-3-8 (Audio)
Cover by SN
Illustrations by Michael W.

SPECIAL MARKET SALES
Organizations, churches, pastors, and small group leaders can receive special discounts when purchasing this book and other resources in bulk. For information, please visit us at revelationriddle.com.
1st Edition – July 4, 2024 (1.1.1)

Contents

Introduction...v

1. Stripped of Glory...1

2. Aborted Destinies...11

3. Deception Quadrella..25

4. Sevenfold Promise...43

5. Thralldom Lease...59

6. Judgment to Victory..79

7. Apokatastasis..105

8. Return to Glory..131

9. YHWY's Divine Timeline...............................159

10. Harvest Before Fire......................................193

11. Back in the Garden..235

12. Prepare to Shine..267

Appendix..293

   Don't Wait, Receive Yeshua Today!.................293

   Prayer of Protection..295

   Banishment of Principalities..........................296

   Warrior's Creed: I Am a Soldier.....................297

   Pride Self-Assessment...................................298

   Glossary of Terms..299

Introduction

God wants people to know His plan for the future. In the Bible, God rewarded His most faithful servants by showing them what happens next for humanity. For Christians who desire to know God's immaculate plan for the future—read this book!

God's plan for our future towers over anything that I ever heard growing up in Sunday school. It involves a divine promotion for followers of Jesus. Unfortunately, now we see the wicked receiving rewards in this age, and the righteous persecuted. Soon however, a dynamic reversal occurs in a series of explosive, supernatural events.

I spent months reading every ancient apocalyptic account available today. The hidden writings of Enoch, Baruch, Ezra, and others all lay out the same story of the future, enumerating vivid texture and detail. When I studied the hidden scrolls, I realized that Jesus, the Apostles, and the early Church held an inimitable advantage over modern-day Christians—they knew God's whole plan. Knowing God's plan gave them supreme courage and boldness, even after losing friends and loved ones to the tyranny of the day.

Once we understand God's plan, the pages of our "short" evangelical Bible pop with clarity and power. Parables and mysteries come to life—confusion and fog end. The veil of deception begins to lift on the Church. The Great Awakening elevates our spirits as old deceits no longer obstruct our thinking. It should not surprise us that the religious establishment, an extension of Ancient Rome, used every tool to prevent Christians from discovering the truth, including hiding the very books that foretold the future and certain demise of religious institutions.

God designed His astronomic blueprint from the very beginning. Even wicked men who thought they stopped God's plan by constructing the Dome of the Rock on the Temple mount actually fulfilled Bible prophecy, down to the year! Evil men who stole time, treasure, and lives of God's people failed to stop God's timeline. This should serve as a sobering reality for *anyone* deceived by Satan. Not only does serving Satan lead to certain and irrevocable destruction, but the intense labor of the wicked only advances God's purposes for the apple of His eye—His righteous remnant.

All destinies of righteous people come to fruition—even if they died. The gifts and calling of God are irrevocable. Not even a misguided mother who aborts her child can stop the plan of God for that child. You see, God plans a divine redemption for humanity—not just a restoration.

Going forward, I refer to Jesus as Yeshua. Yeshua's disciples and followers called Him by that name; It's more respectful. I also refer to God by His name, "Y-H-W-Y" (YAA-way). YHWY signed His name on every human's DNA. YHWY created humanity in His very image and likeness. He now calls His creation back to where everything started for man, in the Garden of Eden. To return, we need to allow our hearts to elevate to new dimensions—this starts by calling our Creator by His real name, YHWY.

Finally, this book includes many capitalized terms. These are defined in a Glossary of Terms in the Appendix.

1. Stripped of Glory

*Bring me everyone who is called by my name, the
ones I created to experience my glory. I myself formed
them to be who they are and made them for my glory.*
— Isa. 43:7 TPT

The Bible chronicles the story of the Glory of YHWY. In the
beginning of the Bible, man wears the Glory of YHWY
effortlessly, like a custom-made suit woven of the finest silk,
flowing seamlessly with every movement. Man walked with
YHWY in the cool of the morning in the Garden of Eden,
enjoying unfettered fellowship (Gen. 3:8). Tragically, high
treason caused man to surrender the "suit" of Glory and lose

direct daily access to YHWY. Thankfully, the biblical story does not end there. At the end of the age in the Bible, man again wears the Glory as clothing, back in the Garden of Eden. This book details when and how that happens.

Once a righteous person experiences the Glory of YHWY, he or she longs to experience it again. A taste of His presence causes people to desire only one thing–more Glory. The "high" of the Glory of YHWY far transcends the temporary ecstasy of illicit drugs, sex, or alcohol. When one partakes of these he or she soon suffers a subsequent low, bodily harm, and feelings of emptiness. The Glory of YHWY changes a person forever. Once one experiences the Glory, he or she draws closer to YHWY and begins to learn of vastness and goodness of our Creator. After truly experiencing YHWY's Glory–you are forever transformed.

The Glory of YHWY fully covered Adam and Eve in the Garden of Eden. Movies and cartoons improperly portray Adam and Eve walking around naked in the Garden, depicting the Garden as a nudist colony! The story books lead us to believe that they simply did not know they were naked, because they had not yet eaten of the fruit of the Tree of Knowledge. Yet, YHWY created Adam in His image. YHWY clothed Himself with Glory as well as man in the Garden. However, this Glory could not stay as a covering for Adam or Eve once they yielded their authority to Satan.

When Adam and Eve committed high treason by partaking of the fruit of the Tree of Knowledge, the Glory stripped off them and they "saw they were naked." However, YHWY already devised a plan for man to once again return to the original glorified state of Adam and Eve in the Garden of Eden. The Bible outlines YHWY's master plan to return man to His Glory in a mystery for His people to seek out.

Since the Fall of Adam and Eve in the Garden, man only witnessed the Glory of YHWY infrequently. Unfortunately, YHWY's Glory never again perpetually clothed man in the manner it did in the Garden of Eden. However, that will soon change.

Visible Glory of YHWY

How do we define YHWY's Glory? Not easily defined by words, referring to YHWY's Glory expresses the magnificence, loveliness, and grandeur of the perfection of YHWY. Most often in the Bible, the Glory indicates YHWY's actual presence, as in the pillars of Glory and of fire which led the children of Israel in the wilderness (Ex. 13:21-22). The manifest presence of YHWY guided them to their destination. The Glory also filled the tabernacle, as an outward and visible sign of YHWY's presence. In Exodus, we read:

> Finally, Moses had the curtain hung around the courtyard. Suddenly the sacred tent was covered by a thick cloud and filled with the glory of the LORD. And so, Moses could not enter the tent (Ex. 40:33-35 CEV).

In this case, the Glory of YHWY manifested as a thick cloud. As long as the Glory covered the tabernacle (the "sacred tent"), Moses could not enter. Here we see a problem. Even a righteous man like Moses could not handle the Glory–he could only get close. The Glory would need to move away from the tabernacle before fallen men could physically move the tent.

The primary Hebrew term for Glory is *kabod*. This word stems from a root that means weight or heaviness. In Greek, Glory is *doxa*, meaning YHWY's manifestation of His person, presence or works, especially His power, judgment, and salvation. In the Bible, the word for the Glory of YHWY is sometimes used as a noun, verb, or even adjective. For instance YHWY reveals His Glory (noun), is glorified (verb) or is glorious (adjective). For the balance of this book, we will focus on YHWY's Glory primarily as the manifest presence of YHWY, in such a way that others *see* it.

The Bible includes examples of visible Glory. For instance, we discussed that Adam and Eve remained clothed with the Glory of YHWY prior to the Fall. After they transgressed, the Glory instantaneously departed, exposing their nakedness for the first time. In another example, when Moses came down from Mount Sinai with the two tablets after having communed with YHWY, the scriptures say, "When Aaron and the others looked at Moses, they saw that his face was shining, and they were afraid to go near him" (Ex. 34:30). Moses himself failed to realize that his face shined. The Glory on Moses' face paled in comparison to the former Glory on Adam and Eve, as only his face shined with Glory. Otherwise, his whole person would glow. Yet even the Glory on his face startled the people around him.

In another instance, when the mob grabbed Stephen in the book of Acts and accused him before the council of priests, his face glowed with a peculiar brightness. Acts 6:15 states, "Then all the council members stared at Stephen. They saw that his face looked like the face of an angel." The visible Glory startled the council, but their relentless pride refused to recognize the Glory on Stephen, and they stoned him.

Only one man fully wore the Glory after the Fall in the Garden. Yeshua briefly displayed the full Glory. We read this account in three of the four gospels. According to one account:

> Six days later Jesus took Peter and the two brothers, Jacob and John, and hiked up a high mountain to be alone. Then Jesus' appearance was dramatically altered. A radiant light as bright as the sun poured from his face. And his clothing became luminescent—dazzling like lightning. He was transfigured before their very eyes. Then suddenly, Moses and Elijah appeared, and they spoke with Jesus.
>
> Peter blurted out, "Lord, it's so wonderful that we are all here together! If you want, I'll construct three shrines, one for you, one for Moses, and one for Elijah."
>
> But while Peter was still speaking, a radiant cloud composed of light spread over them, enveloping them all. And God's voice suddenly spoke from the cloud, saying, "This is my dearly loved Son, the constant focus of my delight. Listen to him!"

The three disciples were dazed and terrified by this phenomenon, and they fell facedown to the ground (Matt. 17:1-6 TPT).

In the presence of the three disciples, Yeshua transformed into a luminescent force whose clothes dazzled like lightning. Just like Adam and Eve in the Garden, Yeshua wore the Glory of YHWY. Yet, it terrified the disciples! Like Adam and Eve before the Fall, Yeshua's seed came directly from YHWY—Mary gave birth as a virgin without the defiled seed of an earthly man. This may explain why the Bible records Yeshua as the only man since Adam to wear the Glory—the curse on Earth must break for others to dress in Glory.

Yeshua ignored Peter's idea to build shrines to commemorate the Glory falling on the mountain and the appearance of the prophets. The disciples' understanding of the Glory related to stories they heard about the Glory in the Temple or within the tent that Moses built. Yeshua showed them a picture, a foretaste of something to come, that did not involve a rock shrine made with hands. Yeshua communed with Moses and Elijah on the mountain when the Glory fell. This also foreshadowed future events, which we will cover later. The passage says Yeshua transfigured *six days later.* Humanity would again wear YHWY's Glory after six biblical days, or six thousand years after the Fall in the Garden.

High Treason

By committing high treason in the Garden of Eden, Adam opened up the door for Satan to "bruise" humanity. When

YHWY spoke to Satan via the serpent in the Garden, He said Satan would "bruise his heel," referring to mankind in general (Gen. 3:15). *Merriam-Webster* defines bruise as crush, or wound, or injure. Also, to batter, dent, or disable. Man became a punching bag for Satan until Yeshua gave us authority over Satan in the spiritual realm.

YHWY required the shedding of blood for man to again draw near to the Glory. You see, when Adam committed high treason in the Garden, he actually gave his authority to Satan. YHWY originally gave the world to human beings, created in His image:

> God created human beings; he created them godlike, Reflecting God's nature. He created them male and female. God blessed them: "Prosper! Reproduce! Fill Earth! Take charge! Be responsible for fish in the sea and birds in the air, for every living thing that moves on the face of Earth" (Gen. 1:28 MSG).

Man retained his crown of authority and wore YHWY's Glory as long as he remained obedient to his Creator. When he yielded to Satan he handed his authority over to Satan. Worse, he separated himself from YHWY. To get back in fellowship with YHWY, a price for the iniquity committed was required—the shedding of blood.

Blood and Mercy

Since the Fall of man in the Garden, the inner longing to once again attain close fellowship with and see YHWY burns in the heart of every righteous person. Moses asked to see YHWY in Exodus, "Moses said, 'Please. Let me see your Glory'" (Ex. 33:18). A few verses later, YHWY honors this request by showing Moses only His back. However, as YHWY passed by Moses, He proclaimed mercy and grace:

> GOD passed in front of him and called out, "GOD, GOD, a God of mercy and grace, endlessly patient —so much love, so deeply true—loyal in love for a thousand generations, forgiving iniquity, rebellion, and sin. Still, he doesn't ignore sin. He holds sons and grandsons responsible for a father's sins to the third and even fourth generation" (Ex. 34:6-7).

To look at YHWY, we must receive His mercy. Man committed high treason in the Garden, we gave our allegiance and our authority to Satan as we doubted the goodness of YHWY. To regain fellowship with YHWY requires mercy and forgiveness, paid for by blood sacrifice.

When YHWY began to show Moses how to build the tent in the wilderness where His Glory would appear, he laid out comprehensive instructions involving sacrificing innocent animals to allow men to once again witness His Glory. "In fact, according to the law of Moses, nearly everything was purified with blood. For without the shedding of blood, there is no forgiveness" (Heb. 9:22 NLT). The sacrifices under the law allowed man proximity to YHWY's Glory with his sins covered for a short time to receive mercy from YHWY. However, the law of Moses and the sacrifice of animals simply foretold of a future day, when the perfect blood sacrifice would come: Yeshua, the spotless Lamb.

Offering Unto Glory

When Yeshua gave His life on the cross as an innocent man, it unlocked man's ability to fellowship with YHWY on an entirely new dimension. Man could once again speak to YHWY without an intermediary, and YHWY's Spirit came to reside in man through the Person of the Holy Spirit. Yeshua's Blood allowed man once more to walk in light. "But if we live in the light, as God does, we share in life with each other. And the blood of his Son Jesus washes all our sins away" (1 John 1:7 CEV). After Yeshua's resurrection, YHWY sent His Spirit to dwell in man, and we see in the Bible the first time a large group of people access the Glory on the day of Pentecost:

> On the day Pentecost was being fulfilled, all the disciples were gathered in one place. Suddenly they heard the sound of a violent blast of wind rushing into the house from out of the heavenly realm. The roar of the wind was so overpowering it was all anyone could bear! Then all at once a pillar of fire appeared before their eyes. It separated into tongues of fire that engulfed each one of them. They were all filled and equipped with the Holy Spirit and were inspired to speak in tongues—empowered by the Spirit to speak in languages they had never learned (Acts 2:1-4 TPT)!

On the day of Pentecost, a measure of the Glory of YHWY returned to men who accepted Yeshua's blood sacrifice and followed His direction to wait for the promise of the Holy Spirit.

What a colossal leap in the right direction toward Glory! After roughly 4,000 years of scarcity, man experienced the presence of YHWY in a way visible to others. The presence of YHWY gave men special languages, called "tongues." All Believers today may request YHWY to baptize them in the Holy Spirit, with the evidence of speaking with other tongues. He won't deny this request (Luke 11:13).

After the Day of Pentecost, the fire of YHWY filled His servants, and they subsequently preached with great boldness—exhibiting fresh zeal for the Lord. The Christian faith spread like wildfire all over the world. If we study the book of Acts, many miracles happened as well as other supernatural events. A measure of the Glory returned to man. But how did this measure compare to what the disciples saw on Yeshua during His transfiguration, when He shined like lightning? Did the Christians who received the baptism of the Holy Spirit, with the evidence of speaking in tongues shine like angels permanently? Obviously not. But why?

2. Aborted Destinies

"NEVER FULFILLED THEIR DESTINY"

...for the gifts and the calling of God are irrevocable.
— Rom. 11:29 NRSV

Have you suffered the loss of a loved one whom you knew "died young?" How about a spouse, child, aunt, sibling or close friend? I lost two older siblings to disease. My eldest sister died at the age of four before my birth. However, I remained close to my oldest brother who died of Lou Gehrig's disease in 2009. He battled the disease for twelve years. During his battle with disease, his wife and two children took care of him, even helping him relieve himself along with getting in and out of bed. My brother's youngest daughter never knew her father in a time of good health.

I believe Yeshua still heals and I prayed long and hard for my brother. In one such time of prayer, I asked the Lord to send my brother an angel to reassure him that Yeshua would heal him. In answer to my prayer, a man named Angel showed up at my brother's doorstep who Yeshua healed of Lou Gehrig's disease. He told my brother how a continual diet of YHWY's medicine (healing scriptures) changed his life, and how Yeshua remains the healer and performs miracles today. Plagued with guilt, my brother never received his healing while in the land of the living. He questioned whether he deserved a healing. I believe my brother died before his time, but do not understand why. I shed bitter tears when my brother died.

Regrets in Heaven

Years ago I read *The Final Quest* by Rick Joyner.[1] In this riveting bestseller, Rick takes readers on a journey through a series of visions of the spirit realm, as he travels up the "mountain of God." I quickly devoured the book's content and still consider it one my favorites. However, one thing about the story bothered me. In the book, Rick meets many, many patriarchs in Heaven, including the acclaimed author C.S. Lewis. Awestruck by whom he meets, Rick sings praises for each person. Yet, everyone he met expressed regrets about what they would do differently on Earth, knowing what they

---

[1]   Joyner, Rick. *The Final Quest*. Fort Mill, SC: MorningStar Publications, 2006.

now know about the nature of YHWY. Until I read Joyner's book, I assumed everyone in Heaven no longer remembered their shortcomings on Earth. Until then, I pictured Heaven as a final destination, a reward for Believers after they died. It never occurred to me that regret lived in Heaven among the saints.

In Revelation chapter 21, we read about the wonderful time of the New Heaven and New Earth. Regardless of personal eschatology, the New Heaven and New Earth represent the furthest description into the future the Bible lays out. Consider the promise:

> Look! God's tabernacle is with human beings. And from now on he will tabernacle with them as their God. Now God himself will have his home with them—'God-with-them' will be their God! He will wipe away every tear from their eyes and eliminate death entirely. No one will mourn or weep any longer. The pain of wounds will no longer exist, for the old order has ceased (Rev. 21:3b-4 TPT).

The scripture illustrates a splendid picture of a day when YHWY dwells with man on an entirely New Heaven and New Earth. At this point, YHWY wipes away every tear from our eyes. The scripture implies that memories of regret, mourning and weeping remain *until that time*. If so, then saints currently in Heaven may hold regrets after all!

Faith Hall of Fame

In most sports leagues, admirers of the sport built "Halls of Fame" to celebrate players exhibiting exceptional talent. The baseball Hall of Fame in Cooperstown, New York honors players and managers that served the sport with excellence. For Christians, our Hall of Fame lies in Hebrews chapter 11, where the author lays out the champions of faith. Hebrews mentions the greats: Enoch, Noah, Abraham, Sarah, and others. Of these "greats," it says:

> These heroes all died still clinging to their faith, not even receiving all that had been promised them. But they saw beyond the horizon the fulfillment of their promises and gladly embraced it from afar. They all lived their lives on earth as those who belonged to another realm. For clearly, those who live this way are longing for the appearing of a heavenly city (Heb. 11:13-14).

Our faith heroes shared one common characteristic—they all died before securing all their promises. They all longed for the appearance of the heavenly city. In Greek, the word for city means "homeland." Which homeland did our patriarchs long for? The scripture says they saw beyond the horizon the fulfillment of *their* promises—promises specific to them finally realized. Does this mean YHWY grants these saints an opportunity to complete their course and attain all the promises? If so, when?

Perhaps most perplexing are the "others" later in Hebrews chapter 11. These saints either died horrible deaths or suffered utter and complete shame by society. The "others" remain unnamed:

> Others were mocked and experienced the most severe beating with whips; they were in chains and imprisoned. Some of these faith champions were brutally killed by stoning, being sawn in two or slaughtered by the sword. These lived in faith as they went about wearing goatskins and sheepskins for clothing. They lost everything they possessed, they endured great afflictions, and they were cruelly mistreated. They wandered the earth living in the desert wilderness, in caves, on barren mountains and in holes in the earth. Truly, the world was not even worthy of them, not realizing who they were (Heb. 11:36-38).

The Bible calls pagan empires "beasts." The prophet Daniel described the Roman system ruling the world in the time of Yeshua's ministry as the Fourth Beast, which followed the third beast, the Greek Empire. Babylon and Medo-Persia represented the first and second beasts, respectively. Scripture clearly describes the Fourth Beast as the most vicious and cruel of the four beasts. The Fourth Beast's brutal reign continues to produce the "others" described in Hebrews chapter 11. *Fox's Book of Martyrs* lays out in excruciating detail the genocide of Christians under the Fourth Beast, mostly at the hands of established religions or governments claiming status as "messengers of god."[2] The

---

[2] Fox, John. *Fox's Book of Martyrs: History of the Lives, Sufferings and Triumphant Deaths, of the Primitive as Well as the Protestant Martyrs, from the Commencement*

Fourth Beast imposed a reign of tyranny on anyone that dared oppose organized religion. For example, the Fourth Beast's minions burned William Tyndale at the stake for translating the Old and New Testaments into English. All of Yeshua's disciples died brutal and painful deaths except for John. Satan continued to bruise the saints long after the Fall, as foretold in Genesis 3:15.

In the final verses of Hebrews chapter 11, we learn that the heroes of the faith achieve finished perfection *alongside of us*. Listen to the last two verses in the chapter:

> These were the true heroes, commended for their faith, yet they lived in hope without receiving the fullness of what was promised them. But now God has invited us to live in something better than what they had—faith's fullness! This is so that they could be brought to finished perfection alongside of us (Heb. 11:39-40).

One might interpret this passage to mean that early saints endured great affliction at the hands of satanic attackers, paving the way for the present generation of saints under the New Covenant. However, this view represents a non-literal interpretation. The passage literally says that these saints are brought to "finished perfection" *alongside of us*. What does this mean?

---

of Christianity to the Latest Periods fo Pagan and Popish Persecutions. Hurst & Co, 1870.

Aborted Children

When we ponder potential unfulfilled destinies, aborted children immediately come to mind. A mother (or in some cases father) decides to end the life of a baby in the womb, for whatever reason. The baby never learns to walk or talk, play with other kids, or grow up to live out his potential. The Bible says "for the gifts and the calling of God are irrevocable" (Rom. 11:29 NRSV). *Oxford Languages* defines irrevocable as not able to be changed, reversed, or recovered; FINAL. So when a woman chooses to abort the baby, what happens to the gifts and calling of that child? Does a parent have the ability to revoke the gifts and calling on that child? Not according to the Bible! A parent can't cancel YHWY's calling. So when would an aborted child fulfill his destiny?

On what grounds would aborted children stand at the final judgment, the White Throne Judgment, and answer to YHWY for their calling? Would they simply say, "YHWY, I would have served you, but I was never born!" If the gifts and calling of aborted children are irrevocable, when will they walk it out? The answer lies in YHWY's immaculate painting of our future.

A Best Friend

I earned an engineering degree at Tulane University in New Orleans. Admittedly, in my first semester, I partied a lot. However, thanks to a praying mother and sister, I felt an irresistible tug on my heart to draw close to YHWY. I knew just enough scripture to know my actions failed to please Him, but not enough of His Word to resist temptation.

Finally, I prayed a simple but rather irreverent prayer, "God, if you want me to serve You, give me the power to stay free. I don't want to live as a miserable Christian, who knows enough rules to suffer condemnation, but lacks power to resist temptation." Many Christians I knew fell into that category, and I didn't envy them.

YHWY supernaturally changed my desires and gave me a great hunger to immerse myself in His Word. I started witnessing to other students. Soon I met a bold young pastor and we worked a campus ministry together, leading worship and prayer services at the on-campus chapel for several years. I witnessed my friend receive numerous prophecies from well established prophetic voices regarding his ministry.

A few years later after I moved to another city, I heard my pastor friend died unexpectedly at the age of 42. I knew this man well, and sensed in my heart his death premature. I organized a few mutual friends to raise our friend from the dead. Yeshua commanded us to, "Heal the sick, raise the dead to life, heal people who have leprosy, and force out demons" (Matt 10:8 CEV). So we descended on a morgue in New Orleans to raise our friend up. The morticians already prepared the body for burial. For eighteen hours, we prayed over the body. Once we saw his eyes flutter, but otherwise, no response. Sixteen hours into our prayer time, the Lord revealed to us why He refused to allow our friend back.

I often think of my dear friend. Super-young, talented, loved YHWY—but he stepped outside his calling. Caught between an overarching desire to please his earthly father and resisting YHWY's calling to pursue a different path, he began to struggle with a wretched demon. I know he lives in Heaven, but I still miss him. Towards the end of those long hours of prayer, the Holy Spirit mercifully showed us things about our friend that none of us knew. YHWY graciously showed us the reason our faith would not work in this instance. You see, the Lord honors bold faith—He kindly showed us *why* our faith failed to work for our dear friend.

When I got back home after that trip, my girlfriend at the time told me that my face glowed brightly. I experienced a taste of YHWY's Glory.

YHWY's Appointed Time

We tend to wonder about YHWY's timing, especially regarding people close to us. My earthly dad died young as well as my granddad—they both knew the Lord. I recently lost a dear friend who suffered heart failure just a few months after taking the Covid-19 vaccine. He left three small children and a heartbroken widow at home. Prior to his death, this friend shared with me prophecies he received regarding his calling—now ostensibly frustrated by death. Earlier I shared how the calling of my friend from New Orleans also appeared truncated.

The prophet Habakkuk expressed frustration with YHWY when the Babylonians attacked Judah. He bitterly complained about how it seems like those who don't know YHWY win more often than His people. He shouts at YHWY, "Will you let them get away with this forever? Will they succeed forever in their heartless conquests?" (Hab. 1:17

NLT). Let's face it, we all experience the same emotions occasionally.

As I write, the world seems acutely dark at the hands of the deep state. Billions woke up in the last couple of years to the abject tyranny imposed by our governments on the people. Christian persecution and martyrdom remains at an all-time high in world history.[3] In the last 100 years, the deep state paved the way for at least a billion aborted children.[4] As I outlined in my book, *Kingdom Age of the Saints* (abbreviated hereafter as *KAS*), the Fourth Beast destroyed another billion people in the last 200 years using war, war-related famine, and new diseases, for a total of nearly 2 billion people, 25% of our present day world population.[5] Many of us also know someone either injured or dead from the Covid-19 vaccine. It *seems* like Satan wins.

The raw emotions oozing from Habakkuk's prayer to YHWY mirror modern-day desperate prayers. YHWY responds to Habakkuk profoundly:

> Write my answer plainly on tablets, so that a runner can carry the correct message to others. This vision is for a future time. It describes **the end**, and it will be fulfilled. If it seems slow in coming, wait patiently, for **it will surely take place. It will not be delayed** (Hab. 2:2-3, emphasis added).

---

[3]   "World Watch List 2023." *Open Doors*. Accessed June 6, 2023, www.opendoors.org/en-US/persecution/countries.

[4]   Johnston, W. Robert. Jacobsen, Thomas. "Abortion Worldwide Report: 100 Nations, 1 Century, 1 Billion Babies." (Colorado Springs, CO: GLC, 2017).

[5]   Thomas, Benjamin. *Kingdom Age of the Saints: End Times for the New World Order*. (San Antonio: Gloriam Media, 2023), 72-73.

Essentially, Habakkuk asks YHWY, "When will evil end?" Have you ever besieged Him with same question? Lately, more ask as circumstances in the world appear dire. YHWY answers Habakkuk by blessing him with a profound vision for the future—He shows him *how* evil ends. Notice YHWY says, "if it seems slow in coming, wait patiently." YHWY promises that His plan will take place and *not be delayed.*

The End of Evil

When Habakkuk asks YHWY when evil ends, YHWY responds with a powerful vision and judgment of evil:

> I, the LORD, refuse to accept anyone who is proud. Only those who live by faith are acceptable to me.
>
> Wine is treacherous, and arrogant people are never satisfied. They are no less greedy than death itself—they open their mouths as wide as the world of the dead and swallow everyone.
>
> But they will be mocked with these words: You're doomed! You stored up stolen goods and cheated others of what belonged to them. But without warning, those you owe will demand payment. Then you will become a frightened victim. You robbed cities and nations everywhere on earth and murdered their people. Now those who survived will be as cruel to you.
>
> You're doomed! You made your family rich at the expense of others. You even said to yourself, "I'm above the law." But you will bring shame on your family and ruin to yourself for what you did

to others. The very stones and wood in your home will testify against you.

You're doomed! You built a city on crime and violence. But the LORD All-Powerful **sends up in flames** what nations and people work so hard to gain. Just as water fills the sea, the land will be filled with people who know and honor the LORD.

You're doomed! You get your friends drunk, just to see them naked. Now you will be disgraced instead of praised. The LORD will make you drunk, and when others see you naked, you will lose their respect.

You destroyed trees and animals on Mount Lebanon; you were ruthless to towns and people everywhere. Now you will be terrorized (Hab 2:4–17 CEV, emphasis added).

YHWY affords Habakkuk an especially precise description of the deep state! YHWY depicts the greed, debauchery, and murder of the elites ruling our society and then forcibly proclaims four different times, "You're doomed!" These four mentions represent judgment of the four successive pagan empires after Habakkuk's day, including the cruel Fourth Beast. YHWY outlines the fate of the satanic governments who ruled the world from the time of Ancient Babylon to present day revived and divided Rome—they all combust in flames. Note "those you owe will demand payment." The entire deep state depends on theft from its citizens. YHWY covenants that a day comes when those debts are *settled in full.*

Did you realize that YHWY officially declared a binding verdict upon the deep state's tyranny? Satan's lease on Earth ends with the Stone Judgment, the second judgment of humanity and the primary focus of this book. It's the End Times for the New World Order, NOT for the Church. In later chapters, we will discover YHWY also plans to make *all* unfulfilled destinies come to fruition in His immaculate redemptive plan.

GLORY OF EDEN

3. Deception Quadrella

Jesus answered, "At that time deception will run rampant. So beware that you are not fooled!"
— Matt. 24:4 TPT

Before we start this chapter, pray out loud: "Father, open my heart, open my eyes, set me free from any deception keeping me from knowing the truth. Grant me discernment in Yeshua's name!"

Yeshua warned His disciples that at the time of the end of the age, *deception would run rampant.* Merriam-Webster defines deception as the act of causing someone to accept as true or valid what is false or invalid: the act of deceiving. Also, something that deceives: TRICK. The same dictionary describes rampant as profusely widespread. Nobody willingly signs up for deception. However once someone consents to deception, breaking he or she from it proves difficult. According to Yeshua, *most* suffer deception in some way in the End Times.

When people get tricked, they often refuse to admit it—it's embarrassing. Mark Twain once said, "It's easier to fool people than to convince them that they have been fooled." Through carefully orchestrated schemes and propaganda, Satan fooled the Church into believing four major deceptions:

a) Church members should not involve themselves in politics.
b) The Rapture saves us during a time of worldwide suffering.
c) YHWY limited His Word to 66 books.
d) Modern-day Jews are "God's chosen people."

You might be offended and tempted to immediately throw this book away or take it to Goodwill. I just shot four sacred cows in less than a paragraph. However, finish this chapter before you do—the truth sets you free.

The Lord instructed me to get His people ready for the Kingdom Age. YHWY yet calls me to write a book that fails to deal with deception. He wants His saints awake so that He can train leaders to rule in the coming Kingdom Age. Would it surprise you if I told you literally billions of dollars of marketing went into convincing each of us that a, b, c and d above are actually true? Satan needed the Church to believe these four deceptions to achieve *his* plan for the End Times.

Other deceptions persist in addition to the four already mentioned, such as false religions, false messiahs, etc. However, the Lord called me to prepare His Church for the

Stone Judgment and Kingdom Age of the Saints. He called others to deal with the deceptions outside the Church.

Most of us bought books reinforcing these false concepts. We love pastors and prophets that preach these impressions, and our favorite Sunday school teachers reinforce these ideas. These things do not make them right. His Word remains the only thing we can trust on these matters, combined with Spirit-led discernment.

My Confession

I am told members of Alcoholics Anonymous start each closed meeting with, "My name is (fill in the blank) and I am an alcoholic." Members acknowledge addiction bondage by making this statement, rather than talking themselves out of the problem. Confessing the quagmire proves instrumental as a first step to attain healing.

Now pretend we form a new group called, "Deceived Christians Anonymous" (DCA). We all show up at the first DCA meeting. For purposes of illustration, let me start: "My name is Benjamin and I accepted *all four* major church deceptions for over 30 years." If you challenged me on any of these topics even three years ago, I would probably have debated you into the ground on them—my "shepherds" taught them to me. Years ago I attended John Hagee's church in San Antonio, Texas, perhaps the most outspoken supporter of the State of Israel, Benjamin Netanyahu, and modern rabbinic Jews in the Church. I also took Jewish studies in college. I refused to read the "extra biblical books," because my shepherds taught me YHWY "limited His Word to 66 books."

I grew up an evangelical Christian, where the church taught the Rapture as orthodoxy. Not one time did I hear a message on the meaning of Ekklesia. *Oxford Languages* defines orthodoxy as authorized or generally accepted theory, doctrine, or practice. All four deceptions aforementioned characterize orthodoxy within the evangelical church. This does not make them true.

Sticky Deception

One of YHWY's greatest personal miracles involved setting me free from the four major deceptions mentioned. Billions of dollars of propaganda vaporized after I studied the Bible for myself and allowed the Holy Spirit to refresh my mind. Behaviorists study why convincing fooled people presents challenges. Common reasons include:

1) *Cognitive dissonance:* When people are presented with evidence that challenges their beliefs or self-image, they experience discomfort and reject new information to protect their beliefs.

2) *Confirmation bias:* People tend to seek out information that confirms their preexisting beliefs, and discount information that contradicts their worldview.

3) *Emotional attachment:* Some people remain emotionally attached to their beliefs, especially if tied to their identity, values, or sense of

belonging. I find this especially true within Christian denominations.

4) *Social influence:* It's uncomfortable for some to challenge mainstream views, particularly if supported by friends, the media, or church community. The risk of losing social connections weighs people down.

5) *Pride:* Our flesh hates to admit we're wrong or misled. People engage in self-justification to maintain a positive self-image, even in the face of contradictory evidence.

6) *Complexity and ambiguity:* Information saturation causes challenges in discerning truth from falsehood. Feeling overwhelmed by conflicting information, some default to their existing beliefs.

While the list above includes legitimate emotions and feelings, these constitute purely flesh reactions. We should live by biblical truths and not feelings. Consider this scripture:

> Christ's resurrection is your resurrection too. This is why we are to yearn for all that is above, for that's where Christ sits enthroned at the place of all power, honor, and authority! Yes, feast on all the treasures of the heavenly realm and fill your thoughts with heavenly realities, and not with the distractions of the natural realm (Col. 3:1-2).

You see, when we focus on the heavenly realm and YHWY's Word, our flesh loses the power to control our lives. Our thoughts are on YHWY, not doctrine.

Orthodoxy Challenger

During Yeshua's earthly ministry, He challenged *every* orthodoxy that failed to line up with YHWY's Word. I believe Yeshua spent most of His teens and 20s in the biblical scrolls, poring over the scriptures and establishing a firm foundation. Yeshua routinely challenged the tradition of the elders—traditions of men and man's biblical commentary that became more important to them than scripture. Yeshua gave zero legitimacy to the tradition of the elders. Yeshua repeatedly challenged false ideas about the Sabbath, regularly healing people and setting them free, recognizing that YHWY made the Sabbath for healing and restoration. Yeshua challenged the hypocritical behavior of the elders, who pompously clung to leadership positions but failed to please YHWY after robbing widows and orphans and operating in greed.

Most importantly, Yeshua knew YHWY's nature. He knew YHWY as healer, as deliverer, and as a tender loving father who authored a flawless redemptive plan for humanity. He knew He came to draw men closer to the Father, to ultimately take them one more step toward the Glory. Yeshua loved the truth. He told us the truth sets us free (John 8:32).

Deception #1: Ekklesia

Occupy till I come (Luke 19:13b KJV).

The word "church" became a catch-all term to describe the Body of Christ, obscuring the true meaning of Ekklesia. Did you know that there are multiple Greek roots describing it? Listen to this quote from the 1915 *Gospel Advocate*:

> The word "Church" is really not a translation of any word that was used by either Christ or His Apostles, but is the Anglican form of a different word which Roman Catholicism substituted in place of the word used by Christ and His Apostles... It is in our english scriptures by order of King James, who instructed his translators of 1611 not to translate the word "Ecclesia" by either "Congregation" or "Assembly" but to use the word "Church" instead of a translation.[6]

According to this article, King James covered over the meaning of Ekklesia with a benign word to mislead Believers. The Greek word *Ekklesia* is correctly defined as the called-out (ones), meaning a civil body of elected people. The *Oxford Universal English Dictionary* defines Ekklesia as a regularly convoked assembly. YHWY intended for us as the Ekklesia to function as called out decision makers, guided by the Holy Spirit. Decision makers define culture—a role the deceived Church relegated to godless bureaucrats long ago.

---

[6]   Jimo, Dr. "Greek root word for church and for 'church'". *Believe Belong Become.* January 7, 2024. https://faith.drjimo.net/greek-root-word-for-church-and-for-church/

Recall the days within the early Church in the book of Acts, when the disciples and other Believers established their own form of government within the Roman Empire:

> A deep sense of holy awe swept over everyone, and the apostles performed many miraculous signs and wonders. All the believers were in fellowship as one body, and they shared with one another whatever they had. Out of generosity they even sold their assets to distribute the proceeds to those who were in need among them...
>
> They were continually filled with praises to God, enjoying the favor of all the people. And the Lord kept adding to their number daily those who were coming to life (Acts 2:43, 47 TPT).

Notice that Believers started taking care of the poor without looking for the help of the government. People received healing without doctors. They operated in a powerful anointing with miracles and daily communion, and began to win the hearts and minds of the people and grow in numbers *daily.* The Ekklesial generosity, miracles and anointing began to threaten the Roman establishment. THIS explains why Rome scattered the Ekklesia. King James feared a repeat of the early Ekklesia, so he ensured the translators hid the meaning of Ekklesia by replacing it with "church."

Yeshua expects us to involve ourselves with leading, making decisions and influencing culture, just as the early Ekklesia did in the book of Acts. Henceforth in this book, I will substitute Ekklesia for Church.

Deception #2: The Rapture

That he might present it to himself the assembly in
glory, not having spot or wrinkle, or any of such things,
but that it may be holy and unblemished
(Eph. 5:27 YLT).

The Rapture remains orthodoxy for millions, particularly within the evangelical church. Distilling the idea to its essence, the world continues to get darker and then YHWY removes His people in a supernatural event, just before the anti-Christ reveals himself and rules the world in utter darkness. After the Rapture, we as a collective Body of Christ, marry our Lord in the Marriage Supper of the Lamb, a heavenly celebration. Thousands of books reinforce the Rapture theory. The *Left Behind* Movie series, starring Kirk Cameron, portrays the Rapture doctrine in graphic detail.[7]

While not explicit, the Rapture doctrine supports the notion that YHWY surrenders this world to Satan. However, adherents to the Rapture orthodoxy fail to provide a *single example* of YHWY acting this way in the Bible. When the world turned to wickedness during Noah's time, YHWY removed the evil people and put Noah in charge of the world. When Egypt persecuted His people, he destroyed evil and later put Israel in charge, transferring the wealth of Egypt to His people. In both cases, YHWY told His people what would happen in advance.

Moreover, Yeshua provided three conditions prior to accepting His Bride in marriage:

---

[7]   Sorbo, Kevin. Baxley, et. al., director. *Left Behind (Series)*. Paul Lalonde, 1994-2023.

1. All things are made right *on Earth*, and all biblical prophecies fulfilled (Acts 3:21).
2. YHWY's enemies are subdued under Yeshua's feet, His Body (Matt. 22:44).
3. The Body of Christ is glorious and without flaw (spot or blemish) (Eph. 5:27).

Not one of these conditions has been satisfied today. Moreover, we read in Habakkuk chapter 2 that YHWY judges evil by fire (after four consecutive pagan empires run their course) ending evil oppression. YHWY's promise to Habakkuk also remains unrealized.

Does the Bible mention a removal of the righteous before the Marriage Supper of the Lamb? Yes. Does YHWY promise in His Word to spare His people from wrath? Definitely! However, lack of understanding of YHWY's complete timeline caused many to isolate certain scriptures and make doctrines out of them. As I began to understand YHWY's immaculate plan for humanity, I understood why the Ekklesia remains confused. Political church leaders hid many of the clearest apocalyptic books from us intentionally. The 66 books of the evangelical Bible contain clues that confirm YHWY's immaculate plan contained in parables and cryptic passages. However, Yeshua and His disciples understood YHWY's plan from other biblical scrolls and assumed readers also understood those texts! In future chapters, I will explain why YHWY's inimitable plan for the Ekklesia overwhelms what we learned in Sunday school!

Deception #3: 66 Books

I testify to everyone who hears the prophetic words of this book: If anyone adds to them, God will add to him the plagues described in this book. And if anyone subtracts from the prophetic words of this book, God will remove his portion from the Tree of Life and in the holy city, which are described in this book (Rev 22:18 TPT).

Scholars defending the 66 book limit of the evangelical "canon" quote Revelation 22:18 as justification. However, let's analyze what this scripture says, as well as the stiff penalty for *subtracting* from the prophetic books!

First, let's look at additions. The Bible includes many imprecations for unrighteous people and no one wants his or her lives cursed. Revelation 22:18 refers to commentaries and writings that contradict the Word of YHWY. For instance, Yeshua taught against the oral tradition of the Pharisees because it clashed with YHWY's Word. These oral traditions later grew into the Babylonian Talmud, a satanic tome that disputes both the Law of Moses and the teachings of Yeshua. Other anthologies, such as the Book of Mormon, also fall into this category.

Revelation 22:18 cannot possibly apply to ancient scrolls that Yeshua Himself quoted from, such as Enoch, Baruch, and others which are even mentioned by name within the Bible. The early Ekklesia arguably demonstrated more fire and anointing in the Holy Spirit than any Christian movement since. One deduces from the writings of the early Ekklesia that they carefully studied the ancient scrolls.

During the course of my research, I discovered many letters, visions and other artifacts written before the third century which are tremendously anointed and are also consistent with our Bible, while also providing more information on End Times events.

Politically motivated men removed many of the "extra-biblical" books as recently as 1885! Up until this year, the King James Version actually contained 80 books—later shortened to 66 by the protestant church.[8]

Notice from the leading scripture passage that "if anyone subtracts from the prophetic words of this book, God will remove his portion from the Tree of Life and in the holy city, which are described in this book." The apocalyptic prophecies of Revelation describe the fate of humanity. So, if men removed other books providing additional detail on the fate of humanity, such as the books of Esdras, Enoch, and Baruch, then the Bible says these individuals won't eat of the Tree of Life or enter the Holy City, referring to the New Jerusalem. Put another way, YHWY cuts them off from His family! This severe punishment should give pause to anyone who attacks the ancient "extra biblical" books that reinforce, supplement, and clarify the apocalyptic prophecy of Revelation.

According to Professor Vincent Marino, the apocalyptic scrolls came into acute focus as the number of volumes within "approved canon" gradually reduced over the centuries following the early Ekklesia. Marino observed, "There always seems to be speculation around apocalyptic

---

8   "English Bible History." *GreatSite*. Accessed June 7, 2024.
     https://greatsite.com/english-bible-history/

writings, and they either barely make it into the canon or are only just excluded."[9]

I discovered in my studies that the "extra-biblical" anthologies provided full color, 3D pictures of the future and answered nearly all my questions about YHWY's timeline. Once I read them, I understood what the passages in the 66 books of the current evangelical Bible meant! The prophet Daniel himself prophesied about the rediscovery of these ancient texts in the End Times:

> But you, O Daniel, shut up the words and seal the Book until the time of the end. [Then] many shall run to and fro and search anxiously [through the Book], and knowledge [of God's purposes as revealed by His prophets] shall be increased and become great (Dan. 12:4 AMPC).

With the resurgence of the book of Enoch and other ancient scrolls, the Ekklesia finally re-discovers the truth about YHWY's immaculate timeline—the chronology that Yeshua and the early Ekklesia assumed readers *already knew*.

Deception #4: Modern-Day Jews

Take note! I will make those of the synagogue of Satan who say they are Jews and are not, but lie—behold, I will make them come and bow down before your feet and learn and acknowledge that I have loved you (Rev 3:9).

---

9   Marino, Vincent (2016). "New Testament Biblical Apocrypha and the Exclusion of Apocalypses from the Canon," *Verbum*. Vol. 13: Iss. 2, Article 6. https://fisherpub.sjf.edu/verbum/vol13/iss2/6

Many Believers remain enamored with modern-day Jews. They believe that they represent "God's chosen people." They believe the State of Israel represents a divine fulfillment of prophecy, that Jews would migrate back to the Holy Land after their scattering. Paraphrasing what Yeshua said, when the branch of the fig tree puts forth leaves, His appearing nears (Matt 24:32-33, Luke 21:29-33).

The fig tree in these verses absolutely applies to biblical Israel. However, the present Jewish leaders in the State of Israel represent mountebanks—pretenders claiming Judean bloodline. Yeshua warned the Ekklesia of these satanic imposters in Revelation 3:9. The progeny of the leadership of the State of Israel originate from Turkic-Ugrians unaffiliated with the seed of Jacob. Rather, they are scions of Khazaria (the region of modern Ukraine). Recent and comprehensive genetic studies conclude that modern-day Jews descended from Khazaria and possess no genetic markers of the ancient Judean tribes whatsoever.[10]

The Babylonian Talmud, not the Old Testament, represents the foundational law of modern-day rabbinic Judaism.[11] The Talmud amounts to a purely satanic book completed in roughly AD 500. The Talmud teaches Jews superior to other races and the goyim (non-Jews) exist for a single purpose—to serve the Jews. The Talmud also authorizes theft and pedophilia and actually demonizes Yeshua and His followers.[12]

---

[10] Venton, Danielle. "Highlight: Out of Khazaria–evidence for "Jewish Genome" Lacking." Europe PMC, (2013). Accessed January 16, 2024. https://europepmc.org/article/PMC/3595031.

[11] Wikipedia. 2024. "Talmud." *Wikimedia Foundation*. Last modified December 7, 2024. https://en.wikipedia.org/wiki/Talmud.

[12] Freedman, Benjamin H. *Facts Are Facts* (Carson City, NV: Bridger House, 1954), 70-72.

I exposed false Israel extensively in Chapter 5 of *Blast of Fire*, providing nearly thirty footnotes to support claims.[13] I encourage you study this resource. Furthermore, I show readers Bible prophecy pertaining to the modern-day State of Israel (Dan. 11:41). The carefully crafted narrative out of the State of Israel causes Christians to unwittingly support their wars and genocide—humiliating any and all detractors with the label "anti-Semitic." Don't fall for this lie any longer. Remember, Satan comes disguised as an angel of light (2 Cor. 11:14). He dresses up like a good angel to deceive us.

Clearly, Christianity remains pro-Hebrew, as we know YHWY promises to ultimately bless the seed of Jacob. YHWY made wonderful and irrevocable promises to the seed of Jacob, the true descendants of Abraham, and for Jerusalem, His "Holy City." I discuss these prophecies in Chapter 7 and Chapter 9.

The Deception Quadrella

Through the four deceptions discussed in this chapter, Satan derailed a large percentage of the Ekklesia. Satan misled many with his poisonous deception quadrella. His master game-plan to derail the Ekklesia summarizes as follows:

a) Cause Christians to believe they should avoid leadership positions impacting culture, allowing Satan's followers to define culture. By changing the Bible, he caused the Church to forget *we are the Ekklesia* and YHWY commands us to lead.

---

[13]   Thomas, Benjamin. *Blast of Fire*. (San Antonio: Gloriam Media, 2024), 85-102.

b) Deceive Christians into believing the Rapture doctrine, where the Ekklesia cedes the world to Satan. This caused the Ekklesia to accept the perversion of our culture without a fight because we guessed YHWY rescues us out of the culture, thus avoiding our responsibility.

c) Mystify Christians on End Times teaching by restricting "extra-biblical" apocalyptic books. Removing important ancient monographs containing biblical prophecies relevant to the future of humanity kept the Ekklesia in the dark. Simultaneously introducing multiple confusing "theories" for YHWY's plan kept many in the Ekklesia subdued, hopeless, and inactive in taking back ground from the enemy.

d) Confuse Christians by causing them to support false Israel, allowing false Israel to carry out the genocide of the seed of Jacob (the real Israel). Satan's objective includes thwarting YHWY's plan for the seed of Jacob. The false Israel deception also caused the Ekklesia to financially support the very satanists trying to destroy us.

Thankfully, the Ekklesia finally begins to wake up at a dramatic pace across the world. Satan's false narratives fall apart at lightning speed. The sleeping giant, the Ekklesia, soon recognizes YHWY's destiny for us.

Lovers of Truth

Decide to crave truth about every question—ask YHWY to show you. I accepted the deception quadrella for most of my adult life. As I snapped out of deceit based on the truth of YHWY's Word, I became angry. None of us enjoy getting lied to!

Years ago I discovered the truth about our Babylonian financial system—a powerful tool created to enslave humanity controlled by the elite. This discovery caused me to question *everything* I learned about our institutions growing up. As a result, I experienced four of the five stages of grief, including denial, anger, depression, and acceptance.

As a Believer, enduring depression for almost two years proved the hardest challenge. The depression came chiefly because I felt helpless to do anything about it. The enemy's systems seemed so ingrained in every aspect of my life, so well-concealed and *so massive* that my intellect failed to process it. For the first time, I became a doomsday prepper, preparing for what appeared inevitable doom.

Looking back, I operated for several years in a dulled state, standing in awe of the plans of the enemy. During that time I decided to take charge and prepare *in my own strength* by stocking up long-life food, camping gear, weapons, and anything else I could find that I thought might protect my family. My faith walk suffered. My relationships suffered. My business suffered.

Isaiah describes a similar situation when YHWY's people feared the enemy, bought into their lies, and failed to acknowledge YHWY's delivering power:

> Don't believe their every conspiracy rumor. And don't fear what they fear—don't be moved or terrified. Fear nothing and no one except Yahweh, Commander of the Angel Armies! Honor him as holy. Be in awe before him with deepest reverence! He will become for you a holy sanctuary but for them a stone people trip over (Isa. 8:12-14a TPT).

After discovering YHWY's amazing plan for humanity in His Word, I became infinitely more impressed with YHWY's plan than Satan's plan. Attempting to compare YHWY's divine blueprint to Satan's futility analogizes to contrasting a planet-hopping antigravity spaceship to a broken bicycle! YHWY not only orchestrated His chess moves thousands of years ago, He knew Satan's every move the entire time! In fact, Satan stepped into *every* trap. I now enjoy a new appreciation for the scripture, "Heaven-throned God breaks out laughing. At first he's amused at their presumption" (Ps. 2:4 MSG).

Obedience entails trusting YHWY by believing His Word. We must no longer express even the slightest hint of respect for Satan. Satan's schemes unravel before our eyes. YHWY's amazing plan for humanity elevates our spirits to the next dimension. We, the Ekklesia, are partners with YHWY in His divine strategy! Soon, we return to the Garden of Eden, clothed in our Glory suits.

4. Sevenfold Promise

Yet if they (thieves) are caught, they will pay sevenfold;
they will forfeit all the goods of their house
— Prov. 6:31 NRSV

In economics one learns there is no "free lunch." This means that there are trade-offs with every decision. For instance, free samples at Costco are not free—someone paid for them. The same applies to retribution related to theft. Even if a thief evades the police, YHWY keeps an account. Regardless of the efficacy of our justice systems, YHWY keeps perfect records.

The deep state controls most justice systems worldwide. Corrupt nations apply unequal justice—for "thee and not for me." If citizens of corrupt nations commit crimes, they are prosecuted to the maximum extent. However, if governments of corrupt nations commit crimes, they evade prosecution. YHWY perfectly describes the behavior of the deep state in the book of Habakkuk:

> You're doomed! You made your family rich at the expense of others. You even said to yourself, "I'm above the law." But you will bring shame on your family and ruin to yourself for what you did to others (Hab. 2:9-10 CEV).

Corrupt political elite may believe they fly above the law and in most cases skirt man's justice. But YHWY notices and adds to their cup of iniquity. When the cup overflows, judgment comes. YHWY moves rapidly in judgment at the tipping point.

Judgment Tipping Point

Understanding YHWY's judgment, equips us to discern our times. YHWY's words to Abram concerning His people speak volumes about His nature:

> Then the LORD said to Abram, "Know this for certain, that your offspring shall be aliens in a land that is not theirs, and shall be slaves there, and they shall be oppressed for four hundred years; but I will bring judgment on the nation that they serve, and afterward they shall come out with great possessions. As for yourself, you shall go to your ancestors in peace; you shall be buried in a good old age. And they shall come back here

in the fourth generation; for the iniquity of the Amorites is not yet complete" (Gen. 15:13-16 NRSV).

What do we learn here? First, YHWY disclosed the future to His man, Abram. YHWY mercifully announced His plan for our day, just like He provided His plan to Abram—with vastly more detail! The religious idea that YHWY hides His plans from His elect amounts to claptrap. Second, we learn Abram's offspring would live as foreigners for four hundred years with people who eventually enslaved them. Third, we learn that YHWY planned to strip Israel's masters of their wealth and convey the fortune to His people after their period of slavery ended. Critically, we learn the iniquity of the Amorites needed to reach a point that justified the judgment by YWHY. In other words, the level of iniquity of YHWY's enemies requires a tipping point.

YHWY purposed to transfer Egypt's wealth to His people, incapacitate their army, and strip the foreigner status from His people by giving them their own land. YHWY is just. For Him to do this work for Israel, the people from whom the wealth and land came needed to commit a specific level of tyranny—reaching the judgment tipping point. Have you ever visited a water park and basked underneath one of those tipping buckets? The bucket slowly fills with water and then, WHOOSH, a soaking deluge plummets down. This provides a fine example of how YHWY's judgment operates in the Bible.

Abuse of Children

YHWY raised up Israel's deliverer after Pharaoh began to murder their children. (See Exodus 1). Moses, YHWY's appointed redeemer, came during the height of the persecution. In a divine chess move, Egypt trained their future enemy in their ways. The crimes against children pushed YHWY's judgment to the tipping point. Today, we live under the Rome-rooted Fourth Beast system. The evil system operated over 2,100 years, since before the birth of Yeshua. In the last 100 years, the Fourth Beast system snuffed out the lives of over a billion children using abortion. Wholesale abortion launched internationally in about 1920 and continued, virtually uninterrupted until now, when crimes against children finally motivated honorable men and women to fight back.

Recently, Kamala Harris made history when she visited an abortion clinic—the first U.S. vice president to do so. She called abortions "vital care." She wants to make sure abortions continue. Murder of children represents unbridled Baal worship—it's nothing new. Pharaoh snuffed out babies because he feared the people who outnumbered the Egyptians and he also worshiped satanic gods. Today, governments around the world desire to depopulate civilization because they fear the people, and they also worship satanic gods. In their depraved minds, it's easier to control societies containing fewer people.

Satan believes he can alter YHWY's plan in the Bible and convinced many to believe he, not YHWY, wins. YHWY debunks this absurd prevarication soon. In *KAS*, I outlined many times when Satan overplayed his hand and YHWY publicly humiliated him. When judgment falls on the current Fourth Beast system, it costs Satan and his minions *everything.*

Sevenfold Return

Joseph, son of Jacob, interpreted Pharaoh's dream and predicted an intense famine in Egypt. Joseph recommended Pharaoh prepare for this event by storing food in times of plenty and his wise plan greatly enriched Egypt. Out of necessity, the entire world came to Egypt to buy food for nearly a decade. As a result, Egypt stockpiled the gold and silver from the entire world, only then did YHWY cause them to hand it over to His people as He freed them from their captivity. Do you see the divine aspects of YHWY's ways here? He orchestrated a stellar plan for His people—their enemies walked right into a trap.

Today, the greedy accumulation of wealth by satanic families around the world provides a repeat of the conditions in Egypt prior to the redemption of YHWY's people. We arrived to the judgment tipping point, where the cup of iniquity overflows. Next, we will experience the largest wealth transfer from the wicked to the righteous in human history—YHWY strips the robber barons of their dirty money.

The term robber baron typically applies to businessmen who use exploitive practices to amass their wealth. This term derives from *Raubritter* (robber knights), the medieval German lords who charged illegal tolls on the primitive roads crossing their lands.[14] One could debate which secret society possesses the most power to rule the world today. I argue the Rothschild clan and by extension, the Jewish Zionists exercise dominion. Others point to the Freemasons. Still others argue hybrid reptilians rule the planet. However, all agree on one thing—the world's financial system currently comprised of private-central-banks remains the means for controlling the world. The system benefits the elites, not the masses.

Private central banks, such as the Federal Reserve system in the United States, are inextricably linked to a related taxation group. In the United States, the Internal Revenue Service (IRS) collects taxes for the Federal Reserve. The IRS incorporated privately in Puerto Rico.[15] A select few ultra-wealthy families own the central banks, which exist in nearly every nation on Earth.[16] The private-central-banking system established a chokehold of modern slavery on humanity. Heavily taxed, citizens can't get ahead by design. Someone who manages to save money suffers value erosion through compounding inflation. For instance, since the passing of the Federal Reserve Act of 1913, the U.S. dollar lost 96% percent of its spending power over the next 107 years.[17] Governments and institutions painstakingly seek to normalize the fractional reserve (FIAT) money system, legitimizing the theft. However, the system's roots originate

---

[14]   Wikipedia. 2024. "Robber baron (industrialist)." *Wikimedia Foundation*. Last modified April 26, 2024. https://en.wikipedia.org/wiki/Robber_baron_(industrialist).

[15]   Federal Register at 36 F.R. 849-890 [C.B 1971 – 1968], 36 F.R I(or 1) 1946 [C.B. 1971 – 2577], and 37 F.R. 489-490; and in Internal Revenue Manual 1100 at 1111.2

[16]   Henderson, Dean. *The Federal Reserve Cartel* (CreateSpace, 2014), Ch. 1.

[17]   O'Neill, Aaron. "Purchasing power of one US dollar (USD) in every year from 1635 to 2020." *Statista*. Accessed June 2, 2024. https://www.statista.com/statistics/1032048/value-us-dollar-since-1640/

from Babylon, an empire that worshiped Mammon, the god of riches and money.

Our enemies who run this plexus largely oppose YHWY or are under the influence of those opposed to Him. It's a win or lose system that extracts value from the vast majority of people in our societies. In a win or lose approach, I win by seeking the best result for me, even if it means my counter-party loses. The system breeds predators who look to take advantage of the weakness or failure of others and exists in every economy on Earth today. Unfortunately, society suffers as a byproduct of concentration of control—the same controllers hold the best position to influence culture, possessing unlimited resources to achieve their sinister goals.[18]

YHWY plans to eradicate evil in the Stone Judgment, an epic event that culminates in a Fire Judgment. According to His promise, the Stone Judgment includes a sevenfold return of stolen goods. Most scholars believe sevenfold refers to seven times. In other words, a thief must pay back seven days of wages for each days' wage stolen. However, another way to interpret the sevenfold return equates to folding of a piece of paper seven times, yielding two raised to the seventh power. Still others interpret sevenfold to mean seven to the seventh power. Figure 1 contains a simple chart illustrating the three methods to calculate a sevenfold return, expressed in U.S. dollars:

18   Nelson, Scott. *The Economic Awakening: Using God's Economics to Change Your Family, Industry, Culture and World.* (Newport Beach: The Economic Awakening Association, 2023). 10-21.

Figure 1: Sevenfold Return

For every $1.00 Stolen...

Method	Calculation	Return ($)
Basic	7 Times	7
Folds	2 to the 7th Power	128
Exponential	7 to the 7th Power	823,543

Per the figure, a sevenfold return potentially yields between seven times and over 823,000 times! Regardless of the calculation YHWY plans to use, our enemy will pay dearly for millenniums of slavery and theft under which YHWY's people suffered. But when the enemy pays out, in what form will he repay? Will this be paid in U.S. dollar equivalent inside of the FIAT complex? No, for this would heap sorrow upon sorrow. To leave the Babylonian network in place would cause billions to end up in the same place in a few years. The sevenfold return requires an entirely new supersystem.

YHWY's Economic System

Before the Babylonian money system came into place, YHWY outlined a biblically-based economy based on Levitical law. Contrary to the Babylonian plexus, which distorts the economy by hoarding wealth, YHWY based His system on love. It rewards producers, not scrapers nor hoarders of wealth. YHWY based His system on four principals:[19]

---

[19] Nelson, *The Economic Awakening, 11.*

1. You own the yield and possession right to the economy and never permanently lose it. It stays in your family.
2. No interest on debt and debt forgiveness occurs within seven years, if not already paid off.
3. 22.33% of gross domestic product (GDP) spent on worship, infrastructure, culture, and dependents.
4. Decentralized economic control; no central bureaucracy.

YHWY's debt-free order allows for modern small-business needs. For instance a cash-flow yielding business, such as a toy manufacturing company, constitutes a possession that stays within your family.

Under YHWY's economy, He owns all the land, and grants men custodial rights. YHWY told Moses, "The land cannot be sold permanently because the land is mine and you are foreigners—you're my tenants" (Lev. 25:23 MSG). Governments and feudal lords sought to interject substitute laws giving them ownership, creating distortions in YHWY's economy. Legal processes, including bankruptcy, injunctions, synthetic entities, etc. effectively stole people's land or producing assets and concentrated wealth in the hands of a few. If we acknowledge that YHWY owns the land and His law reigns supreme, then other court systems fail to possess jurisdiction.

The Year of Jubilee remains a central tenet of YHWY's economic plan. Every 50 years the economy resets. Two things happened in the Year of Jubilee:

1. You received your family's productive land back —even if sold or lost.
2. Indentured servants were released and set free.

In economic terms your means of production return during the Jubilee, and you were freed from being a slave or the requirement to work for someone else. If by foolishness or calamity a person lost fields, orchards, or vineyards or was sold into slavery, everything reset during the Jubilee. YHWY based His order, from top to bottom, on love and forgiveness!

In ancient Israel, righteous kings honored the Year of Jubilee. Unrighteous kings, lobbied by greedy landowners, ignored YHWY's laws and once again introduced distortions into YHWY's economic system. I believe this explains why YHWY did not want His people to choose a king (1 Sam. 8:18). YHWY provided the perfect order for His people. He knew kings who relied on taxation to support their reign would distort YHWY's economic order.

The 7th Week of Enoch

In my book *Blast of Fire*, I explained that when we enter YHWY's Kingdom Age, everything is *already built*. Soldier Saints began preparing the systems, the currency, and the laws for the Kingdom Age years ago. But how? I found the secret in the book of Enoch. Yeshua Himself referred to passages from the book of Enoch dealing with marriage after the resurrection of the dead, providing legitimacy to this remarkable book (Matt. 22:29). Enoch represents the only place in scripture dealing with marriage among glorified beings (1 Enoch 15). In addition, the New Testament contains many stark and uncanny references to the book of Enoch. In some cases, the early Ekklesia directly quoted Enoch in the New Testament, such as in Jude 1:14-15, which quotes 1 Enoch 1:9.

Enoch contains a remarkable summary of all humanity, from after the Fall of man in the Garden to the end of time, contained in ten apocalyptic weeks. In a recent podcast on *rumble*, I taught on each of the apocalyptic weeks of Enoch and connected the dots to world history and our future.[20] I explained how humanity currently lives in week seven of Enoch's weeks—with three more weeks to come—for a total of ten weeks. Listen to the description of week seven in the book of Enoch:

> And after that in the seventh week shall an apostate generation arise, and many shall be its deeds, and all its deeds shall be apostate. And at its close shall be elected the elect righteous of the eternal plant of righteousness, **to receive sevenfold instruction concerning all His creation** (1 Enoch 93:9-10, emphasis added).

---

[20] "Enoch's Apocalyptic Weeks: Part 1 of 2." rumble.com/c/revelationriddle. May 12, 2024. Video, https://rumble.com/v4ue2jn-enochs-apocalyptic-weeks-part-1-of-2-end-times-kingdom-age-stone-judgment.html. "Enoch's Apocalyptic Weeks: Part 2 of 2." rumble.com/c/revelationriddle. May 12, 2024. Video, https://rumble.com/v4ufd8o-enochs-apocalyptic-weeks-part-2-of-2-rapture-end-times-kingdom-age-stone-ju.html.

Notice in week seven, YHWY gives His elect "sevenfold instruction concerning all His creation." You see, YHWY already spoke to men and women about the future, and leads them to build out systems, laws, etc. for implementation during the Kingdom Age of the Saints!

For instance, He led Scott Nelson to write the book *Economic Awakening* and put together "virtual nations" to implement YHWY's laws across economies. He led Chris Larsen and Jed McCaleb to launch Ripple Labs in 2012, creating an institutional token called XRP, designed to someday move large amounts of wealth, based on tokenized commodity collateral. McCaleb also founded Stellar Labs in 2014 to ultimately replace the stock market with digitized, fraud-free tokens on a distributed ledger. YHWY led John F. Kennedy and other leaders to begin to lay out plans to topple the deep state over 50 years ago. He also led President Trump to craft numerous executive orders during his first term to strip assets from the cabal and eliminate human trafficking.[21] He impressed upon the U.S. military to update the Department of Defense Law of War Manual to allow for military intervention to enforce YHWY's plan. He leads many patriots to form new political parties in Canada, Australia and other countries to take back nations for the people.

Our Father planned our generation *before creation*. He instructed His servant Enoch to write it down *before* the Great Flood! Saints, be encouraged. YHWY already determined His reset plan for humanity! He forcibly extracts

---

[21] "Executive Order Blocking the Property of Persons Involved in Serious Human Rights Abuse or Corruption." *White House Archives*, December 21, 2017. "https://trumpwhitehouse.archives.gov/presidential-actions/executive-order-blocking-property-persons-involved-serious-human-rights-abuse-corruption/

from Satan *everything* he stole and reboots the earth—on YHWY's Kingdom operating system.

YHWY's World Reboot

When YHWY judges the Fourth Beast in the Stone Judgment, a major financial reset occurs. However, His plan far exceeds simply replacing stolen wealth—YHWY now speaks to wise men and women to replace the current insidious Babylonian network with a YHWY-designed supersystem.

Calculate all the wealth stolen from you over your lifetime. As an example, let's say the enemy robbed you of $10 million when considering unlawful taxes, lending on your birth certificate, interest, fees, etc. Using the basic method in Figure 1, determining a thief must repay seven times, your enemy owes you $70 million as biblical reparations. Would YHWY pay this to you in U.S. dollars? No! U.S. dollars (and other FIAT money across the world) represent paper money backed by nothing! Since 1971, no assets back U.S. dollars. So, what currency would YHWY demand as repayment?

YHWY promises, "The blessing of the LORD makes a person rich, and he adds no sorrow with it" (Prov. 10:22 NLT). If YHWY enforced reparations on our enemies in U.S. dollars, we would all land back on square-one in just a few years. FIAT money represents a Babylonian construction. It penalizes savers and enriches a small group self-entitled to print the money. When YHWY delivered Israel from Egypt, He gave them real prosperity—silver, gold, and health. "And he brought them forth with silver and gold; And there was not one feeble person among his tribes" (Ps. 105:37 ASV).

Gold and silver coins, ancient money, embodies impractical currency given the billions of people on Earth. However, gold and silver backed digital currency, redeemable by the physical metal, remains a very useful method to restore fiscal security to our currency. Our Father bases reparations on real value.

Panoramic Redemption

In my prayer journal, I maintain a list of all things stolen over my lifetime by the modern Babylonian bondage. I knew YHWY promised in Proverbs 6:31 to enforce reparations on enemies that stole from me. My list includes:

1. Stolen tax money from an illegal system (income, property, inheritance, capital gains, etc.).
2. Legal expenses related to the Babylonian legal system.
3. Stolen company equity by hostile, demonic forces.
4. Uncovered insurance claims.
5. Fees on *everything.*
6. Interest on mortgages.
7. Inheritances stolen by banks.
8. Stolen time, based on the rat-race of the Babylonian system.
9. Unfulfilled dreams due to setbacks in business caused by bad people.
10. Health issues related to poisoned medicine, food, and water.

11. Miscarried children and infertility, doubtless due to a poisoned environment.

12. People close to me that died young.

For items one through seven in the list above, I managed to reduce the damage to a dollar amount, apply a sevenfold reparation promise, and come up with a clean "amount owed" figure.

However, I struggled with items eight through twelve. How could Satan repay these items? Could he restore time wasted, unfulfilled dreams or bring people back to life? I noticed as I prayed through the list, I subconsciously began to skip over these items. One day, I felt the Lord say, "Why do you ignore these?" Subsequently, when YHWY showed me His astounding plan for humanity, I understood His redemptive plan leaves out *nothing!* Our Father's amazing plan includes panoramic redemption, not simply restoration.

GLORY OF EDEN

5. Thralldom Lease

The last enemy to be destroyed is death.

— 1 Cor. 15:26 ESV

On the Day of Pentecost, YHWY baptized His people with the Holy Spirit and with fire. Why did this not immediately clothe YHWY's people with perpetual Glory, which we wore in the Garden of Eden? For answers, let's return to the Garden of Eden and explore what actually happened.

YHWY created man in His image, in His likeness. YHWY clothed men with Glory, just as He remains clothed with Glory. YHWY equipped man with complete authority over Earth's kingdoms, which at that time included all animal kingdoms. YHWY endowed a beautiful earth to man, which produced fruit and provision for man on its own. Consider the description of the Garden:

> The LORD made a garden in a place called Eden, which was in the east, and he put the man there. The LORD God placed all kinds of beautiful trees and fruit trees in the garden. Two other trees were in the middle of the garden. One of the trees gave life—the other gave the power to know the difference between right and wrong.
>
> From Eden a river flowed out to water the garden, then it divided into four rivers. The first one is the Pishon River that flows through the land of Havilah, where pure gold, rare perfumes, and precious stones are found. The second is the Gihon River that winds through Ethiopia. The Tigris River that flows east of Assyria is the third, and the fourth is the Euphrates River (Gen. 2:8-14 CEV).

The Garden of Eden contained everything man needed; a gorgeous home, amazing food, clean water, gold, precious stones and even perfume for the ladies! However, the Tree of Life represented the ultimate trophy in the Garden of Eden. This tree gave man immortality. Man would never die as long as he could access the fruit of this tree. However, in reality unhindered fellowship with our Creator transcended any other treasure—man walked and talked with YHWY in the cool of the morning. When YHWY recognized man needed something, He provided it. "The Lord God said, 'It isn't good for the man to live alone. I need to make a suitable partner for him'" (Gen 2:18). He then made a beautiful helpmate for Adam—Eve. Our Father gave man absolutely everything anyone could want or need.

Man's Original Assignment

YHWY gave man work to do. Man's work involved ruling and reigning with the Father. For instance, YHWY gave Adam the important assignment of naming all the animals (Gen. 2:20). He then told man to spring forth many children and fill the earth with people (Gen. 1:27).

YHWY said, "Now we will make humans, and they will be like us. We will let them rule the fish, the birds, and all other living creatures" (Gen. 1:26). Note the passage gave man no license to rule over other men, although man did rule the animals and other living creatures. Satan imparted his evil desire on man to exercise rule over other men. YHWY never intended for kings to enrich themselves by oppressing people. When the Hebrew people demanded a king like other nations, the prophet Samuel warned them that kings lay heavy burdens on nations, and they did not need a king (1 Sam. 8:18). YHWY originally destined each man to fellowship with Him and to trust Him for protection and guidance. We worship YHWY, not government.

YHWY put man on Earth to look after it and have righteous dominion over it. "And God blessed them, and God said unto them, 'Be fruitful, and multiply, and replenish the earth, and subdue it: and have dominion over the fish of the sea, and over the fowl of the air, and over every living thing that moveth upon the earth'" (Gen. 1:28 KJV). YHWY commanded man to dress and keep the Garden of Eden (Gen. 2:15). While YHWY gave man the earth and the kingdoms of the earth, He knew of potential trouble. Satan lurked in the shadows, which explains why He told Adam to subdue the earth. *Merriam-Webster* defines subdue as to conquer and bring into subjection: VANQUISH. From the beginning, YHWY's assignment for man involved exercising authority over Satan.

YHWY gave man a will and destined him to become greater than the angels (Heb 1:14). Our God-given free will necessitated the presence of the Tree of Knowledge in the Garden, for without it, no choice existed for man to demonstrate obedience. The Lord told him, "You may eat fruit from any tree in the garden, except the one that has the power to let you know the difference between right and wrong. If you eat any fruit from that tree, you will die before the day is over!" (Gen 2:16-17 CEV). When man ate the fruit of the Tree of Knowledge, he immediately died spiritually and separated himself from YHWY. He no longer enjoyed close fellowship. Man indeed selected a new master—Satan.

Meet the New Boss

When Adam and Eve transgressed, they disobeyed YHWY's command and immediately died spiritually. Within milliseconds of their treason, YHWY's Glory stripped off of man. The human race woke up to a stark new reality. By choosing to obey a different master, they cursed themselves and brought a curse upon their domain—Earth. YHWY told Adam:

> You listened to your wife and ate fruit from that tree. And so, the ground will be under a curse because of what you did.
>
> As long as you live, you will have to struggle to grow enough food. Your food will be plants, but the ground will produce thorns and thistles. You will have to sweat to earn a living; you were made out of soil, and you will once again turn into soil (Gen. 3:17-19).

YHWY understood the fullness of what happened when Adam and Eve chose Satan's lordship instead of His. Three curses landed on Adam and his progeny. One, the earth became cursed and crops would suffer under weeds and thorns. Two, man became cursed and would live by the sweat of his brow to earn a living. And three, man died spiritually, and thus death and decay came to his body for the first time —one day he would indeed die a physical death. No longer clothed in righteousness and Glory, man also needed to secure a different covering for his body.

In the first recorded bloodshed, YHWY killed an animal to make skins for Adam and Eve to cover their nakedness (Gen. 3:21). This act showed the necessity of shedding blood to cover man's sin. What a hideous substitute for the righteous Glory that formerly adorned this couple!

Before YHWY spoke the words of the curse over Adam, He also spoke to Satan (through the serpent), saying "And I will put enmity between thee and the woman, and between thy seed and her seed; it shall bruise thy head, and thou shalt bruise his heel." (Gen. 3:15 KJV). This passage articulates YHWY's plan that *through man* Satan would be struck down. Most scholars agree the portion of scripture, "it shall bruise thy head" speaks of Yeshua. Yeshua stripped Satan of spiritual authority after His resurrection and give His followers authority over sickness, disease, as well as the ability to receive the Holy Spirit, achieving a *giant* step closer to the Glory of Eden. In addition, man's spirit could now become white and clean by accepting Yeshua as his Savior.

The Life of Adam and Eve,[22] an ancient text providing more texture to the story of Adam and Eve, offers a slight expansion of Genesis 3:15 by adding five words. "I will put enmity between thee and his seed: he shall bruise thy head and thou shalt bruise his heel **until the day of Judgment**" (1:26b, emphasis added). Here we get a clue as to how long Satan would bruise, or injure, man. Satan would possess the ability to bruise man until the day of judgment. As we cover in later chapters, Satan's ability to bruise humanity and

---

[22]   Charles, R.H. (translator). The Greek Life of Adam and Eve, 1913.

exercise dominion on Earth lasts 6,000 years. But which judgment ends Satan's lease of authority on Earth?

Water and Fire

The Bible mentions several judgments while the earth (as we know it) remains. The Great Flood represents the first judgment of mankind, which drowned nearly everyone on Earth with water. (See Genesis 7). The entire earth turned to wickedness after rebellious sons of God, who the prophet Enoch calls "Watchers," mated with women and produced Nephilim offspring who terrorized humanity. If you look carefully at the account in Enoch, *mankind faced an existential threat;* The Nephilim ran out of resources and began eating men and all the animals until the earth cried out for judgment. (See 1 Enoch 7). YHWY found the few remaining righteous, namely Noah and his family, and provided a way of escape for them through Noah's obedience in building the Ark, despite lack of rain. After YHWY flooded the earth with water, He promised never to judge the earth again in this manner (Gen. 9:15).

Before the Great Flood destroyed the majority of humanity, YHWY showed mercy on the wicked by warning them. The *Book of Jasher* explains:[23]

> In that time, the Lord said to Noah and Methuselah, Stand forth and proclaim to the sons of men all the words that I spoke to you in those days, peradventure they may turn from their evil

---

[23]   Samuel, Moses. *The Book of Jasher FIRST EDITION.* IAP, 2017.

ways, and I will then repent of the evil and will not bring it.

And Noah and Methuselah stood forth, and said in the ears of the sons of men, all that God had spoken concerning them.

But the sons of men would not hearken, neither would they incline their ears to all their declarations (Jasher 5:22-24).

YHWY's mercy before the Great Flood included warning humanity about His plan and providing them an opportunity to repent. Unfortunately, they declined YHWY's mercy and suffered complete annihilation. Before the finality of the Stone Judgment, the Ekklesia again warns humanity.

Satan continued to plague man after the Great Flood. Evil empires grew up and afflicted YHWY's people. His people suffered greatly under Egypt, Assyria, Babylon, Persia, Greece, Rome and others. Today, Christian persecution continues, with 13 Christians a day dying for their faith.[24] Clearly, the judgment by water did not end Satan's tyranny on Earth. However, the Bible prophesied a second judgment sets men free from Satan's tyranny—a judgment of fire. We read about this judgment in Malachi:

> The day of judgment is certain to come. And **it will be like a red-hot furnace with flames** that burn up proud and sinful people, as though they were straw. Not a branch or a root will be left. I,

---

[24] "World Watch List 2023," Open Doors, accessed June 6, 2023, www.opendoors.org/en-US/persecution/countries.

the LORD All-Powerful, have spoken! But for you that honor my name, victory will shine like the sun with healing in its rays, and you will jump around like calves at play. When I come to bring justice, you will trample those who are evil, as though they were ashes under your feet. I, the LORD All-Powerful, have spoken! (Mal. 4:1–3 CEV, emphasis added).

Will the judgment of fire in Malachi end Satan's ability to injure and/or destroy YHWY's people? From the passage we learn that the judgment of fire leads to a victory for YHWY's people, who then shine like the sun. This judgment of fire (subsequently, the "Fire Judgment") paves the way again for YHWY's Glory to rest on His people! Note YHWY reinforces His promise, "The day of judgment is certain to come."

But what is the Fire Judgment, and when does it happen? My church taught about the Great Flood as a worldwide judgment, about YHWY's deliverance from Egypt of His people, and about a future Battle of Armageddon when Yeshua would judge the anti-Christ. Growing up in the evangelical church and reading many books on End Times, I never once heard about a Fire Judgment or the Stone Judgment. Now, I realize the Bible contains *scores* of references similar to the passage we read in Malachi.

The Stone Judgment

If you read either of my prior books, *KAS* or *Blast of Fire,* recall that I devoted considerable effort to explaining the

Stone Judgment. However, my prior description proved grossly inadequate upon further revelation—it's massively greater in scope and impact! The Stone Judgment adjudicates *all humanity and demon forces*. The Stone Judgment *precedes* the battle of Armageddon. The Stone Judgment contains three phases, climaxing with the Fire Judgment. References to the Stone Judgment *are all over* the Bible. Yet, few Bible scholars discuss or teach on the Stone Judgment. Precious few books currently on the market explain the Stone Judgment, although I became aware of a forthcoming book by Mark Eaton on the Stone Judgment. A lawyer who read my book *KAS* told a relative that he always read the passage in Daniel about the Stone Judgment but could not find anything written concerning it, and so with much excitement he dove into my teaching on the Stone Judgment.

We should welcome teaching on the Stone Judgment, because it marks the end of Satan's dominion lease on the earth, ending his ability to bruise YHWY's people. The Stone Judgment ushers in an age of Glory for YHWY's people like what Adam and Eve originally experienced in the Garden of Eden! However, the Stone Judgment also completely removes evil empires, demons and wicked people from Earth. The following summarizes the key points of the Stone Judgment:

- It begins at the end of the reign of the Fourth Beast— Rome. In the modern era, revived and divided Rome (Dan 2:33-34).
- Starts slowly at first, then ends in a single day (Dan. 7:26).

- Includes a Shaking of Nations, which ends the power structure of the Fourth Beast and completes the "Times of the Gentiles," that Yeshua spoke about (Luke 21:24, Heb. 12:26-29).
- Includes a Fire Judgment, which destroys any leftover elements of modern Rome and the pagan remnants of Babylon, Medo-Persia, and Greece (Dan. 7:11).
- Removes demonic forces and all evil people from the earth (Isa. 34:1-4).
- Yeshua appears during the Stone Judgment to usher in the Glory of YHWY and raise the righteous dead (1 Cor. 15:52-53).
- Includes many alarming signs in the heavens (Rev 6:12-17).
- After the Stone Judgment, YHWY restores the dominion and kingdoms on Earth to His people, restoring man's authority lost after the Fall (Dan 7:18, 22, 27).

I cover additional aspects of the Stone Judgment in later chapters within this book, and provide a great number of supplementary scripture references.

As in the Great Flood, the Stone Judgment comes at a time when Satan's forces threaten to destroy all humanity. The New World Order, the modern face of Rome, crafted a plan to depopulate the world by 90%, as displayed publicly on the Georgia Guidestones for over 40 years until their destruction in 2022.[25] The modern deep state attempted to change the genetic structure of humanity through a

---

[25] Wikipedia. 2024. "Georgia Guidestones." *Wikimedia Foundation*. Last modified May 15, 2024. https://en.wikipedia.org/wiki/Georgia_Guidestones.

bioweapon called the Covid-19 vaccine.[26] Already 17 million people died after billions of doses administered, worldwide.[27] The more we learn about the Covid-19 shot, we more we realize it's a gene-altering, military-grade bioweapon, designed to remove the "God gene" from our DNA. Had Soldier Saints not interrupted the Fourth Beast's insidious plan to destroy humanity, you would not be reading this book. Once again, YHWY intervenes to save humanity. Only this time, He promotes His people to total victory and Glory through the Stone Judgment.

Immaculate Painting of the Future

YHWY showed His prophets the future using harmonious dreams and visions. Have you ever seen a beautiful painting that displays slight variations from different angles? This reflects how YHWY showed His prophets the future of His creation and how He would redeem humanity. YHWY revealed to multiple prophets the same story: four pagan empires would come to power, followed by a mighty judgment that would redeem YHWY's people and usher in YHWY's Kingdom on Earth.

For instance, He showed Daniel the interpretation of Nebuchadnezzar's dream of a statue with a gold head, silver arms, bronze body, legs of iron, and feet of iron and clay. Each of these parts of the statue represented the pagan empires

---

[26] Cohen, John. "Further evidence supports controversial claim that SARS-CoV-2 genes can integrate with human DNA." *Science*, May 6, 2021. https://www.science.org/content/article/further-evidence-offered-claim-genes-pandemic-coronavirus-can-integrate-human-dna

[27] Redshaw, Megan. "Researchers Find COVID Vaccines Causally Linked to Increased Mortality, Estimate 17 Million Deaths." *Epoch Times*, October 2, 2023. https://archive.ph/4PCBk#selection-409.0-409.98

that would come to rule. A succession of pagan empires, namely Babylon, Medo-Persia, Greece, Rome, and divided Rome, comprised the head, arms, breastplate, legs, and feet of the statue, respectively. In the dream, a stone made without hands (Yeshua) comes from Heaven and crushes the entire statue, representing the amazing sequence of events within the Stone Judgment. (See Daniel 2).

Later in Daniel 7, YHWY showed Daniel another depiction of the same events. Only this time, a winged lion represented Babylon, a bear represented Medo-Persia, a tiger represented Greece, and a terrible beast with iron teeth represented Rome. The Most High judges the beast in the Court of Heaven (in the dream) and burns the beast with fire.

In Revelation 6, YHWY gives John the Revelator the same vision He gave Daniel, only this time seals on scrolls unlock to unleash the four beasts, now represented by four horsemen. The white horse represents Babylon, the red horse represents Medo-Persia, the black horse represents Greece, and the pale horse represents Rome. This passage also ends with a judgment event, in the form of the sixth seal described in Revelation 6:12-17. YHWY showed John the Revelator the same story! But wait, some say, I thought the book of Revelation only dealt with the future?

Many believe the book of Revelation only covers the future after Yeshua's resurrection. However, Revelation 1:19 states, "Write the things which thou hast seen, and the things **which are**, and the things which shall be hereafter" (KJV, emphasis added). The Bible links the Fourth Beast, the

Rome-rooted system that now controls our world, with the former beasts, namely Babylon, Medo-Persia, and Greece. Each of these pagan empires adopted the practices of the former evil empire, and built upon them. When the Stone Judgment occurs, *all four* pagan empires are judged, starting with the most vicious beast of all, the Fourth Beast.

YHWY showed the prophet Isaiah the same picture of the four reigning empires in Isaiah chapter 5. Only in this picture, a warrior represents Babylon, an archer represents Medo-Persia, a horse represents Greece, and a strong lion represents Rome. In the next chapter of Isaiah (chapter 6), we are shown the Fire Judgment, accompanied by YHWY's Glory—a picture of the Stone Judgment once again.

As we soon see, YHWY showed His immaculate plan for the future of His people not just to Habakkuk, Malachi, Daniel, Isaiah, and John the Revelator—prophets I already mentioned. YHWY also showed His plan to Ezekiel, Micah, Jeremiah, Ezra, Baruch, Enoch, Haggai, Obadiah, Joel, Nahum, Peter, Paul, and of course, Yeshua. Each account unveils slightly different elements of the same future prophecy. Taken all together we see the whole picture in vivid detail.

The Fourth Beast and Little Horn

The Bible refers to pagan governments as "beasts." The fourth and last pagan empire, Rome, represents the most vicious, bloodthirsty and dangerous empire in human history. YHWY showed this empire to Daniel as the legs and feet of the statue as well as a terrible beast with iron teeth. The vision of the Fourth Beast terrified Daniel (Dan. 7:19). In the book of Revelation, YHWY showed John the Revelator the Fourth Beast as a pale horse. "Its rider was named Death, and Death's Kingdom followed behind" (Rev. 6:8b CEV). The Bible also depicts the Fourth Beast as an evil three-headed eagle described by the prophet Ezra, which I covered in my book *Blast of Fire.*[28] The Fourth Beast unleashed many destructive powers over humanity, and also:

- Is ruled by Leviathan, the Demon-god dragon of the sea (Isa. 27:1-2, Rev. 13:1).
- Has ten horns and teeth of iron (Dan. 7:7, Rev 13:1).
- Is worshiped by the godless (Rev 13:4, 8).
- Devours, breaks into pieces, and stamps out the residue (Dan. 7:7).
- Has a body of a leopard, feet of a bear, and mouth of a lion (Rev 13:2).
- Destroys 25% of the earth. This includes both arable farmland and population (Rev. 6:7).
- Destroys people with war, famine, disease, and wild animals (Rev. 6:7).
- Makes war with and prevails against the saints (Dan. 7:21-22, Rev 13:7).
- Attempts to change the seasons and law of YHWY (Dan. 7:25).
- Reigns for a time, two times, and half a time [2,150 years, *see below*] (Dan. 7:25; 12:7).

---

[28] Thomas, *Blast of Fire*, 147-157.

- And finally, yields all its authority to a Little Horn, which subdues three of its ten horns (Dan. 7:8, 7:24).

The Little Horn eventually gains control of the Fourth Beast by subduing three of its ten horns, or power centers. The Little Horn:

- Comes from an insignificant race [not the seed of Jacob] (Dan. 11:21).
- Receives help by a foreign god [Behemoth] and partners with Leviathan (2 Bar. 29:4, Dan. 11:39).
- Makes a covenant with false Jews (Dan. 11:30).
- Removes YHWY's chosen high priest [Yeshua] (Dan. 11:22).
- Suddenly appears and gains control through infiltration, *with no army* (Dan. 11:21).
- Acts with great authority for forty-two months [1,260 years, *42 months times 30 days/month*] (Rev 13:5).
- Entices with flattery those who betray YHWY's covenant (Dan. 11:32).
- Invades many wealthy countries (Dan. 11:42).
- Rewards his followers with great wealth (Dan. 11:39).
- Installs the Dome of the Rock (Dan. 11:31).
- Takes over and destroys the roots of three powerful horns of the Fourth Beast (Dan. 7:8, 7:24).

- Has eyes like a man [I believe this represents the "eye of god" on top of the pyramid, the symbol of the New World Order] (Dan. 7:8).
- Has a mouth speaking great lies [the mainstream media] (Dan. 7:8).
- Overtakes Jerusalem, murdering many (Dan. 11:41).
- Defeats Ethiopia, Libya, and Egypt (Dan. 11:43).
- Controls the gold and silver market (Dan. 11:43).
- Dies after a final battle between the armies of the north and east (Dan. 11:44).
- Is completely isolated with no allies when he dies (Dan 11:45).

As discussed in *KAS*, the Little Horn represents the false Jews —the Khazarian mafia—who effectively rule the Fourth Beast system through three city-states: the City of London, the District of Columbia, and the Vatican.[29] These three modern city-states represent the three subdued nations and the governance of the contemporary Fourth Beast. These three seats of power also represent three heads of the eagle YHWY showed to Ezra in 2 Esdras chapter 11. The Little Horn controls the rest of the world through an intricate network of finance and private-central-banking. He also currently controls Jerusalem, although this soon will change.

The Little Horn suffers utter destruction in the Stone Judgment, including a plague among their leaders (Isa.

---

[29]   Thomas, *Kingdom Age of the Saints*, 52-60.

10:16). All Nazi-Zionists perish. Peace on Earth cannot exist unless the Little Horn is completely eradicated.

Rome's Lease is Up

The Lord revealed to me by revelation that the Fourth Beast's lease on Earth lasts 2,150 years. The prophecy that the Fourth Beast possesses authority for "a time, two times, and half a time" in the Bible indeed tells us how long the Fourth Beast reigns (Dan. 7:25, 12:7). To explain, "times" equals 1,000 years (two times equals 2,000 years), while "time" equals 100 years, and "half a time" equals 50 years. If you ask historians when Rome began, they give you several possible answers. Some say 146 BC, when Rome sacked Athens. Some say as early as 201 BC after the Roman victory in the Second Punic War. While other historians quote 27 BC, when power consolidated under Caesar Augustus.

However, In YHWY's eyes, Rome began when the Roman deep state started assassinating political opponents. In June 133 BC, the Roman deep state assassinated a tribune by the name of Tiberius Gracchus.[30] His "crime" included passing a significant law favoring the people over the government. The law transferred land from the Roman state and wealthy landowners to poorer citizens. Tiberius represented a man of the people. After his brutal assassination, his younger brother Gaius picked up the charge and also represented the people. The Roman deep state assassinated Gaius as well. This reminds me of John F.

---

30   Brittanica. 2024. "Tiberius Sempronius Gracchus." *Encyclopedia Britannica.* Last modified May 28, 2024. https://www.britannica.com/biography/Cornelia-Roman-aristocrat

Kennedy and Robert Kennedy, whom I also believe the deep state assassinated, roughly 2,100 years after the Gracchus brothers. Nothing really changed. As long as the deep state remains in charge, the people's voice doesn't count.

The impact of these murders in Ancient Rome started a cycle of increased aristocratic violence to suppress popular movements. By introducing violent repression, the senatorial oligarchy created norms making future deep state repression more acceptable. Prior to the assassination of the Gracchus brothers, negotiation resolved political disputes, not murder. The death of Tiberius Gracchus in 133 BC was viewed both in the Roman period and modern scholarship, as the start of a new period in which politics remained polarized and political violence became normalized. I believe YHWY saw the Fourth Beast rising in 133 BC, and considers this year as the first year of the Fourth Beast system, when big government and big business ruled. If political figures got in the way, the deep state simply terminated them. The deep state's power to kill and defy the will of the people ends imminently.

In 2 Esdras chapter 11, YHWY gave Ezra an elaborate vision of the Fourth Beast, represented by an evil three-headed eagle, guided by a demonic voice. The Bible provides a blow-by-blow analysis of how the Fourth Beast dies, which I covered extensively in *Blast of Fire*.[31] His death begins with a judgment by Yeshua, represented by a lion from the forest. The Lion speaks to the Fourth Beast and pronounces judgment. Then the Bible introduces us to the man-from-the-

---

[31]   Thomas, *Blast of Fire*, 187-210.

sea, who based on prophecies undoubtedly represents President Trump. A military alliance destroys the head of the Fourth Beast, the Little Horn, and the Whore of Babylon using force and the law. Angel armies assist and protect the military alliance on their mission. What the military starts, Yeshua then finishes supernaturally in the Fire Judgment.

You see, YHWY *wants* His people to know the game plan. He cares about us, and already blueprinted a mighty deliverance. Each aspect of YHWY's immaculate painting as revealed to His prophets contains unique features that, taken together, give us the complete story of the future. As I uncovered YHWY's immaculate painting of hereafter, I discovered elements that amazed me—invigorating my soul such that I shouted to YHWY in praise!

The demise of the Fourth Beast, Little Horn and Whore of Babylon mark the launch of YHWY's amazing plan for His people, when He begins to return His people to the Garden of Eden. YHWY planned all along to restore the Glory of Eden lost after the Fall. What occurs afterward will truly shock and amaze you!

6. Judgment to Victory

A bruised reed shall he not break, and smoking flax shall he not quench, till he send forth judgment unto victory.

— Matt. 12:20 KJV

Judgment leads to victory. When Christians think of judgment, many think of the final judgment, the White Throne Judgment, when YHWY judges the dead (Rev 20:12). Others think of the judgment of the anti-Christ, when Yeshua comes from Heaven riding on a white horse and judges the dragon in the Battle of Armageddon (Rev 19:11-21). Some Christians recall when fire from Heaven consumes Gog and Magog's armies (Rev 20:7-10). Still others think of the past judgment of humanity by water in the Great Flood (Gen. 6-9). However, most Christians neglect to recognize humanity soon faces a *second* judgment, the Fire Judgment, which occurs as the last phase of the Stone Judgment. The Stone Judgment represents one of five major judgments described in the Bible and is arguably the most important within scripture. The Stone Judgment already began!

The Bible describes two major "shaking(s) of nations." Shaking of nations depict a type of YHWY's judgment limited to evil empires—they don't constitute a judgment of entire humanity. The first shaking occurred when YHWY judged Egypt and set the Israelites free. (See Exodus 7-11). YHWY dealt with an evil world empire enslaving His people, Israel. However, He did not deal with the giants in other lands at that time—also enemies of Israel. YHWY commanded Joshua to methodically destroy these giants to enter the land of Canaan, the land YHWY promised to His people.

The second shaking of nations occurs as I write, as YHWY empowers mighty Soldier Saints to topple the New World Order, the modern name for the Roman system we live under today—the Fourth Beast. Listen to the words of Haggai:

> Soon I will **again** shake the heavens and the earth, the sea and the dry land. I will shake the nations, and their treasures will be brought here. Then the brightness of my glory will fill this temple. All silver and gold belong to me, and I promise that this new temple will be more glorious than the first one. I will also bless this city with peace (Hag. 2:6-9 CEV, emphasis added).

Haggai prophesied during the time of the return of YHWY's people to Jerusalem after King Cyrus defeated Babylon. Yet, the prophecy in the scripture above remains unrealized. The second Judaic Temple did not contain more Glory than the first (Ezra 3:12-13). The nations did not bring their treasure to Jerusalem. In fact, funding remained tight and efforts to rebuild the second Temple frustrated. Many Judeans failed to get onboard the reconstruction effort. No, this promise of the second shaking referred to the future—our time.

The scripture in Haggai clearly describes a shaking of expanded scope, greater than the shaking of nations that delivered Israel from Egypt. The scripture mentions a shaking of the heavens, Earth, the sea and dry land. Haggai describes a return of the Glory more significant than the Glory of Solomon's Temple or Moses' tent. It describes how treasures of the nations flood into YHWY's house. The shaking within the prophecy of Haggai brings peace. What Haggai described appears monumental—pivotal to YHWY's purposes for His people.

Figure 2 summarizes the five major judgments of YHWY and the two shaking of nations. Figure 2 shows us Judgment #1, the past judgment of all wicked on the earth by water in the Great Flood. Only Noah, his family, and the animals survived. Humanity faced an existential threat due to the rise of the Nephilim, genetically defiled giants— offspring of fallen sons of God and women. YHWY intervened with the Great Flood and both wicked men and the giants perished. While the giants' physical bodies died, their spirits lived on as Evil Spirits, as we will cover later in this chapter.

Figure 2: *Major Judgments and Shakings*

Description	Name	Included
SATAN'S DOMINION LEASE (6,000 YEARS)		
JUDGMENT #1	**Great Flood**	- All Wicked Men - The Giants (Nephilim)
SHAKING #1	**Egyptian Plagues**	- Egyptian Empire
THE STONE JUDGMENT		
SHAKING #2	**Shaking of Nations**	- Fourth Beast - Little Horn - Whore of Babylon - First three Beasts
JUDGMENT #2	**Fire Judgment**	- Demon-gods (Watchers) - Evil Spirits (demons) - All Wicked Men
KINGDOM AGE OF SAINTS (1,000 YEARS)		
JUDGMENT #3	**Battle of Armageddon**	- All Wicked Men - anti-Christ - Satan (Dragon) - Unclean Spirits (angels)
MILLENNIAL REIGN OF CHRIST (1,000 YEARS)		
JUDGMENT #4	**Battle of Gog & Magog**	- All Wicked Men - Satan
JUDGMENT #5	**White Throne Judgment**	- All Wicked Men - All Wicked Principalities
NEW HEAVEN AND EARTH ∞		

In the first shaking of nations in Figure 2, marked by Shaking #1, YHWY judged the Egyptian Empire, who enslaved YHWY's people. The first shaking of nations did not represent a judgment of humanity, but rather a removal of the power of Egypt. The first shaking of nations did not remove demonic forces, but it did set up YHWY's people to establish their own kingdom on Earth for a brief time. This serves as a type and shadow of YHWY's Kingdom Age on Earth.

Both the Great Flood and the first shaking of nations *led to victory*. After the Great Flood, Noah and his family ruled the world after evil people and the hybrid Giants drowned. After the shaking of Egypt, YHWY's people possessed the wealth of the nations and later went on to form the Kingdom of Israel and Judah.

As indicated in Figure 2, the Stone Judgment includes both a Shaking of Nations, marked as Shaking #2, as well as a Fire Judgment, indicated as Judgment #2. The Stone Judgment ends Satan's tyrannical 6,000-year lease on Earth and his power to "bruise" YHWY's people! During the Stone Judgment, the Fourth Beast, the Little Horn and the Whore of Babylon all die in the shaking. In addition, remnants of prior pagan empires perish, including Ancient Babylon, Medo-Persia, and Greece. Watchers and Evil Spirits are banished from Earth by the Ekklesia. The subsequent Fire Judgment removes all wicked people from the earth, as well as all remaining Watchers and Evil Spirits. Once humanity is set free from evil principalities, Satan's power on Earth wanes dramatically. The Stone Judgment launches the Kingdom Age of the Saints, an era when YHWY restores to His people rule over the kingdoms of Earth, renewing man's authority he possessed in the Garden of Eden before the Fall.

Figure 2 also lays out future judgments, such as the Battle of Armageddon (marked as Judgment #3), when Yeshua returns to rule the nations and kingdoms of Earth in the flesh during the Millennial Reign of Christ. The

Millennial Reign of Christ occurs after Yeshua marries His Bride, the perfected Ekklesia. Thankfully, Satan and his remaining forces, the Unclean Spirits (fallen angels) are bound during this stage in the next age. Figure 2 lists the Battle of Gog and Magog as Judgment #4, after YHWY releases Satan for a short while. The fifth and penultimate judgment is the White Throne Judgment. After the White Throne Judgment, YHWY creates a New Heaven and New Earth.

During the Stone Judgment, the primary topic of this book, Watchers and Evil Spirits are bound until the White Throne Judgment, setting humanity free from the vicious destructive powers of these evil beings. But how did Watchers and Evil Spirits get here?

Watchers and Evil Spirits

The book of Genesis affords scant detail on the conditions leading up to the Great Flood:

> WHEN MEN began to multiply on the face of the land and daughters were born to them, the sons of God saw that the daughters of men were fair, and they took wives of all they desired *and* chose. Then the Lord said, My Spirit shall not forever dwell *and* strive with man, for he also is flesh; but his days shall yet be 120 years. There were giants on the earth in those days—and also afterward—when the sons of God lived with the daughters of men, and they bore children to them. These were the mighty men who were of old, men of renown.

The Lord saw that the wickedness of man was great in the earth, and that every imagination *and* intention of all human thinking was only evil continually (Gen. 6:1-5 AMPC).

The earth was depraved *and* putrid in God's sight, and the land was filled with violence (desecration, infringement, outrage, assault, and lust for power). And God looked upon the world and saw how degenerate, debased, *and* vicious it was, for all humanity had corrupted their way upon the earth *and* lost their true direction. God said to Noah, I intend to make an end of all flesh, for through men the land is filled with violence; and behold, I will destroy them and the land (Gen. 6:11-13).

In just a few verses of scripture, the Word provides us with the backstory on what caused humanity to fall into abject depravity. "Sons of God" (or "Watchers") mated with women and bore genetically defiled Giants, otherwise known as Nephilim.

We garner far more information from the book of Enoch. Enoch wrote that the sons of God taught men "eternal secrets that were (preserved) in heaven, which men were striving to learn" (1 Enoch 9:6). These included the making of weapons, metalworking, chemistry, magic, root-cuttings, constellations, and signs of the Earth, Moon and Sun. Ultimately, the use of this knowledge for violence created extreme scarcity, and the Nephilim offspring began to eat men. The Flood destroyed the flesh of the Nephilim, yet their spirits remained. Of these spirits, the book of Enoch says:

> And now, the giants, who are produced from the spirits and flesh, shall be called evil spirits upon the earth, and on the earth shall be their dwelling. Evil spirits have proceeded from their bodies; because they are born from men and from the holy Watchers is their beginning and primal origin; they shall be called evil spirits on earth, and evil spirits they shall be called.
>
> As for the spirits of heaven, in heaven shall be their dwelling, but as for the spirits of the earth which were born upon the earth, on the earth shall be their dwelling.
>
> And the spirits of the giants afflict, oppress, destroy, attack, do battle, and work destruction on the earth, and cause trouble: they take no food, but nevertheless hunger and thirst, and cause offences. And these spirits shall rise up against the children of man and against the women, because they have proceeded from them (1 Enoch 15:8-12).

The passage indicates that the Evil Spirits of the Nephilim, offspring of the Watchers, would rise up against humanity, work destruction, and cause trouble. Most Christians believe Evil Spirits are fallen angels, but in fact, they are the defiled evil offspring of the Nephilim. YHWY pronounced the same future on both the Watchers and their offspring:

> Bind them fast for seventy generations in the valleys of the earth, till the day of their judgment and of their consummation, till the judgment that is forever and ever is consummated. In those days they shall be led off to the abyss of fire; and to the torment and the prison in which they shall be confined forever (1 Enoch 10:12-13).

Initially the Evil Spirits are confined in the "valleys of the earth" until the day of their first judgment. Their final verdict occurs at the last judgment, the White Throne Judgment. In the next chapter of Enoch, YHWY provides more detail regarding Evil Spirits:

> From the days of the slaughter and destruction and death of the giants, from the souls whose flesh the spirits, having gone forth, shall destroy without incurring judgment—thus shall they destroy until the day of the consummation, **the great judgment in which the age shall be consummated**, over the Watchers and the godless, shall be wholly consummated (1 Enoch 16:1, emphasis added).

The initial judgment of the Watchers and their offspring, the Evil Spirits, occurs when the age consummates. *Merriam-Webster* defines consummation as the ultimate end: FINISH. So the first judgment of Watchers and Evil Spirits occurs when *the age ends*. YHWY shows us in scripture the precise year the age ends! I cover this in greater detail within Chapter 9.

Demons Flee

Judgment of the Watchers and Evil Spirits represents an epic development for humanity. Humanity wrestled with these troublemakers since shortly after the Garden of Eden. Listen to what Paul tells us in Ephesians:

> Your hand-to-hand combat is not with human beings, but with the highest principalities and authorities operating in rebellion under the heavenly realms. For they are a powerful class of **demon-gods and evil spirits** that hold this dark world in bondage (Eph. 6:12 TPT, emphasis added).

In this passage, Demon-gods refer to the Watchers, and Evil Spirits their offspring—two powerful classes of principalities and authorities who currently cause mayhem. As they did in ancient times, they provide instruction to satanic world leaders to accomplish evil. In addition, Believers battle them in our everyday lives when we encounter demon-possessed people. Many wicked world leaders completely submit to these principalities and authorities. These leaders believed a lie, that Satan wins. Boy are they wrong!

The most substantial power of the Demon-gods (synonymous with Watchers) and Evil Spirits relates to their ability to "hold this dark world in bondage," according to the passage above. Mass deception of false religions represent one example through which mass deception occurs. When a false religion takes root, such as Hinduism, then it's difficult to cause enthusiastic adherents to see the truth—there are not thousands of gods, just one true God—YHWH. I picture whole regions of the earth with powerful Demon-gods holding that particular geography in bondage. When the Demon-gods and Evil Spirits are judged, they no longer can hold people in captivity—people more clearly discern righteousness. The riddance of Demon-gods and Evil Spirits also paves the way for YHWY's people to once again wear His Glory as clothing.

Yeshua encountered two demonized men in the region of the Gadarenes. The name of the region stems from Gadara, which means "thorn hedge." These demon-possessed men wandered in a cemetery. Demons seem to enjoy hanging out among dead bodies. In the Old Testament, a person who touched dead bodies was considered unclean and needed to go through a ceremonial purification (Num. 19:13). Today, many are attracted to skeletons and other images of death. Every altar within the Catholic Church contains bone fragments of dead saints, called "relics"—evidencing current-day demonic activity![32] When the Gadarene demoniacs encountered Yeshua, their response confirmed the scriptures we read in Enoch:

> They lived among the tombs of a cemetery and
> were considered so extremely violent that no one

---

32 Pekarek, Nancy. Diocesan News. "Faithful Gifts: The Church and relics of the saints." *Catholic Diocese of Raleigh.* December 15, 2022. https://dioceseofraleigh.org/news/faithful-gifts-church-and-relics-saints#:~:text=Once%20Emperor%20Constantine%20legalized%20Christianity,relic%2C%20on%20pain%20of%20excommunication.

felt safe passing through that area. The demons screamed at Jesus, shouting, "Son of God, what do you want with us? Leave us alone! Have you come to torment us **before the appointed time**?" (Matt. 8:28b-29, emphasis added).

Notice the demons asked Yeshua if He planned to torment them "before the appointed time." You see, the demons knew they faced a future of torment—a time when they no longer possess authority to terrorize people.

The demons asked Yeshua to allow them to go into a herd of pigs. He gave them permission. "Then the entire herd of crazed pigs stampeded down the steep slope and fell into the water and drowned" (Matt. 8:32b). Pigs are intelligent creatures and animals instinctively want to live. Once the demons entered into the herd of pigs, the pigs all killed themselves by drowning. People that unwittingly accept demons remain tormented by them and many commit suicide, just like the herd of pigs.

So, what fate awaits the Watchers and Evil Spirits after their first judgment? According to Enoch, they both are confined to a dark prison until the great day of judgment, the White Throne Judgment. Enoch describes the initial resultant of the Evil Spirits, offspring of the Watchers and men:

And those men took me and led me up on to the second heaven, and showed me darkness, greater than earthly darkness, and there I saw prisoners hanging, watched, awaiting the great and boundless judgement, and these angels were dark-looking, more than earthly darkness, and incessantly making weeping through all hours.

And I said to the men who were with me: Wherefore are these incessantly tortured? They answered me: These are God's apostates, who obeyed not God's commands, but took counsel with their own will, and turned away with their prince, who also is fastened on the fifth heaven (2 Enoch 7:1-2).

Likewise, the Watchers themselves, fathers of the Evil Spirits, are confined after the first judgment. YHWY confines them to a place called the "fifth heaven":

The men took me on to the fifth heaven and placed me, and there I saw many and countless soldiers, called Grigori, of human appearance, and their size was greater than that of great giants and their faces withered, and the silence of their mouths perpetual, and there was no service on the fifth heaven, and I said to the men who were with me: "Wherefore are these very withered and their faces melancholy, and their mouths silent, and wherefore is there no service on this heaven?"

And they said to me: These are the Grigori, who with their prince Satanail rejected the Lord of light, and after them are those who are held in great darkness on the second heaven, and three of them went down on to earth from the Lord's throne, to the place Ermon, and broke through their vows on the shoulder of the hill Ermon and saw the daughters of men how good they are, and took to themselves wives, and befouled the earth with their deeds, who in all **times of their age** made lawlessness and mixing, and giants are born and marvellous big men and great enmity.

And therefore God judged them with great judgement, and they weep for their brethren and they will be punished on the Lord's great day (2 Enoch 18:1-4, emphasis added).

In the passage, we learn the Watchers, also called Grigori, came down to Earth on Mount Hermon ("hill Ermon" in the passage). Located in the Golan Heights between the current State of Israel and Syria, the peak reaches an altitude of 2,814 meters (9,200 feet). Since 1967, the United Nations (UN) operates a permanent base here, nicknamed "Hermon Hotel," the highest UN position on Earth.[33] I am curious to know what goes on there!

Significantly, the passage above indicates that the prince of the Grigori (Watchers) is Satanail, indicating Satan's supremacy over the clan of Watchers and Evil Spirits. As discussed earlier, Satan tempted man in the Garden of Eden. He later tempted Yeshua himself, although He passed the test. I emphasized in bold the phrase "times of their age" in the passage from Enoch. After Adam relinquished his

---

[33] Wikipedia. 2024. "Mount Hermon." *Wikimedia Foundation*. Last modified March 6, 2024. https://en.wikipedia.org/wiki/Mount_Hermon).

authority to Satan in the Garden of Eden, Satan became the god of the age. Listen to this passage:

> Even if our gospel message is veiled, it is only veiled to those who are perishing, for their minds have been **blinded by the god of this age**, leaving them in unbelief. Their blindness keeps them from seeing the dayspring light of the wonderful news **of the glory of Jesus Christ**, who is the *divine* image of God (2 Cor. 4:3-4, emphasis added).

Many translators refer to Satan as "god of this world" in the same verse. This mistranslation gives Satan more power than he deserves in the minds of Christians. Adam's sin gave Satan the power to rule the age, not the power to permanently rule Earth! As "god of this age," Satan's henchmen possessed the ability to blind only those who already perish, to keep them from understanding the wonderful news of the *Glory* of Yeshua! You see, not everyone hungers for the Glory. Not everyone wants to serve YHWY. Those that do want YHWY find Him regardless of any veil put in place upon them by Satan. *Satan loses his ability to rule at the end of the age.*

Many scholars agree that YHWY transfigured Yeshua into a glorious state on the top of Mount Hermon. This transfiguration serves as a sign of the future destiny of YHWY's people. YHWY promises to fill the earth with His Glory and His people are once again clothed in Glory at a time when Demon-gods and Evil Spirits no longer rule the age. The veil of deception on man shatters! The Stone Judgment ushers in the next age.

A-Team and B-Team Vanish

Like many in Texas, I played high school football. I played offensive line even though I only weighed about 185 pounds. I compensated for my lack of mass with speed and wit! On most football teams, "starters" are the best players who play the A-team. Behind the A-team falls the B-team, C-team and so forth, depending on the size of the overall team. When the team scores a substantial lead, the coach may play the B-team players or even the C-team. However, typically the non-starters don't play unless a player on the A-team receives an injury.

The Demon-gods and Evil Spirits represent Satan's A-team and his B-team, respectively. They have unique powers to cast veils over whole territories on Earth and keep vast numbers of people deceived. Because the Evil Spirits are part-human and part-sons of God, they possess a unique understanding of the human condition and can easily take over and transform people into evil monsters. When YHWY imprisons them in the fifth and second heavens, Satan cannot exercise the same level of deception on humanity through them—he's left with his C-team, the Unclean Spirits.

A passage in Revelation describes all three classes of fallen spirits, "Fallen, fallen is Babylon the great! She has become a demonic dwelling place, a prison for every unclean spirit, unclean bird, and every unclean, detestable beast" (Rev 18:2). The unclean bird in this passage refer to Evil

Spirits, spirits of the Nephilim who—like vultures—ate carcasses of men in ancient times. Detestable beasts refer to Demon-gods, the spirits of the Watchers, or fallen "sons of God." Finally, Unclean Spirits refer to fallen angels, who defected alongside Satan when he rebelled against YHWY.

Satan himself and his Unclean Spirits won't be bound until the Millennial Reign of Christ, the second period in the Kingdom Age when Yeshua rules as King on Earth. However, Satan loses his A-team and B-Team in the Stone Judgment. When this happens, mass deceptions and false religions simply fall apart. We already see some of this happening today!

The King Stone

I wrote extensively concerning the Stone Judgment in my books *KAS* and *Blast of Fire.* However, I now realize the Stone Judgment is vastly more eventful than I previously understood. The Stone Judgment includes a Shaking of Nations, a shaking of Earth and the heavens, and the release of YHWY's consuming fire, all happening in a short period of time. We encounter Yeshua in the clouds at the end of the Stone Judgment. The Stone Judgment begins with a Shaking of Nations and ends with a Fire Judgment. The Stone Judgment encompasses all wicked people, Watchers and Evil Spirits. It ushers in the fullness of our salvation and YHWY's Kingdom Age on Earth. The old age ends with the Stone Judgment.

The Stone Judgment event in the Bible arguably reigns supreme over the Great Flood. For one, it adjudicates a longer period of evil—roughly 5,000 years. The Great Flood only judged evil committed over a thousand years or so by the Watchers, who mated with women and corrupted society. In addition, the Great Flood failed to restore man to the state of Glory. The Stone Judgment ends the current age and ushers in the Glory.

The Bible contains *scores* of scriptures on the Stone Judgment! We call it the Stone Judgment because of the original reference in the book of Daniel. King Nebuchadnezzar of Babylon dreamed a dream and could not remember it. The prophet Daniel explained to the king his dream:

> Your Majesty, what you saw standing in front of you was a huge and terrifying statue, shining brightly. Its head was made of gold, its chest and arms were silver, and from its waist down to its knees, it was bronze. From there to its ankles it was iron, and its feet were a mixture of iron and clay.
>
> As you watched, a stone was cut from a mountain—but not by human hands. The stone struck the feet, completely shattering the iron and clay. Then the iron, the clay, the bronze, the silver, and the gold were crushed and blown away without a trace, like husks of wheat at threshing time. But the stone became a tremendous mountain that covered the entire earth (Dan. 2:31-35 CEV).

Daniel interpreted the first part of the dream, the statue, as a series of four successive empires. These included Babylon, Medo-Persia, Greece and Rome. The feet of iron and clay represent revived and divided Rome and a unification of false religion (clay) with a warlike state (iron). Rome represents the Fourth Beast, the fourth and most deadly empire.

The clay feet of the statue represent the religious foundation of revived Rome, namely false Christianity and false Judaism inextricably linked to a warlike government. It also symbolizes an unstable, crumbling union between two incompatible kingdoms, just as iron and clay don't stick together (Dan. 2:43). Daniel plainly interprets the last part of the dream:

> In the days of those kings *of iron and clay*, the God of heaven will set up an eternal kingdom that will never be destroyed nor ruled by other people. It will shatter and bring all other kingdoms to an end, and it will stand forever! This is the meaning of what you saw in your vision: a rock cut out of a mountain—but not by human hands—a rock that shattered the iron, the bronze, the clay, the silver, and the gold to pieces is *his eternal kingdom* (Dan. 2:44-45a TPT).

The Stone Judgment represents the coming of the Kingdom of YHWY (the "eternal kingdom"). The advent of the eternal kingdom judges and replaces the old system of demonic rule on Earth and ends Satan's unrestrained dominion.

The stone made without hands depicts Yeshua. Peter describes Yeshua as "the stone you masons threw out, which is now the cornerstone" (Acts 4:11 MSG). Yeshua reigns as the cornerstone of the Kingdom of YHWY. Yeshua stands as the rock of our salvation (Ps. 62:6). When Daniel prophesied the rock would shatter the statue, he referred to Yeshua judging the world system—the corrupt Fourth Beast. Furthermore, the stone then grows into a large mountain and fills the earth, symbolizing the gradational development of the Kingdom of Heaven on Earth. In *Blast of Fire*, I detailed how Yeshua judges the Fourth Beast as the lion from the forest.[34] Yeshua judging the Fourth Beast on behalf of the Most High fulfills the scripture:

> Thrones were set up while I was watching, and the Eternal God took his place. His clothing and his hair were white as snow. His throne was a blazing fire with fiery wheels, and flames were dashing out from all around him. Countless thousands were standing there to serve him. The time of judgment began, and the books were opened.
>
> I watched closely to see what would happen to this smaller horn because of the arrogant things it was saying. Then before my very eyes, the fourth beast was killed and its body destroyed by fire (Dan. 7:9-11 CEV).

---

[34] Thomas, *Blast of Fire*, 123-144.

According to this passage, the Most High (the "Eternal God") convenes in the Court of Heaven. Then He judges the Fourth Beast—the time of judgment *begins*. The Fourth Beast subsequently dies and his body destroyed by *fire*. Note Daniel references the Little Horn, which controls the Fourth Beast. This horn comes from an insignificant race and defeats three mighty horns of the ten-horned Fourth Beast with *no army*.

Devastation of the Fourth Beast happens slowly at first, and then culminates in a single day. "But the judgment shall be set [by the court of the Most High], and they shall take away his dominion to consume it [gradually] and to destroy it [suddenly] in the end" (Dan. 7:26 AMPC). But when does the Stone Judgment begin? I believe the judgment of the Fourth Beast in the Court of Heaven occurred on September 23, 2017, as evidenced by a rare alignment of the stars.

A Sign in the Stars

On September 23, 2017, a few months into President Trump's first term, the heavens showed us an extremely rare sign involving the constellations Virgo and Leo.[35] Many believe the alignment of the stars, Sun, and Moon on this day pointed to the woman in Revelation 12 now wearing a fully formed crown with 12 stars, about to give birth. When His disciples asked Yeshua the signs of the end of the age in Matt 24:3, Yeshua explained that wars, rumors of wars, and other signs are really birth pangs of something new. The something new alludes to the next age—the Kingdom Age.

---

[35] "Solar Eclipse, September 23, 2017 and Celestial Signs of Revelation 12." *Prayer in Every City.* August 19, 2017. https://prayerineverycity.com/2017/08/19/solar-eclipse-september-23-2017-celestial-signs-of-revelation-12/

The sign in the heavens depicting the woman in Revelation 12:1-2 is significant. Revelation chapter 12 describes the Blood Wars that would endure between Mary's seed (the seed of Jacob), Believers in Yeshua—and Satan. The time frame given for the persecution in Revelation 12:14 (CEV) includes "a time, two times, and half a time"—the same time frame as the rule of the Roman system, the Fourth Beast. So when we saw the signs in the constellations in 2017, what did YHWY show us?

The Bible says after the judgment of the Fourth Beast in the Court of Heaven, he dies slowly at first, then suddenly, ending in a single day. In the book of 2 Esdras, YHWY gave Ezra a dream of the three-headed eagle, representing the Roman system, the Fourth Beast. In 2 Esdras 11, we learn that Yeshua, the lion of the tribe of Judah, judges the Fourth Beast face-to-face on behalf of the Most High. In the next couple chapters of 2 Esdras, YHWY gives Ezra another vision. Here, he sees the man-from-the-sea, a man who comes out of the world and ushers in peace. Prophetically, I believe this man-from-the-sea points to President Trump.

In Chapter 5, I explained the term of the Fourth Beast lease to exercise tyranny on Earth lasts 2,150 years. The sign in the heavens on September 23, 2017 occurred in the 2,150th year after the Roman deep state assassinated Tiberius Gracchus, marking the beginning of the Fourth Beast in the eyes of YHWY. This demonstrates YHWY's precision regarding His immaculate plan for humanity!

Seven Year Shaking

When YHWY gave Ezra the vision of the lion judging the Fourth Beast, he told him to wait seven days before He showed him the vision of the man-from-the-sea. During the seven days, YHWY instructed Ezra to roam the fields and eat flowers (2 Esd. 12:39-51). In other words, Ezra should rest. Also, during the seven days, the townspeople came out and wailed at their condition and Ezra did his best to calm them down. The wailing masses indicate the condition of many in the Ekklesia today—panicked by circumstances. The Father mercifully gives prophetic words almost daily through His vessels Julie Green, Donna Rigney, Barry Wunsch and others to settle the Ekklesia during this trying time—however, the saints are tired and worn out. In contrast to the way circumstances appear, we live in the best time ever. Don't panic! Biblical prophecy plays out in front of our very eyes with our best days ahead of us!

In Ezra's next vision after the seven days, YHWY showed him how the man-from-the-sea leads humanity into great victory and peace. I believe the seven days between the initial judgment of the Fourth Beast and the final victory represent seven years. If the heavenly sign on September 23, 2017 represented the day that Yeshua judged the Fourth Beast in the spirit realm, then this would mean that September 23, 2024 would signal the time of defeat in the natural of the Fourth Beast, when the man-from-the-sea comes out of the mountain and declares peace. This would partially complete the Shaking of Nations, a first step towards the completion of the Stone Judgment.

The Shaking of Nations initiates with military forces, assisted by angelic hosts. However, the Stone Judgment ends with a supernatural, angelic judgment of all evil in the Fire Judgment.

Evil "Raptured"

The evangelical church teaches that the Rapture removes the righteous from the earth. However, the opposite stands true —evil people are removed from Earth. YHWY removes all unrighteous men and women from Earth during the Stone Judgment. Consider this passage:

> Concerning that day and exact hour, no one knows when it will arrive, not even the angels of heaven—only the Father knows. For it will be exactly like it was in the days of Noah when the Son of Man appears. Before the flood, people lived their lives eating, drinking, marrying, and having children. They didn't realize the end was near until Noah entered the ark, and then suddenly, the flood came and took them all away in judgment. It will happen the same way when the Son of Man appears.
>
> At that time, two men will be working on the farm; one will be taken away **in judgment**, the other left. Two women will be grinding grain; one will be taken away **in judgment**, the other left. This is why you must stay alert: because no one knows the day your Lord will come (Matt. 24:36-42 TPT, emphasis added).

Many churches teach that *Christians* get taken from the field and the granary in the Rapture. However, The Passion Translation accurately explains the ones taken represent *non-Believers*, removed in judgment. Note the circumstance mirrors the time of Noah before the Great Flood. Men live their lives normally, then the judgment comes. The Son of YHWY, Yeshua, appears around the same time!

Earlier in the same chapter in Matthew, Yeshua explains the signs of His appearing:

> The appearing of the Son of Man will burst forth with the brightness of a lightning strike that shines from one end of the sky to the other, illuminating the earth. How do birds of prey know where the dead body is? They just know instinctively, and so you will know when I appear. (Matt. 24:27-28).

The word "appearing" in the passage also means presence. Yeshua does not come back to rule the earth in the flesh at this time. He comes bringing the Glory and performs a mighty miracle—the resurrection of the dead.

The book of Malachi describes the final day of the Stone Judgment, especially highlighting how it ends with the consuming fire of YHWY. This passage also confirms the removal of evil and the Glory and ecstatic victory that follow:

> The day of judgment is certain to come. And it will be like a red-hot furnace with flames that **burn up proud and sinful people**, as though they were straw. Not a branch or a root will be left. I,

the LORD All-Powerful, have spoken! But for you that honor my name, **victory will shine like the sun with healing in its rays**, and you will jump around like calves at play. When I come to bring justice, you will trample those who are evil, as though they were ashes under your feet. I, the LORD All-Powerful, have spoken! (Mal. 4:1–3 CEV, emphasis added).

As with all other judgments in the Bible, the Stone Judgment leads to victory. However, the Stone Judgment leads to complete victory—victory over death. In future chapters, I cover the complete timeline of events during the Stone Judgment, including the final event—the Fire Judgment.

7. Apokatastasis

For he must remain in heaven until the restoration of
all things has taken place...

— Acts 3:21 TPT

I grew up in an evangelical church that taught me soon the
Rapture takes out fellow Believers. The Rapture describes an
event when Yeshua brings His bride to Heaven for the
Marriage Supper of the Lamb celebration. After this, those
that remain on Earth suffer a brutal time of persecution,
called the Great Tribulation. During the Great Tribulation, an
anti-Christ rules the world and causes extreme devastation. I
agree with everything taught with one important exception

—the Rapture occurs in a time of great victory, not defeat. The Rapture does not rescue Christians from defeat at the hands of a cruel world. The Ekklesia does not surrender the earth to Satan in the Rapture.

The Rapture of the righteous in times of duress represents a relatively recent teaching that goes back to 1839 —codified in the footnotes of the Scofield Bible. Currently, over 60% of the evangelical church believes the biblical rapture event happens next. However, most believe the Rapture occurs in times of defeat for the Ekklesia, during the time of an evil, exceedingly dark world. In a recent interview with Eric Metaxas, I discussed the fruit of this teaching— how it took the Ekklesia out of the game in the geopolitical arena.[36] If we await a rescue, then most don't bother to engage geopolitically. Several pastors openly criticized both of us for discussing an alternative to the pre-tribulation rapture doctrine. Pastor Rob McCoy of GodSpeak church in California, observing the visceral reaction by some, preached a Sunday morning sermon calling for peace, and also pointing out that a super-majority within the evangelical church don't even bother to vote, much less get involved on school boards or in politics.[37]

The early Ekklesia focused on when Yeshua would establish His Kingdom *on Earth*. When Yeshua appeared to the disciples after His resurrection they clearly asked Him when He would establish His Kingdom, for it says, "During

---

[36] "Benjamin Thomas: The Sixth Seal in Revelation & The Next MAJOR Biblical Event." https://www.youtube.com/@EricMetaxasTBN. February 13, 2024. Video, https://www.youtube.com/watch?v=SfhwpYJ6-bs.

[37] "Endeaver To Unify." https://www.youtube.com/@GodspeakCalvaryChapel. February 25, 2024. Video, https://www.youtube.com/watch?v=Rn-peAHiMV8

these encounters, he taught them the truths of God's kingdom realm" (Acts 1:3b). They did not ask Him when He would rescue them from evil. They had no concept of a surrender to Satan. After spending time with Yeshua face-to-face after His resurrection, the disciples experienced the infilling of the Holy Spirit and then became emboldened, mighty warriors for Christ.

Peter, now transformed from a Christ denier to a Soldier Saint, preached a fiery message in Acts chapter three that infuriated the Jews, particularly the politically oriented Sadducee elders who demonstrated a cozy relationship with the Roman leaders at the time. Consider Peter's message to this class of politically connected Jewish leaders:

> My fellow Jews, I realize that neither you nor your leaders realized the grave mistake you made. But in spite of what you've done, God has fulfilled what he foretold through the prophets long ago about the sufferings of his Anointed One. And now you must repent and turn back to God so that your sins will be removed, and so that times of refreshing will stream from the Lord's presence. And he will send you Jesus, the Messiah, the appointed one. **For he must remain in heaven until the restoration of all things has taken place,** *fulfilling everything that God said* **long ago through his holy prophets**. For has not Moses told us:
>
> "The Lord your God will raise up a prophet from among you who is like me. Listen to him and

follow everything he tells you. Every person who disobeys that prophet will be cut off and completely destroyed" (Acts 3:17-23, emphasis added).

We discover in the next chapter of Acts that Peter's message angered the priests, the captain of the temple police, and the Sadducees so much they arrested Peter and John during their message! What angered them so much? Something triggered these politically motivated religious teachers—they refused to hear Peter and John. Was it the part about Yeshua establishing His Kingdom and restoring all things? Or perhaps the part about all disobedient people facing destruction? Religious people love to hear about a future rescue. They hate to hear about a judgment and a kingdom here on Earth. Satan *loathes* hearing about the future when his kingdom goes away, he loses his followers, and YHWY establishes the Kingdom of the righteous.

In Acts 3:21, the Bible says that Yeshua *remains in Heaven* until the restoration of all things has taken place. In The Passion Translation, a footnote elaborates on the word restoration. It says:

> The word *restoration* in Greek is *apokatastasis*, which infers the restoration of creation to the state of existence **before the fall**, but also Davidic covenant being restored. Luke's choice of the Greek word found only here in the New Testament is noteworthy. It is a medical term that means

"restoration of perfect health" (Acts 3:21, TPT commentary, emphasis added).

Some say restoration also applies to Satan and his angels—a false doctrine. From Acts 3:23, in the final part of the passage describing the restoration, evil ones are destroyed.

Does the passage we read in Acts even faintly resemble the Rapture in times of duress currently taught in the evangelical church? It says that Yeshua *remains in Heaven* until the restoration of all things has taken place, a word meaning total restoration on Earth—a restoration to the time *before the Fall in the Garden of Eden!* This happens *before* He returns to rule Earth in the flesh! Then in Acts 3:23 it says that those who disobey are cut off and completely destroyed. Could this passage refer to the Stone Judgment spoken of by Daniel, when the Roman system under which we suffer receives judgment and a mountain made without hands fills the earth? How about the sixth seal in the book of Revelation 6:12-17, when the evil nobles of the earth are judged by the lamb of YHWY *before* the seventh seal, the time of the Great Tribulation?

Folks, it's obvious the message of restoring the earth and making things right *before* Yeshua returns to rule made the religious people furious in the book of Acts. Nothing has changed. The religious today also resist when we talk about YHWY's Kingdom on Earth.

Early Ekklesia Understanding

The early Ekklesia understood YHWY intended to establish His Kingdom on Earth before returning to rule physically. Many promises made to Adam, Moses, Abraham, David, Daniel, and others remained unrealized, and they knew YHWY kept ALL His promises. For instance, in Hebrews we learn "that there is still a full and complete 'rest' waiting for believers to experience" (Heb. 6:9). The "complete rest" refers to the Sabbath rest for humanity, the seventh day of humanity.

The early Ekklesia studied many prophetic writings of which the evangelical church today remains ignorant. These include the books of Enoch, Esdras, Baruch, Jubilees and others. Recently I enjoyed rapport over dinner with a Greek Orthodox priest. I asked him which books the Greek Orthodox Bible contained. It surprised me to learn that the Greek Orthodox Bible contains 79 books, compared to the evangelical church's 66! But what do the other 13 books say about End Times?

I decided to study all the "extra-biblical books" to discern what they said about End Times. I focused my energies on passages that foretold the future. After reading literally hundreds of pages, many passages jumped out at me —the Holy Spirit wanted me to see them. I noticed passages that Yeshua quoted, like "The last shall be first, and the first last" (Matt 20:16 ASV) likely came from 2 Baruch 30:2. While these books are not "canon" for evangelicals, Yeshua read and knew them! I decided to follow Yeshua's lead and read the books.

I discovered *all* these books told the same remarkable story concerning the end of the age. The old age ends, and a new one begins. At the end of the old age, a judgment occurs. This judgment removes pagan governments and replaces them with the Kingdom of YHWY. Evil people are removed. Demon-gods and Evil Spirits are bound. The dead in Christ are resurrected. The Glory of YHWY clothes His people once again. We encounter Yeshua in the clouds (He later comes to Earth on a white horse). Many signs in the sky accompany the judgment. Wow, what a story, right? The early Ekklesia knew this story because they read the ancient scrolls.

The apostles, Paul, John the Revelator and others wrote about YHWY's amazing future plan and provided fragments and clues in the 66 books of the evangelical church "canon." The book of Revelation, which church leaders almost didn't include in our "canon," tells this story accurately, although not in sequential format. However, without the benefit of the other books, it's somewhat difficult to comprehend. So why did past leaders remove the books from canon?

When Christianity became the state religion of the Roman Empire in the fourth century, the Roman church began to teach the state's official version of Christianity represented the Kingdom of God, the "Divine institution." I believe the Roman church needed the "extra-biblical books" removed from circulation to remove challenges to the deception that the "infallible" Roman church represented God's Kingdom on Earth.

In addition, the Pharisees rejected Yeshua when He appeared. Many of the "extra-biblical books" provided concise messianic prophecies further proving that Yeshua is the anointed Messiah. To hang onto power, the Pharisees needed to propagate doubt regarding specific books pointing to Yeshua. At the same time, Jewish elders gave ever increasing credence to their traditions and commentary (that Yeshua openly criticized during His earthly ministry) and began to point to the Talmud as the supreme law.

During an evil era, religious leaders made decisions to omit ancient scrolls from "canon." During this era, known as the Middle Ages, the same religious leaders made it difficult for humanity to access *any* biblical texts. The Bible foretold the very power structure of the Fourth Beast, including the false shepherds of Christianity and Judaism, would face judgment and disintegrate during the Stone Judgment. Many of the apocalyptic scrolls clearly outlining the demise of the religious institutions constitute the very volumes missing from the evangelical Bible today. It should come as no surprise to the awakened Ekklesia that men made decisions to eliminate important books that described their own demise prior to YHWY's Kingdom Age.

Esau's Age of Days

The early Ekklesia knew the present age would end, and a new one would begin *on the same earth*. It's clear from their writings they studied the books of Esdras, Enoch, Baruch, and others. The old age contained 12 parts, or days. We live in the *final seconds* of the old age. Listen to how Ezra described the age:

The age has lost its youth, and the times begin to grow old. For the age is divided into twelve parts, and nine of its parts have already passed, as well as half of the tenth part; so two of its parts remain, besides half of the tenth part. (2 Esd. 14:10-12 NRSV).

We learn that the age has 12 parts, or days. We know that days in the Bible can mean 1,000 years, according to 2 Peter 3:8. During the first six days, or 6,000 years of the age, YHWY created life on Earth. (See Genesis 1). The last six days of the age are days of humanity. Following Adam's transgression in the Garden of Eden, Satan ruled for the next six days, or 6,000 years of humanity. However, Satan's rule ends when the old age ends. The next age represents YHWY's Kingdom Age.

YHWY told Ezra that only two and half parts (or days) remained—2,500 years. YHWY spoke to Ezra about 2,500 years ago! In my book, *Blast of Fire*, I lay out a timeline of all 12 days of the age along with important biblical and prophetic events for each day of the age.[38] Ezra describes how the world gets more evil as the age progresses:

For evils worse than those that you have now seen happen shall take place hereafter. For the weaker the world becomes through old age, the more shall evils be increased upon its inhabitants. Truth shall go farther away, and falsehood shall come

---

[38] Thomas, *Blast of Fire,* "Figure 3: Days of the Current Age, Followed by Stone Judgment and Kingdom Age of the Saints." p. 168.

near. For the eagle that you saw in the vision is already hurrying to come (2 Esd. 14:16-18).

In the passage we learn that the older the age becomes, the more evil it becomes—more and more deception comes over the people. At the end of this passage, it says the eagle hurries to come. This eagle in the passage points to the evil three-headed eagle that represents the Roman Empire. Folks, Rome *never died*. We still suffer under a Roman system, led by three city-state heads, representing the three heads of the evil eagle.

So when we talk about the "last days," we actually refer to the last days of the 12-day age YHWY spoke to Ezra about. Evil did increase towards the end of the age! However, the declining evil age imminently ends. We live in the last seconds of the last day of an old age, and the end of the sixth day of humanity, about to start our seventh day rest. When the age ends, the times of the Gentiles ends. Satan's ability to afflict YHWY's people ends at the end of the current age!

Esau leads the current age of bondage. The Bible says the present age ends with Esau, and the age that follows begins with Jacob:

> He said to me, "From Abraham to Isaac, because from him were born Jacob and Esau, for Jacob's hand held Esau's heel from the beginning. Now Esau is the end of this age, and Jacob is the beginning of the age that follows" (2 Esd. 6:8-9).

Esau, also known as Edom, despised his birthright and traded it to Jacob, despite firstborn status. He rejected YHWY's ways, and instead chose Satan's ways. Esau's offspring ultimately became arch enemies of the seed of Jacob, the Edomites. Isaac's blessing of Esau foretold Esau's future, that he would break free from Jacob's yoke, live by the sword, and live away from the richness of the earth or the dew of heaven (Gen. 27:39-40). According to the *Apocalypse of Abraham*, YHWY applies the dew of Heaven to awaken the dead (vs. 25). So in Isaac's blessing of Esau, he actually pronounced a curse on Esau's seed, because of his unrighteous heart toward YHWY. Under this curse, Esau's descendants would not participate in the resurrection of the righteous dead, which I discuss in Chapter 10.

The prophet Obadiah prophesied the curse of Edom (or Esau) breaks when YHWY judges the nations:

> The day is coming when I, the LORD, will judge the nations. And, Edom, you will pay in full for what you have done. I forced the people of Judah to drink the wine of my anger on my sacred mountain. Soon the neighboring nations must drink their fill—then vanish without a trace.
>
> The LORD's people who escape will go to Mount Zion, and it will be holy. Then Jacob's descendants will capture the land of those who took their land. Israel will be a fire, and Edom will be straw **going up in flames**. The LORD has spoken! (Obad. 15-18 CEV, emphasis added).

Notice Obadiah also mentions a judgment of fire on Edom, and that Israel (the seed of Jacob) represents the fire that burns up the "straw" of Edom! When YHWY speaks of judging Edom, He also refers to Rome. Roman leadership originate from Edomites, descendants of Esau.[39]

A worldwide awakening occurs as I write this book that correctly identifies the seed of Jacob among us. The masses rapidly "rediscover" the lost tribes of Israel. Society soon discovers many great leaders serve Yeshua as they wage a fierce battle to overturn the seed of Esau. Many of these leaders originate from the seed of Jacob. Soldier Saints courageously expose the false Israel narrative, and the truth swiftly spreads throughout the Ekklesia.

Yeshua called Esau's age the Times of the Gentiles in the Gospel of Luke. Speaking of the seed of Jacob, He said:

> They will fall by the mouth and the edge of the sword and will be led away as captives to and among all nations; and Jerusalem will be trodden down by the Gentiles **until the times of the Gentiles are fulfilled** (completed) (Luke 21:24 AMPC, emphasis added).

The Passion Translation ends Luke 21:24 with, "And Jerusalem shall be trampled down by nations until the days of world empires come to an end." Gentile means pagan, or people without YHWY. The nations of the earth today represent pagan nations. The treachery of the nations pummeled the Ekklesia for the last two thousand years.

---

[39] Beeston, William. *The Roman Empire of the Edomite* (np: 1858), 4.

Rome successfully quenched the revival in the book of Acts, scattering the early Ekklesia. The same wicked players destroyed the Judean temple in AD 70.

True saints of YHWY experienced brutal persecution for the last two thousand years. The seed of Esau continues to trample Jerusalem even until now. As discussed in Chapter 3, modern-day Pharisees currently governing the State of Israel are not the true seed of Jacob, but rather usurpers and impostors. This soon changes when the era of evil world empires wraps up at the conclusion of the age.

Everything that God Said

Earlier we read, "For he must remain in heaven until the restoration of all things has taken place, *fulfilling everything that God said* long ago through his holy prophets" (Acts 3:21 TPT). So what did the prophets' presage that needs to come to pass before things are made right?

Many unrealized prophecies found in scripture relate to YHWY's judgment. Saints should embrace judgment, because judgment in the Bible leads to victory. YHWY's judgment leads to a redemption of His people—setting us free from bondage. We should not fear judgment, but rather extol judgment. If we desire YHWY's Glory, we must embrace His judgment. If we want true revival, we must allow YHWY to purify our hearts and destroy the corrupt institutions around us quenching the revival. YHWY says, "For a day of vengeance was in my heart, and the time for my redeeming work had come" (Isa. 63:4). This scripture couples vengeance with redemption!

YHWY ushers His people into the next age by first purifying His body and ridding the world of evil. *Many unfulfilled prophecies link YHWY's judgment with His coming Glory!* Let's discuss six unfulfilled promises YHWY made through the prophets of old.

Purification of YHWY's Household

For the time has come for judgment, and it must begin with God's household (1 Pet. 4:17).

YHWY's judgment begins in His own household. Pastors, teachers and other church leaders tied up in sexual sin or the exploitation of children are exposed. *No one* involved in child-trafficking will survive. Churches that yielded to the demonic LGTBQ+ agenda don't survive. Churches that received funds to promote the poisonous Covid-19 vaccine or other sinister government programs are exposed. Churches that deny the power of the Holy Spirit and miracles will either wake up to the revival or dwindle in attendance—surviving churches must satisfy people's hunger for the power of YHWY.

Although already begun, I believe the purification of YHWY's household heats up in the Summer of 2024 and continues for the next couple of years. The fall of prominent ministers and denominations represents a sign that judgment in the "house of the Lord" begins.

Judgment of the Whore of Babylon

*Fallen, fallen is Babylon the great! She has become a
demonic dwelling place, a prison for every unclean
spirit, unclean bird, and every unclean, detestable
beast. All the nations have drunk of the wine of her
immoral passion, and the kings of the earth have
committed fornication with her, and merchants of the
earth have grown wealthy because of her power and
luxury (Rev 18:2b-3).*

The Catholic Church, the state church of Rome, represents an
ungodly alignment between a warlike state and religion, iron
and clay, respectively. History proves the church squashed
revival, hid the Bible from the people, and became wealthy
beyond imagination through sinister alliances with
governments and commercial interests around the world.
From the beginning, the Catholic Church mixed paganism
with Christian practice, and foisted it on the people as the
"true" Ekklesia.

Revelation 18:2-3 indicates every type of evil demonic
force dwells within the Whore of Babylon. It mentions that
"all nations" drank her wine and merchants of the earth
grew wealthy because of her power. These scriptures point to
businesses aligned with the sinister objectives of the Fourth
Beast and Whore of Babylon, which profit from destructive
practices—religion became a business under the Fourth
Beast.

The pope sits under a gigantic sculpture called "The
Resurrection" in the Vatican. This sculpture represents not

the resurrection of Christ (He's already risen), but the rising of a disfigured Demon-god surrounded by other spirits. This sculpture sits within the jaws of a gigantic serpent. Despite commentary on the Internet normalizing this sculpture, even a child recognizes the evil nature of the symbolism. I showed my 10-year-old a picture of "The Resurrection" sculpture and he said, "What *is* that?!" Other Vatican chambers feature sculptures to honor murderous leaders such as Adam Weishaupt, founder of the Bavarian Illuminati and notorious Satan-worshiper.[40]

Yet, many faithful Catholics know Yeshua, and will suffer confusion during the judgment of the Catholic Church leadership. They will need our help to recover—we need to serve them as tender guides after judgment falls on their religion.

Judgment of False Shepherds of Israel

Woe to those who drag behind them their guilt with ropes made of lies—straining and tugging, harnessed to their bondage! They say, "May God hurry up and bring his judgment so that we can see it once and for all! Let the prophetic plan of the Holy One of Israel quickly come to pass so that we can see what it is!
(Isa. 5:18-19)

The Chabad and other senior leadership within modern Rabbinic Judaism hatched a plan years ago to make the end of the age come in the form of their liking, with them still in

---

[40] Windrod, Gerald B. *Adam Weishaupt: A Human Devil.* Wichita: Defender Publishers, 1935.

control. Carefully hidden in the Babylonian Talmud remains a plan to dominate all other races. The New World Order reflects a plan of destruction for the human race *hatched by* Jewish leaders. Klaus Schwab, Noah Harari and countless others devising the evil plan claim Judaism as their faith. Communism, a wicked construct fathered by atheist Jew Karl Marx, murdered nearly 150 million people in the last century alone in "revolutions" within Russia and China.[41]

The words of Jewish leaders explain the sinister nature of the death-cult perfectly. At the funeral of Grand Rabbi Simeon Ben-Judah in 1869, Rabbi Reichorn made the following revealing statement:[42]

> Thanks to the terrible power of our International Banks, we have forced the Christians into wars without number. Wars have special value for Jews, since Christians massacre each other and make more room for us Jews. Wars are the Jews' Harvest, the Jew banks grow fat on Christian wars. Over one hundred million Christians have been swept off the face of the earth by wars, and the end is not yet.

The average person cannot comprehend the breathtakingly evil agenda of false Jews. YHWY exposes every lie that induced nations to send their young people into banker's wars.

---

[41]   Valerie Strauss and Daniel Southerl, "How Many Died? New Evidence Suggests Far Higher Numbers for the Victims of Mao Zedong's Era," *Washington Post*, July 17, 1994, and Alexander Solzhenitsyn, Gulag Archipelago Two (1918-1956) (New York: Harper & Row, 1975), 10.

[42]   Hitchcock, Andrew Carrington. *The Synagogue of Satan*. (Austin: RiverCrest Publishing, 2009), 73.

Benjamin Netenyahu represents the modern-day king of Assyria. Genetically, Netenyahu and others in the Khazarian mafia come from an Ugrian-Turkic race, with no Hebrew blood whatsoever.[43] The Bible spells out their doom in the Stone Judgment:

> But when the Lord has carried out his purpose on Mount Zion and Jerusalem, he will punish the king of Assyria because of his overbearing arrogance and unrestrained pride! He boasted, "Look what I have done by the strength of my hand and by my wisdom. See how clever I am! I have erased the borders of nations and plundered their treasures. I have been like a mighty conqueror, subduing those in strong fortresses. I seized their wealth as one who found an *unprotected* nest. As one who gathers eggs that have left behind, so I gathered the wealth of the world. And the young birds could neither move a wing nor even open their mouths to peep!"...
>
> Therefore, the sovereign Lord YAHWEH, Commander of Angel Armies, will send a **devastating plague** among Assyria's proud warriors. Yes, the "glory" of Assyria will be burned and go up in smoke! For the light of Israel will become a **fire in their midst, and the Holy One will become a flame**! He will consume the

---

43   Ofer Aderet, "The Jewish People's Ultimate Treasure Hunt," *Haaretz*, December 28, 2012, www.haaretz.com/2012-12-28/ty-article/.premium/the-jewish-peoples-ultimate-treasure-hunt/0000017f-f70a-d47e-a37f-ff3e820d0000.

thorns and thistles of the Assyrian king in one day! (Isa. 10:12-14, 16-18, emphasis added).

The description above offers a detailed overview of the Khazarian mafia's agenda, which includes erasing national borders, plundering the treasures of nations, and placing humanity under brutal control. YHWY sends a deadly plague among the Khazarian leadership. Those who survive the plague are destroyed by the Fire Judgment.

The false Jews of today handsomely compensate pastors, politicians, and others to promote their false "God's chosen people" narrative. It's time for church leaders to publicly repent for assisting in this sinister agenda or potentially face the same fate.

Lifting of the Veil of Deception

And on this mountain he will destroy the shroud wrapped around all the people, the veil spread over all nations. It is the gloom of death (Isa. 25:7-8a)!

A veil of deception currently surrounds the nations. It allows massive deceit, false religions and other forms of hypnosis to remain in place and fool people. Recall from 2 Esdras that at the end of the old age, "Truth shall go farther away, and falsehood shall come near" (2 Esd. 14:18 NRSV). Yeshua warned at the end of the age, "deception will run rampant. So beware that you are not fooled!" (Matt. 24:4 TPT). The veil of deception currently blankets the eyes of men and nations with falsehood. In the passage above, Isaiah foretells the shroud wraps around *all the people* and spreads over *all nations*! If you are like me, and recognize you once believed lies, rejoice! Be thankful that YHWY set you free.

The mountain of the Kingdom of YHWY destroys the veil, or shroud of deception. In the TPT footnotes on Isaiah 25:7, the shroud translates to "face of the shroud." Who is the face of the shroud of deception? As discussed in Chapter 6, the Demon-gods and Evil Spirits are judged and removed in the Stone Judgment. Their removal permanently destroys the shroud of deception. The names of the Demon-gods behind the Fourth Beast and Little Horn are Leviathan and Behemoth, respectively. The judgment of both in the Court of Heaven and the subsequent demolition of their power structures, including the mainstream media, initiates the relaxation of the grip of deception, even before the final Fire Judgment.

Already, it feels like the shroud dissolves. Billions of people worldwide are waking up to deception and formerly taboo topics (like the tyranny of nations, private-central-banking, bankers' wars, etc.) the masses begin to comprehend. The enemy lost his cover, and now defeat closes in. Later in this book, I describe our role in accelerating the removal of deception.

Once the veil completely dissolves, all falsehood flees. In one remarkable promise, the ancient schism between Ishmael and Isaac, the source of many Middle East wars, ends in a single year! (Isa. 21:16-17).

YHWY's Glory Fills the Ekklesia

Then Yahweh will create over all of Mount Zion and over every gathering a cloud of smoke by day and a glow of flaming fire by night. And all this manifestation of dazzling glory will spread over them like a wedding canopy (Isa. 4:5).

The Lord promised His visible Glory will appear all over His Ekklesia, spreading over us like a wedding canopy. The promise calls for every gathering of Believers to enjoy the dazzling, wonderful Glory of YHWY. While this occurred a handful of times over the course of history, Isaiah 4:5 promises the Glory over *every* gathering—clearly an unrealized promise for the Ekklesia.

The Holy Spirit descended upon the 120 followers of Yeshua in the upper room and the fire of YHWY appeared on each of them. Peter stood up and quoted the prophet Joel, saying, "this is [the beginning of] what was spoken through the prophet Joel" (Acts 2:16 AMPC). He goes on to quote Joel:

'This is what I will do in the last days—I will pour out my Spirit on everybody and cause your sons and daughters to prophesy, and your young men will see visions, and your old men will experience dreams *from* God. The Holy Spirit will come upon all my servants, men and women alike, and they will prophesy.

I will reveal startling signs and wonders in the sky above and mighty miracles on the earth below. Blood and fire and pillars of clouds will appear. For the sun will be turned dark and the moon blood-red before that great and awesome appearance of the day of the Lord. But everyone who calls on the name of the Lord will be saved.' (Acts 2:17-21 TPT).

The baptism of the Holy Spirit and visible fire on the 120 in the upper room in Acts 2 represents a sign indicative of the future for the Ekklesia. We learn from the passage in Joel, the Glory intensifies into great signs in Heaven and the appearance of the day of the Lord. The End Times revival, accompanied by visible Glory on every gathering of Believers, remains an unfulfilled sign. We have a lot to look forward to, Soldier Saints!

Defeat of the Curse of Death

...the last enemy to be destroyed is death
(1 Cor 15:26 ESV).

Physical death connects directly to the curse pronounced on man after the treasonous mutiny in the Garden. The Bible says Yeshua must "reign until he has put all his enemies under his feet. The last enemy to be destroyed is death" (1 Cor 15:25-26). Death remains the last enemy set for destruction. Most remain aware of human fragility and know that, unless something changes, we will all die a physical death. Yet Yeshua told John the Revelator, "I am the living one. I died, but look—I am alive forever and ever! And I hold the keys of death and the grave" (Rev 1:18 NLT). When does Yeshua plan to use these keys? He apparently used them on His own body, when He rose from the dead. Yeshua promised a day, however, when He will defeat physical death for His people.

If Yeshua stays in Heaven until all things are set right on Earth, including unrealized prophesies declared by the holy prophets, when does He defeat the curse of death? Many say these prophecies don't occur until Yeshua returns to rule in the Millennial Reign of Christ. However, in 1 Corinthians 15:25-26, the Bible classifies death as an enemy and Yeshua stays in Heaven until His enemies defeated! In the book of Hebrews, we learn:

> But our High Priest offered himself to God as a single sacrifice for sins, good for all time. Then he sat down in the place of honor at God's right hand. There he waits until his enemies are humbled and made a footstool under his feet (Heb. 10:12-13).

So, if the Bible classifies death as an enemy, and also promises Yeshua stays at the right hand of the Father *until* His enemies are made a footstool under His feet, when does physical death end? Yeshua must defeat death BEFORE the Millennial Reign of Christ, when He returns from Heaven riding on a white horse to rule Earth for 1,000 years (Rev 19:11-18).

In addition, we know that Yeshua presents to Himself a bride, "not having spot or wrinkle, or any of such things, but that it may be holy and unblemished" (Eph. 5:27 YLT). If decaying flesh leading to physical death represents an enemy, then does not death need to end for the Ekklesia to qualify as a bride "holy and unblemished?" If so, then Yeshua defeats death BEFORE the Marriage Supper of the Lamb!

Redemption, not Restoration

In *KAS*, I predicted a return to the "good old days" in America and in other nations, the days before satanic forces perverted our culture. I now see YHWY designed something far superior to restoration—He plans a monumental redemption. You see, YHWY plans to take His people back to the time before corruption put humanity in slavery to Satan —the very era of the Garden of Eden. YHWY intends to crown His people with Glory!

Oxford Languages defines redemption as the action of saving or being saved from sin, error, or evil. Also, the action of regaining or gaining possession of something in exchange for payment, or clearing a debt. In YHWY's mighty redemption, He clears the debt of the transgression by Adam in the Garden of Eden. He saves us from evil forces by removing them. He defeats the last enemy—death.

In Eden, YHWY provided everything man could need or want. Earth worked for man by providing food and nutrients on its own. No death existed. Man also experienced inimitable fellowship with YHWY, walking with Him in the cool of the morning. Man possessed authority over all the kingdoms of Earth. When Adam committed treason, everything changed. At the end of the present age, we return to the Garden!

When YHWY redeems humanity, He restores everything we lost in Eden, including our authority over the kingdoms of Earth. Once again, we shine like lightning, clothed with Glory! We enjoy closer fellowship with YHWY. The earth produces wonderful fruit with no curse. YHWY restores everything stolen from us by Satan—even stolen destinies.

However, in the Garden, man still chose to serve YHWY. The mere existence of the Tree of Knowledge proves this. YHWY told men not to partake of this fruit, and we disobeyed. However, we don't have a record of man considering partaking of the Tree of Knowledge until Satan gained access to the Garden through the serpent. Satan needed a body of an animal to yield its authority for him to gain access to the Garden to tempt Eve. Until Eve faced the possibility of free-will choice presented so succinctly by the serpent, no real struggle for obedience existed.

The Garden of Eden represents a type and shadow of the Kingdom Age of the Saints. The Garden did not represent Heaven. Satan cannot tempt anyone in Heaven. Nor did the Garden represent the Millennial Reign of Christ—Yeshua binds Satan during His reign on Earth. When we return to the Eden and the Tree of Life in the beginning of the Kingdom Age, temptation still exists—YHWY preserves our free will. Satan remains free, although his A-team and B-team of Demon-gods and Evil Spirits are bound during the Kingdom Age—the face of the shroud removed.

8. Return to Glory

Then GOD's bright glory will shine and everyone will see it. Yes. Just as GOD has said.

— Isa. 40:5 MSG

The Glory of the Lord filling the earth remains a critical promise to YHWY's people. So what event must happen for YHWY's Glory to fill Earth? Do we need a major revival? Onlookers saw glimpses of tangible Glory during famous past revivals, such as the New York City revival of 1857, the Azusa Street revival in 1906, and the Hebrides revival in 1949. However, these occurrences appeared in isolation. Isaiah promises that "everyone will see it."

In Chapter 1, I discussed how the tangible Glory appeared in the Judean tabernacle and later in the Temple. On the Day of Pentecost, onlookers saw cloven tongues of fire on the 120 men and women of the upper room. The disciples saw the Glory on Yeshua when YHWY transfigured Him on the mountain. These examples give us a glimpse of the return of Glory. However, none of these instances fulfilled Isaiah 40:5 or other scriptures about the Glory that "*all* will see."

In the Garden of Eden, Adam and Eve wore the Glory of YHWY as their clothing. In Eve's account of what happened in the Garden of Eden after she ate of the Tree of Knowledge, she says:

> And in that very hour my eyes were opened, and forthwith I knew that I was bare of the righteousness with which I had been clothed (upon), and I wept and said to him: "Why hast thou done this to me in that thou hast deprived me of the glory with which I was clothed" (*Apocalypse of Moses*, v. 20).

Eve calls the Glory that formerly clothed her "righteousness." There remains a connection between the righteousness of YHWY, and the Glory. When Adam and Eve sinned, their bodies immediately started to decay, because YHWY's righteousness departed from them and sin nature entered their bodies. Adam and Eve died spiritually and brought a curse upon Earth.

Our decaying bodies serve as a constant reminder of the curse pronounced on man after he lost his privileges in the Garden. YHWY would not allow him to eat of the Tree of Life and live forever because he yielded to Satan's authority and took on his nature. So how do we get back to wearing the Glory of YHWY?

The Curse Broken

Yeshua must defeat death, the last enemy, before we can again wear the Glory of YHWY permanently. Yeshua rose from the dead as a demonstration of the first man to defeat death; He reclaimed and raised His own body. However, Yeshua promised others would follow Him. Consider this passage:

> He is the Head of his body, which is the church. And since he is the beginning and the firstborn heir in resurrection, he is the most exalted One, holding first place in everything. For God is satisfied to have all his fullness dwelling in Christ. And by the blood of his cross, everything in heaven and earth is brought back to himself— *back to its original intent, restored to innocence again* (Col. 1:18-20 TPT)!

Here Paul refers to Yeshua as the "firstborn heir in resurrection." If a firstborn exists, then a secondborn, and thirdborn, etc. come in the future! Yeshua raised several people from the dead during His ministry on Earth. The most notable example includes Lazarus, whom Yeshua rose from a sealed tomb after four days. The thought of opening the tomb horrified Lazarus' sister Martha who said, "But Lord, it's been four days since he died—by now his body is already decomposing!" (John 11:39b). At this stage, Lazarus' internal organs suffered complete decomposition and his body began to bloat and leak foam from the nose and mouth!

In response to Martha, Yeshua said, "Didn't I tell you that if you will believe in me, you will see God unveil his power?" (John 11:40b). Resurrection of the dead, particularly of those cremated, lost at sea, etc. represents an unveiling of YHWY's power. *Merriam-Webster* defines unveil as to remove a veil or covering from, or to make public: DIVULGE, REVEAL. The ultimate public revealing of YHWY's power involves the resurrection of the dead.

Earlier in the conversation, Yeshua told Martha, "Your brother will rise and live," to which she responded, "Yes, I know he will rise with everyone else on resurrection day" (John 11:23-24). Martha knew one day Lazarus would rise from the dead, on resurrection day. However, Yeshua planned a surprise. He told Martha:

> 'Martha,' Jesus said, 'You don't have to wait until then. I am the Resurrection, and I am Life Eternal. Anyone who clings to me in faith, even though he dies, will live forever. And the one who lives by believing in me will never die. Do you believe this?' (John 11:25-26).

Here Yeshua settled once and for all that "He is the Resurrection and the Life Eternal," that His power raises the dead. Yeshua also speaks about two groups in the passage: Those who already died physically, and those who never died. But to whom does Yeshua refer that never died physically?

Many are familiar with the scripture, "Every human being is appointed to die once, and then to face God's judgment" (Heb. 9:27). The word "judgment" in this scripture can literally be interpreted as "a court trial" in the Greek. In another place, Paul explains, "I was once alive apart from the law, but when the commandment came, sin came alive and I died" (Rom. 7:9 ESV). Every child that comes into the world begins innocent and pure. Then a day comes that they must choose whether or not to serve YHWY—by losing their innocence they die once. Some refer to the age when a child loses his or her innocence as "the age of accountability." *Merriam-Webster* defines accountability as an obligation or willingness to accept responsibility or to account for one's actions—much like a court hearing. When children lose their innocence, they die the First Death.

The Second Death describes physical death. In the book of Revelation, we read "Whoever wins the victory will not be hurt by the second death" (Rev. 2:11b CEV). In *KAS*, I explain that a number of scriptures in Revelation combine to provide a riddle that fully describes the Kingdom Age of the Saints.[44] Many saints in the Kingdom Age won't taste of the Second Death. However, this only happens *after* Yeshua defeats

---

[44] Thomas, *Kingdom Age of the Saints*, 151-162.

death, the last enemy, in the resurrection, when all the righteous rise from the dead—reunited with their bodies.

The curse YHWY pronounced over man after the Fall breaks simultaneously with death's defeat. When man yielded his authority to Satan by partaking of the Tree of Knowledge, a curse resulted. To paraphrase the curse over men and women:

Curse over Men

- The ground (Earth) will be under a curse and will bring forth thorns and thistles.
- Men will have to sweat and struggle to earn a living or grow food.
- Men (and women's) bodies would die. (See Gen. 3:19).

Curse over Women

- Multiplication of hardship, toil.
- Extreme pain in giving birth.
- She would desire to control her husband.
- Her husband would rule over her. (See Gen. 3:16).

The curse came upon Earth because man yielded his authority over Earth to Satan. The curse came over the woman because she convinced her husband to disobey YHWY, although He also held man responsible because he listened to her. The curse must break to achieve the defeat of death. YWHY breaks the curse on man resulting from the Fall at the end of the current age, when Yeshua appears and causes us to inherit our full salvation—once again allowing the Glory to reside on man.

Full Salvation and the Butterfly

As Christians, we know we experience salvation when we accept Yeshua as Lord and Savior. We receive salvation by believing in our hearts that YHWY raised Yeshua from the dead and confessing Yeshua as Lord:

> And what is God's "living message?" It is the revelation of faith for salvation, which is the message that we preach. For if you publicly declare with your mouth that Jesus is Lord and believe in your heart that God raised him from the dead, you will experience salvation (Rom. 10:9 TPT).

This "living message" represents the very core of the Gospel of Yeshua, the very basis of Christianity. Every person on Earth must receive Yeshua to experience salvation and the promise of everlasting life with the Heavenly Father. Receiving salvation wipes away past sins and puts us in right standing with YHWY. But did you know the Bible also talks about *full salvation*?

The early Ekklesia wrote extensively on the triumphant hope of Yeshua's second appearing, resulting in *full salvation*. Listen to Peter's description:

> Through our faith, the mighty power of God constantly guards us until our **full salvation** is ready to be revealed in the last time. May the

137

thought of this cause you to jump for joy, even though lately you've had to put up with the grief of many trials. But these only reveal the sterling core of your faith, which is far more valuable than gold that perishes, for even gold is refined by fire. Your *authentic faith* will result in even more praise, glory, and honor when Jesus the Anointed One is revealed (1 Pet. 1:5-7, emphasis added).

In the passage, Peter spoke to Believers who already accepted the Lord as Savior. They endured many trials, as the Fourth Beast (Rome) scattered the Ekklesia, killing many. Peter encouraged the Ekklesia to look to their *full salvation*, which he said comes when Yeshua appears a second time, or is "revealed." Peter compared the trials under the Fourth Beast to refiner's fire, yielding gold with greater purity.

The unveiling, or revealing of Yeshua connects to the Glory. "Now, I encourage you as an elder, an eyewitness of the sufferings of Christ, and one who shares in the **glory that is about to be unveiled**" (1 Pet. 5:1, emphasis added). Later in the same chapter, Peter explicitly states, "And when the Shepherd-King appears, you will win the **victor's crown of glory** that never fades away" (1 Pet. 5:4, emphasis added). We receive the victors crown of Glory when Yeshua appears!

Paul describes the "hope of our salvation" as the knowledge of what YHWY plans for His people, that one day our physical bodies are glorified and death defeated. Consider this passage in Romans:

... We who have already experienced the firstfruits of the Spirit also inwardly groan as we passionately long to experience our full status as God's sons and daughters—including our physical bodies being transformed. For this is the hope of our salvation.

But hope means that we must trust and wait for what is still unseen. For why would we need to hope for something we already have? So because our hope is set on what is yet to be seen, we patiently keep on waiting for its fulfillment (Rom. 8:23-25).

Paul clearly outlines in the passage that the hope of our salvation, the transformation of our physical bodies, constitutes a *future event*. He says, "why would we need to hope for something we already have?" When Yeshua came, our spirits became white, new and refreshed. Remember that we are spirits, we live in a body, and we have a soul (our mind, will and emotions) (1 Thess. 5:23). However, our bodies bear the corruption of the original transgression of Adam. Adam's transgression gave Satan dominion over the kingdoms of the earth and gave man a sin nature as long as he possessed a physical body that came from a now cursed Earth. Death reigned as king, a temporary monarch.

YHWY provided the butterfly in nature as a perfect example of our glorious transformation into full salvation. The caterpillar's job includes feasting prior to weaving its cocoon. Between dinner sessions, the caterpillar sheds his skin four or five times. Believers feast on YHWY's Word, allowing it to transform them into YHWY's image bit by bit, shedding their worldly nature. The caterpillar then weaves silken threads around itself forming a cocoon. While in the cocoon, the caterpillar actually breaks apart and becomes a pulpy, mushy soup—similar to what occurs after physical death. Inside the cocoon, the caterpillar awaits its transformation. Eventually, Believers die a bodily death, and await their full salvation—the resurrection from the dead.

The caterpillar finally breaks out of the cocoon and emerges as a glorious butterfly, symbolic of our full salvation. The complete metamorphosis of the caterpillar inside the cocoon into a colorful, flying creature shows the re-emergence of Believers into their glorified bodies. Paul describes the transformation:

> The body is "sown" in decay, but will be raised in immortality. It is "sown" in humiliation, but will be raised in glorification. It is "sown" in weakness but will be raised in power. If there is a physical body, there is also a spiritual body (1 Cor. 15:43-44).

It's nearly impossible to recognize the caterpillar after he metamorphoses into a butterfly. The caterpillar has a few tiny eyes, stubby legs and very short antennae. While the butterfly (an adult caterpillar) has long legs, long antennae, and compound eyes.[45] The caterpillar's death reigned only

---

[45] "Butterfly Life Cycle." The Academy of Natural Sciences of Drexel University. https://ansp.org/exhibits/online-exhibits/butterflies/lifecycle/#:~:text=The%20adult %20stage%20is%20what,long%20antennae%2C%20and%20compound%20eyes.

temporarily. His death leads to a glorious transformation into arguably one of the most beautiful creatures in nature—the butterfly.

Death and Sin

Paul describes death as a king in his letter to the Romans:

> When Adam sinned, the entire world was affected. Sin entered human experience, and death was the result. And so death followed this sin, casting its shadow over all humanity, because all have sinned. Sin was in the world before Moses gave the written law, but it was not charged against them where no law existed. Yet death reigned as king from Adam to Moses even though they hadn't broken a command *the way Adam had*. The first man, Adam, was a picture of the Messiah, who was to come (Rom. 5:12-14).

Note Paul mentions that Adam's transgression impacted the entire world, causing sin to "enter the human experience." In a later verse, Paul says, "death reigned as king over humanity" (Rom. 5:17). Just as a man caused death to reign as king for all humanity, the man Yeshua would one day defeat death.

Until Yeshua defeats death, we all die a physical death. I know friends in the funeral business and sales boom for them! The Covid-19 pandemic and more specifically, the vaccine, continues to cause excess death rates to soar worldwide. While Paul acknowledged death still reigns, he calls sin a "dethroned monarch." It reigned as king until Yeshua came. By accepting Yeshua, and relying on His righteousness, we overcome sin. However, we must not give sin any opportunity in our lives:

> Sin is a dethroned monarch; so you must no longer give it an opportunity to rule over your life, controlling how you live and compelling you to obey its desires and cravings. So then, refuse to answer its call to surrender your body as a tool for wickedness.
>
> Instead, passionately answer God's call to keep yielding your body to him as one who has now experienced resurrection life! You live now for his pleasure, ready to be used for his noble purpose. Remember this: sin will not conquer you, for God already has! You are not governed by law but governed by the reign of the grace of God (Rom. 6:12-14).

While the wicked world normalizes sin, YHWY doesn't. As I drew closer to YHWY over the past few years, He convicted me of things that needed addressing in my own life. He provoked me to deal with old grudges and unforgiveness. You see, if we love the Lord, we obey His commandments. Now remains a particularly important time to purge sin from your life, and ready yourself for His "noble purpose." The time of Yeshua's appearing comes soon—we need to be ready!

Yeshua Thrice Appears

Growing up in the evangelical church, I remained confused about the appearance of Yeshua. Of course, I knew that He came to Earth, died, and rose again to bring us salvation as the perfect sin offering, eliminating the need for animal sacrifices under the law and ushering in the New Covenant. The first appearance of Yeshua as Messiah remains clear. However, from there, things began to get murky.

I would see bumper stickers that said, "Jesus is Coming Back Soon!" I would see other bumper stickers that said, "When the Rapture Comes, You Can Have My Car." In most churches I attended, teachers taught that Yeshua first appears, and we meet Him in the sky for the Rapture. According to these teachers, during the Rapture, Christians are removed from the earth. The anti-Christ then comes and rules in absolute tyranny during the Great Tribulation. A few years later, Yeshua comes back on a white horse, defeats the anti Christ, and then rules the world for a 1,000 years in the Millennial Reign of Christ. Most End Times debate centered not so much on the prevailing narrative about the Rapture— meaning that *Christians* disappear from Earth—but *when* they disappear; Meaning, at what stage during the Great Tribulation.

The Bible does not say the second appearance of Yeshua signifies a removal of the Ekklesia from Earth. Contrary to thousands of End Times books, the second appearance of Yeshua reveals our "full salvation" and ushers in the Kingdom Age, full of the Glory of YHWY. The only people "raptured" out of this world are people that don't know

143

YHWY! After the second appearance of Yeshua, Soldier Saints rule the nations with a rod of iron (Dan. 7:18, 21-22, 27; Rev 2:25-28). The first chapter of the next age is the Kingdom Age of the Saints, when YHWY's saints not only rule but also become the perfected Bride of Christ.

The third appearance of Yeshua relates to His coming from Heaven on a white horse to defeat the anti-Christ (Rev 19:11-21). After Yeshua defeats the anti-Christ, Yeshua rules the nations Himself on Earth (Rev. 20:4). Yeshua binds Satan, and he remains bound during the Millennial Reign of Christ —the second chapter of the next age (Rev. 20:2). Visit *revelationriddle.com* for a timeline and sequence of events.

The Perfect Bride

The first chapter of the Kingdom Age, the Kingdom Age of the Saints, finalizes the preparation for the Ekklesia to marry our Lord in the Marriage Supper of the Lamb:

> And to the husbands, you are to demonstrate love for your wives with the same tender devotion that Christ demonstrated to us, his bride. For he died for us, sacrificing himself to make us holy and pure, cleansing us through the showering of the pure water of the Word of God.
>
> *All that he does in us is designed* to make us a mature church for his pleasure, until we become a source of praise to him—glorious and radiant, beautiful and holy, without fault or flaw (Eph. 5:25-27).

The footnote of The Passion Translation elaborates on the Greek word for radiance. *Endoxos* can also mean gorgeous, honorable, esteemed, splendid, infused with Glory. The Greek text includes "without any wrinkle." The Aramaic translates the same word, "without chips or knots." Ask yourself, does this describe the Ekklesia today? Let's face reality—we are not ready to marry our Lord. Yeshua designed the Kingdom Age of the Saints to get us ready.

As Christians, we know our own spirits are made perfect and clean by His Blood (Heb. 10:14). However, Yeshua plans to marry His Body, not an individual. He plans to marry the collective holy, righteous, and *glorified* Ekklesia. What's more, even if we fast and pray, win souls, walk in perfect love toward others, do everything right—we all still fall short. Why? Because we live in sinful flesh and don't wear YHWY's Glory—we won't achieve this until Yeshua conquers death, the last enemy, and gives us our glorified bodies. Paul describes it perfectly: "Now, I tell you this, my brothers and sisters, flesh and blood are not able to inherit God's kingdom realm, and neither will that which is decaying be able to inherit what is incorruptible" (1 Cor. 15:50). The Bride cannot marry the Lord until we receive our glorified body!

Romans 3:23 represents one of the most quoted scriptures from the Bible. With our fresh understanding about what Yeshua requires of His bride, let's review it. Romans 3:23 says, "for all have sinned, and **come short of the glory of God**" (KJV, emphasis added). Said another way, "for we all have sinned and are **in need of the glory of God**" (TPT, emphasis added). Do you now understand the importance of the Glory? The Glory completes Christians! Salvation deals with the "sin problem" if we accept YHWY's forgiveness and Yeshua's perfect sacrifice for our sins. However, *full salvation* completes YHWY's plan of redemption, defeats death, and clothes His children in Glory once again!

Once the Ekklesia bathes in YHWY's Glory we transfigure into a state qualifying the Body of Christ to marry our Lord. We are then taken into Heaven for the Marriage Supper of the Lamb. However, this does not happen until the Body of Christ achieves perfection. For the individual Christian, this involves receiving *full salvation*, including our glorified bodies. For the collective, the Body of Christ, this means *learning to rule and reign on Earth as the Ekklesia*. When we do translate to Heaven for the Marriage Supper of the Lamb, we go the way the prophet Enoch went.

Hebrews 11 chronicles the "faith Hall of Fame" stories of those who went before us, including the prophet Enoch. Consider the account:

> Faith lifted Enoch from this life and he was taken up into heaven! He never had to experience death; he just disappeared from this world because God promoted him. For before he was translated to the heavenly realm his life had become a pleasure to God (Heb. 11:5).

Enoch simply disappeared from this world—never experiencing death! The Bible says Enoch "was translated to the heavenly realm." Why did YHWY translate Enoch from

Earth to the heavenly realm? Enoch's life became a pleasure to YHWY, so He promoted him.

Saints, do you see that the Ekklesia's translation to Heaven, or "rapture" represents a promotion? *Merriam-Webster* defines promotion as the act or fact of being raised in position or rank: PREFERMENT. *Webster* defines preferment as advancement or promotion in dignity, office, or station. You see, translation of the Body of Christ represents an advancement, an increase in rank. Until we transform to our glorified state, experience *full salvation*, and learn to lead Earth as the unified Ekklesia, we don't qualify to marry our Lord!

Thy Kingdom Come

In Chapter 6, we read from Daniel 2 about the stone made without hands coming from Heaven—smashing evil empires. The stone represents Yeshua. The judgment described in Daniel 2 represents the Stone Judgment. In the passage, after the evil empires are smashed we read, "But the boulder that hit the statue grew into a massive mountain that covered the whole earth" (Dan. 2:35b TPT). Daniel interprets this portion of the dream later in the chapter by saying, "the God of heaven will set up an eternal kingdom that will never be destroyed nor ruled by other people" (Dan. 2:44b). In the footnotes for the verse, the last portion of the scripture also means, "be left to another people [or other kingdoms]." Only YHWY's people rule His Kingdom on Earth, not usurpers or the unrighteous.

Most interpret this passage to mean that Yeshua comes to reign in person, during the Millennial Reign of Christ. However, as we discussed in the prior chapter, Yeshua remains in Heaven until all things are made right on Earth and the curse of death defeated. The prophet Zechariah makes it clear the curse lifts *after* the Stone Judgment:

> For behold, upon the stone which I have set before Joshua, upon that one stone are seven eyes or facets [the all-embracing providence of God and the sevenfold radiations of the Spirit of God]. Behold, I will carve upon it its inscription, says the Lord of hosts, and I will remove **the iniquity *and* guilt of this land in a single day.**
>
> In that day, says the Lord of hosts, you shall invite each man his neighbor under his own vine and his own fig tree (Zech. 3:9-10 AMPC, emphasis added).

Removing the iniquity and guilt of the land refers to the curse after the Fall, when Earth became cursed and physical death and corruption entered the human condition. The sevenfold radiations of the Spirit of YHWY are seven spirits who have a mission on Earth, related to the seven mountains of YHWY, representing power and authority in all areas. They *also* descend on Earth during the Stone Judgment. The phrase "under his own vine and fig tree" appears only three times in the Bible, and refers to the prosperity and Glory of the Kingdom of YHWY. In Micah we read:

In the last days, the mountain of the LORD's house will be the highest of all—the most important place on earth. It will be raised above the other hills, and people from all over the world will stream there to worship.

People from many nations will come and say, "Come, let us go up to the mountain of the LORD, to the house of Jacob's God. There he will teach us his ways, and we will walk in his paths." For the LORD's teaching will go out from Zion; his word will go out from Jerusalem.

The LORD will mediate between peoples and will settle disputes between strong nations far away. They will hammer their swords into plowshares and their spears into pruning hooks. Nation will no longer fight against nation, nor train for war anymore.

Everyone will live in peace and prosperity, enjoying their own grapevines and fig trees, for there will be nothing to fear. The LORD of Heaven's Armies has made this promise!

Though the nations around us follow their idols, we will follow the LORD our God forever and ever (Mic. 4:1–5 NLT).

The passage begins by describing a time on Earth that the mountain of YHWY reigns as the highest place—the most important. The Lord's teaching going forth "out from Zion" includes His Ekklesia, the Body of Christ. We also learn that the "word will go out from Jerusalem," indicating peace in the region. No more wars occur in the Kingdom Age—YHWY's people live in peace and prosperity.

Note from the passage some nations continue to serve idols in the next age. Satan remains unbound in the first phase of YHWY's Kingdom on Earth. Yeshua binds Him in the second phase of YHWY's Kingdom, when Yeshua rules in the flesh: The Millennial Reign of Christ. Yet, even in the Millennial Reign of Christ, some choose not to serve YHWY.

Reversal of Fortune

During the current evil age, many observe the wicked appear to prosper and the righteous don't. Yes, a few times YHWY's people prospered, such as in the early days of the Kingdom of Israel under David and Solomon. But for the most part, it appears the wicked receive rewards in this age. As Christians, we know we possess an eternal reward in Heaven, and the wicked are subject to eternal punishment in Hell. However, in the Kingdom Age, the roles are reversed. We read about this in Isaiah:

> Woe to those who, *in their greed*, buy up house after house to make one grand estate until there is no place for anyone else and only the landowner is left! This is what YAHWEH, the Commander of Angel Armies, said in my ears: Truly many of your houses will become devastated and your large, impressive mansions will have no one living in them!

Indeed, even a vast vineyard will produce only a few gallons of wine, and several bushels of seed will produce only a bushel of harvest! (Isa. 5:8-10 TPT).

In the passage above YHWY describes the monopolists, the industry titans like Blackrock that buy up massive tracts of real estate to force whole communities into a "rental economy." During the Stone Judgment, these globalist titans fall on hard times and sell their mansions. Already, we see signs of this. The homes of many Hollywood elite are up for sale, as well as massive estates of the Rothschild family, formerly titans of the FIAT banking system.

However, in the second part of the passage, notice that a perpetual curse now resides on the wicked. A vast vineyard only produces a few gallons of wine! Now the wicked endure a curse—Satan no longer possesses the ability to reward the wicked with extreme wealth. YHWY's judgment continues later in the same chapter of Isaiah:

The people will be humiliated, all of humanity humbled, and the arrogant will be brought low.

With Justice the Lord YAHWEH, Commander of Angel Armies, displays his greatness, and righteousness sets him apart as the holy God. Then lambs will graze, as if in their own pastures, and the refugee will eat in the ruins of the rich (Isa. 5:15-17).

In the passage, the reversal of fortune for YHWY's people occurs after "all of humanity humbled," pointing to the Stone Judgment. YHWY's lambs graze in their own pastures, and the evil are now refugees of the rich, referring to YHWY's people. What a mighty and glorious reversal of fortune!

I used to get frustrated about how the wicked prosper and belong to the "right clubs" but those of us excited about Yeshua and the things of YHWY get cast out of their circles. While I earned many of the same credentials that the world respects, I still felt like an outsider. I graduated from a top business school. I helped cofound a chapter of an elite business group called the Young Presidents Organization. Invariably, once I shared my testimony of Yeshua to leaders in these secular organizations, things simply changed—I stopped receiving the invites to the elite parties. Yeshua explains what YHWY's people experience in the old age:

> If you were to give your allegiance to the world, they would love and welcome you as one of their own. But because you won't align yourself with the values of this world, they will hate you. I have chosen you and taken you out of the world to be mine (John 15:19).

When I began to understand the old age we endure today soon ends as YHWY's immaculate plan for the future unfolds, my perspective completely changed. The wicked actually help fulfill YHWY's immaculate plan for humanity:

> For to the one who pleases him God has given wisdom and knowledge and joy, but to the sinner

he has given the business of gathering and collecting, only to give to one who pleases God. This also is vanity and a striving after wind (Eccles. 2:26 ESV).

YHWY's purpose for the wicked includes gathering and collecting—only to give to one who pleases Him! The wicked actually work for YHWY's people! All the sinister banking empires, monopolistic satanists, and elite families who for centuries piled up the real assets of gold, silver, and real estate simply fulfilled YHWY's purpose. His purpose includes giving this wealth to His people!

Author W.D. Wattles understood this concept vividly—way ahead of its time. He wrote a book in the early 1900s and spoke about the wealthy working for the righteous in his book, *The Science of Getting Rich*:

> Rockefeller, Carnegie, Morgan, *et al.*, have been unconscious agents of the Supreme in the necessary work of systematizing and organizing productive industry; and in the end, their work will contribute immensely toward increasing life for all. Their day is nearly over; they have organized production, and *will soon be succeeded by the agents of the multitude, who will organize the machinery of distribution.*
>
> The multi-millionaires are like the monster reptiles of the prehistoric eras; they play a necessary part in the evolutionary process, but the same Power which produced them will dispose of

them. And it is well to bear in mind that they have never been really rich; a record of the private lives of most of this class will show that they have really been the most abject and wretched of the poor.[46]

The multi-millionaires in Waddles book represent the multi-billionaires of today. A million dollars in 1910, when Waddles wrote his book, equates to $33 billion today.[47]

Recall from scripture the story of Pharaoh. Pharaoh enslaved YHWY's people, achieving great wealth on their backs. His empire benefited tremendously from the revelation of Joseph, that Egypt should store up in times of plenty because a famine came soon. Egypt became extraordinarily wealthy as an empire, with gold and silver reserves swelling after the entire world came to buy food from them during the famine. YHWY gave all this wealth to His people when they left! Egypt represents the first shaking of the nations within the Bible, where YHWY decimates the power of an empire and transfers their wealth to His children. YHWY plans another wealth transfer after the second Shaking of Nations, the one we experience right now!

The Wealth Transfer

Wealth represents a type of glory in the Bible. The word glory describes material possessions and wealth in Genesis 31:1. YHWY plans a wealth transfer representing the *largest in*

---

46   Wattles, W.D. *The Science of Getting Rich*. (Holyoke: Elizabeth Town, 1910). 49-50.
47   CPI Inflation Calculator. Accessed May 22, 2024.
      https://www.in2013dollars.com/us/inflation/1910?amount=1000000

human history. The modern system of debt slavery consolidated vast and durable wealth of gold, silver, natural resources, businesses and real estate into the hands of a few at the expense of many. Humanity unwittingly assumed the role of sharecroppers in the fields of the wicked. Taxes, fees, interest, rent, inflation, insurance bills, legal bills, healthcare expenses and other frictional costs steadily depleted the masses and enriched the governments and institutions aligned with the Fourth Beast. At the top of the pyramid of theft a handful of families benefited—enriched by Satan as a reward for serving him.

Humanity labored to aggregate paper money—not worth the paper used for printing it. We willingly traded our precious time to accumulate paper money or other goods traded for paper money, while mega-controllers stockpiled real money—gold. The world worships the Babylonian money system, the tool and creation of the Fourth Beast:

> And all the people who belong to this world worshiped the [fourth] beast. They are the ones whose names were not written in the Book of Life that belongs to the Lamb who was slaughtered before the world was made (Rev 13:8 NLT).

It's tempting for Believers to also get sucked into and worship the Babylonian money system. Have any of you used debt, an enslavement instrument of the Fourth Beast, to buy things you could not afford on credit? I know I have!

In the scripture, we read both a promise and an omen as it relates to the coming wealth transfer:

> The benevolent man leaves an inheritance that
> endures to his children's children, but the wealth
> of the wicked is treasured up for the righteous.
>
> The lovers of God will live a long life and get
> to enjoy their wealth, but the ungodly will
> suddenly perish (Prov. 13:22-23 TPT).

In the Aramaic, verse 23 says, "Those who don't find the way of life destroy many years of wealth, and some are utterly destroyed." So, after the asset transfer from the wicked to the righteous, some squander the fortune and some are destroyed by riches. This constitutes the first test after the second Shaking of Nations. When YHWY blesses us with extreme wealth, we must remain obedient and walk out our calling with the new prosperity.

Recall from the first major wealth transfer after Israel's deliverance from Egypt, that YHWY blessed all former slaves with great fortunes. However, some used their newfound riches to build a golden calf (a pagan god) in the desert. As punishment, Moses ground up the calf into powder and fed it to them (Ex. 32:20). These children lost some or all their gold and suffered humiliation. They gave thanks to the wrong god, and became impatient waiting for new instructions from YHWY.

Every promise YHWY made comes to pass. "God is not a man, so he does not lie. He is not human, so he does not change his mind. Has he ever spoken and failed to act? Has he ever promised and not carried it through?" (Num. 23:19 NLT). Many are weary. Many are tired. The Fourth Beast wore out the Ekklesia with 2,000 years of torment and oppression. However, soon *everything* changes.

I sense from scripture that YHWY eagerly awaits this day, and it thrills Him to give His children a biblical day of rest. We live in the most exciting time ever, saints!

9. YHWY's Divine Timeline

Seek for Yahweh's book and read it carefully. You will learn that none of these prophecies will fail; none will lack a fulfillment as its companion. For the Lord has issued his decree.

— Isa. 34:16a TPT

YHWY's flawless blueprint of the future continues to amaze me. It stands vastly superior to anything I ever learned in Sunday school! The Stone Judgment begins with a Shaking of Nations and ends with a mighty resurrection of the dead. His plan includes a remarkable redemption of His people, placing us back in the Garden of Eden, shining in His Glory!

YHWY designed a future so splendid, many won't believe it. However, Believers that love truth and His Word will immerse themselves in the Bible and allow the scripture to ignite their spirits with the immaculate vision of our future—the story of the return of Glory and deep fellowship with our Creator.

In past chapters, I covered many of the high points of YHWY's immaculate and inimitable plan. Now I lay out His timeline. YHWY gave us the year for the end of the age—the end of Satan's lease on Earth. Knowing the year the old age ends provides clear guidance on *when* everything happens!

The End of the Age

In Chapter 7, I outline how YHWY showed the prophet Ezra the old age lasts 12,000 years. The first six days of the age included the days of creation, or 6,000 years. YHWY showed Ezra the age gets darker and more and more evil until it ends. I asked the Lord to show me the year the old age ends. YHWY showed me through revelation that He gave us the *exact year* the age ends in our modern timeline based upon a simple passage in the book of Daniel!

Confusion abounds within the Ekklesia about the "end of the age." Many Bible translations inappropriately substitute "world" for "age." For instance, in Matthew 24:3, the disciples asked Yeshua to tell them the signs of the end of the "age," not "world." In the verse, the New Revised Standard Version translates "age" properly, while the King James

Version does not. When we think of "end of the world," we usually think of one of many apocalyptic films about the end of Earth. They usually depict mass-casualty events or alien invasions. Hollywood's depiction purposely horrifies the masses regarding the end of the world. However, YHWY's story ends in a *completely* different way. You see, the present age ends and then a new era begins on the *same earth*. According to YHWY's timeline, Earth ends *much* later, *after* He establishes His Kingdom on Earth and restores order.

YHWY showed Daniel when the old, dark age ends. The timing centers on the construction of the Dome of the Rock, the "abomination that brings destruction." Let's read from Daniel 12:

> Between the end of the continual burnt offering and the abomination that brings destruction will be 1,290 days. Blessed are those who wait and faithfully endure to the end of the 1,335 days. As for you, be at peace and rest; and you will rise for your reward at the end of the age (Dan. 12:11-13).

In these two verses, the angel of the Lord gives Daniel the timeline of the completion of the age. Evil men built the Dome of the Rock on top of the Temple Mount in Jerusalem in AD 691-692.[48] The "days" in Daniel 12:11-12 correspond to years in our timeframe.

Between 600 and 599 BC, continual burnt offerings in the First Temple likely ceased, 1,290 years prior to the construction of the Dome of the Rock, explaining the first

---

48   Wikipedia. 2024. "Dome of the Rock." *Wikimedia Foundation*. Last modified May 22, 2024. https://en.wikipedia.org/wiki/Dome_of_the_Rock.

part of the passage we read in Daniel 12. King Josiah, a righteous king of Judah most certainly offered sacrifices before his reign ended in 609 BC. The Bible indicates he walked in *all* the ways of King David (2 King 22:2). Josiah's fourth son and successor, Jehoahaz, reigned for only three months before his capture by Pharaoh Necho.[49] Necho installed Johoahaz's brother, Jehoiakim, who did evil in YHWY's sight and reigned until 598 BC. It's very likely that Jehoiakim ended the Temple offerings before his reign ended. At the time, both Egypt and Babylon vied to control Jerusalem. Until 605 BC, Jehoaikim paid heavy gold tribute to Egypt for protection against Babylon. In the same year, the battle of Carchemish led to Babylonian victory and the king began to pay tribute to Babylon, including giving Babylon Temple treasure. Given Johoaikim's unrighteous nature, he likely raided the Temple and shut down offerings between 600 BC and 599 BC. Babylon laid complete siege over Jerusalem in 598 BC, the next year.

Daniel gave us a second important number, when he said, "Blessed are those who wait and faithfully endure to the end of the 1,335 days" (Dan. 12:12). Using the same methodology of days equating to years, we add 1,335 years to AD 691-692, arriving at AD 2026-2027. The masons stamped "AH 72," within the walls of the Dome of the Rock, indicating the completion year. AH 72 represents a year in the Islamic lunar calendar, which crosses two Gregorian calendar years; AD 691 and 692. Figure 3 shows the range of dates corresponding to the end of the age, based upon adding 1,335

---

49   Wikipedia. 2024. "Kings of Judah." *Wikimedia Foundation*. Last modified May 19, 2024.
      https://en.m.wikipedia.org/wiki/Kings_of_Judah.

years to both the starting and ending date of AH 72, corresponding to the Gregorian calendar.

Figure 3: *Date Range for End of the Age*[50]

Completion of the Dome of the Rock	1335 Year Anniversary
AH 72 Start: June 4, 691 AD	Sunday, June 7, 2026 AD
AH 72 End: May 23, 692 AD	Thursday, May 27, 2027 AD

As shown in Figure 3, the 1,335th year following the completion of construction of the Dome of the Rock spans between June 7, 2026 and May 27, 2027 in our calendar— only a couple of years from now!

Note the last promise in the scripture passage above, "As for you, be at peace and rest and you will rise for your reward at the end of the age" (Dan. 12:13). This scripture confirms the earlier calculation represents the end of the age. YHWY also promises Daniel a beautiful and personal promise, that he will rise for his reward at the conclusion of the age, forecasting the glorious resurrection of the righteous dead! After the resurrection of the dead during the Kingdom Age, I look forward to having dinner with the prophet Daniel!

The Third Day of the Ekklesia

If the old age ends in the year range of 2026 to 2027, then how does this relate to YHWY's overall timeline? I wrote extensively in *Blast of Fire* of the third-day redemption. Yeshua rising on the third day represents a dual promise. The first meaning relates to Yeshua Himself rising on the third day physically. However, the promise *also* signifies the

---

[50] 1,335 year anniversary calculated by adding 487,599 days (1,335 * 365.2425 days per year) to start date on timeanddate.com. Initial date conversion from Islamic Lunar Calendar (AH) to Gregorian calendar performed on https://www.muslimphilosophy.com/ip/hijri.htm

Ekklesia rises after two biblical days, or two thousand years. A day often means a thousand years in scripture (2 Pet. 3:8). The Bible includes numerous examples of third day redemption, including:

- Yeshua went to the grave for two days and rose on the third day (Luke 24:6, 1 Cor. 15:4, Mark 9:31).
- Yeshua spoke to Herod, the Rome-appointed King of Israel and told him He would finish his course against Rome on the third day (Luke 13:32).
- Yeshua said He would be delivered into the hands of sinful men for two days, and rise on the third day (Luke 24:7).
- The Lord told Moses to have the people cleanse and prepare themselves for two days, before witnessing the Glory on the third day (Ex. 19:10-11).
- Yeshua turned water into wine on the third day (John 2:1-10).
- Hosea says the Lord revives us on the third day (Hos. 6:1-3).

If Yeshua resurrects the Ekklesia on the third millennial day after His resurrection, when does the third day start? Despite centuries of debate, no unanimous agreement exists for the actual date of the Crucifixion. However, the date of Yeshua's birth appears relatively straightforward. I believe His birth occurred in 6 BC, based on biblical records:

- Matthew indicates Yeshua's birth occurred in the days of Herod the Great. Historical records show that Herod died in 4 BC, dating Yeshua's birth on or before 4 BC (Matt. 2:1).
- Because Yeshua's birth occurred two years before Herod died, this dates Yeshua's birth to 6 BC. (See Matthew 2:13-16).

Most scholars agree the only dates astronomically and calendrically plausible for the Crucifixion fall on three possible dates, as shown in Figure 4. Also shown are conceivable dates reflecting the beginning of the third millennial day following Yeshua's resurrection, based on adding 2,000 years to His resurrection date, assuming He rose the Sunday following the Crucifixion. The three probable start days of the third millennia all fall on a Sunday on either April 11, 2027, April 7, 2030, or April 3, 2033.

Figure 4: *Possible Crucifixion Dates & Third Millennial Day*[51]

Possible Crucifixion Dates of Yeshua	Third Millennial Day Beginning
Friday, April 11, 27 AD	Sunday, April 11, 2027 AD
Friday, April 7, 30 AD	Sunday, April 7, 2030 AD
Friday, April 3, 33 AD	Sunday, April 3, 2033 AD

---

[51] Humphreys, Colin J., Waddington, W.G. "The Jewish Calendar, a Lunar Eclipse And the Date of Christ's Crucifixion." *Tyndalebulletin.* Vol. 43. Issue 2. 1992 November 1, 1992. https://www.tyndalebulletin.org/article/30487-the-jewish-calendar-a-lunar-eclipse-and-the-date-of-christ-s-crucifixion. Third millennial dates calculated by adding 730,485 days years (2,000 * 365.2425 days per year) to Sunday following resurrection, using timeanddate.com.

If Yeshua's birth occurred in 6 BC and His ministry spanned three years, then the most probable date of the third millennial launch of the Ekklesia based on the dates given in Figure 4 occurs on April 11, 2027. This date falls *46 days* before the finality of the old age on May 27, 2027!

In 2027, remarkable alignment exists between the third millennial day of the Ekklesia and the date the age ends, based upon Daniel 12:12. Notwithstanding this, remain aware scholars don't agree on the date of Yeshua's resurrection. Many believe that 2030 represents a likely year the third millennial day begins after His resurrection, when considering all the evidence given in scripture.

Seventh Day Rest

YHWY rested on the seventh day after six biblical days of creation, or 6,000 years. After committing treason in the Garden of Eden, a curse came to man. Subsequently, YHWY's people endured many ups-and-downs over the next 6,000 years, during a time when Satan ruled Earth's kingdoms. However, in the seventh day of humanity, YHWY gives us rest. The book of Hebrews describes a Sabbath rest for YHWY's children:

> If Joshua had really given the people rest, there would not be any need for God to talk about another day of rest. But God has promised us a Sabbath when we will rest, **even though it has not yet come**. On that day God's people will rest from their work, just as God rested from his work (Heb. 4:8-10 CEV, emphasis added).

The true rest of YHWY comes during the Kingdom Age of the Saints and the Millennial Reign of Christ, both chapters in the next era. When YHWY rested after He created the world, He simply enjoyed His creation. A day comes soon when we can enjoy YHWY's creation in the divine rest of YHWY—the seventh day of humanity and the Kingdom Age of the Saints.

Transition to the Next Age

As we transition to the first chapter of the next age, many events occur in sequence during the Stone Judgment. This book focuses primarily on the biblical events during the Stone Judgment, when Yeshua establishes the first phase of His Kingdom on Earth. The Stone Judgment encompasses three distinct phases, including: a) the Shaking of Nations, b) an End Times Harvest, and c) a Fire Judgment. Figure 5 shows the three phases of the Stone Judgment.

Figure 5: Sequence of Events in Stone Judgment

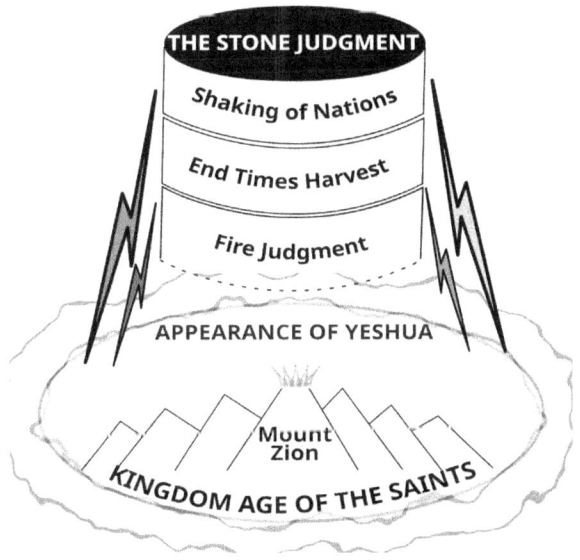

The Shaking of Nations occurs in the first phase of the Stone Judgment. In this phase, Yeshua judges the Fourth Beast in the Court of Heaven. Then the man-from-the-sea appears (President Trump) and, with YHWY's help, decapitates the leaders of the Fourth Beast. The Ekklesia rises up to usher in the Kingdom Age by expelling the Demon-gods and Evil Spirits from Earth. The Whore of Babylon dies and connected deception revealed. The Little Horn, the controller of the Fourth Beast, also succumbs in the Shaking of Nations. The destruction of Jerusalem likely occurs in this phase as well, and the land around Jerusalem finally granted to the rightful heirs, the seed of Jacob. During the shaking, the assets of the wicked are confiscated and re-distributed to those from whom the theft occurred. The Shaking of Nations represents both a military operation and a spiritual awakening. The man-from-the-sea and the military alliance execute the military component, assisted by supernatural angelic hosts. The Ekklesia rising up to expel principalities shatters once and for all time the deception blinding humanity by removing demonic oppression. Satan loses his most powerful forces during the Shaking of Nations.

Shaking of Nations

The modern Shaking of Nations represents the second in human history. The prophet Haggai speaks about the second shaking, "Soon I will again shake the heavens and the earth, the sea and the dry land" (Hag. 2:6). The book of Hebrews references Haggai and gives us more context on the second shaking:

The earth was rocked at the sound of his voice from the mountain, but now he has promised, "Once and for all I will not only shake the systems of the world, but also the unseen powers in the heavenly realm!" Now this phrase "once and for all" clearly indicates the final removal of things that are shaking, that is, the old order, so only what is unshakeable will remain.

Since we are receiving our rights to an unshakable kingdom we should be extremely thankful and offer God the purest worship that delights his heart as we lay down our lives in absolute surrender, filled with awe. For our God is a holy, devouring fire (Heb. 12:26-29 TPT)!

In the passage, we learn all the systems of the world are shaken, as well as the evil principalities, referring to the Demon-gods and Evil Spirits, who we discussed in Chapter 6. Note the passage indicates not just a shaking but a "final removal" of shakable things. The passage describes the entire Stone Judgment at a high level as the last sentence refers to YHWY's devouring fire, the last phase of the Stone Judgment. We should worship during this time of shaking, in reverential awe of our Lord!

Righteous men and women of YHWY, helped by the angelic host, execute the Shaking of Nations. YHWY gives these Soldier Saints the anointing, strategic vision, and supernatural protection to implement His plan. King Cyrus, a pagan king, commanded over the fall of Ancient Babylon in the Bible. However, King Cyrus followed a playbook designed by YHWY which involved draining the Euphrates river to infiltrate Babylon. I wrote extensively on King Cyrus and the miraculous defeat of Babylon in *KAS* and *Blast of Fire.*

Figure 6: *Events During the Shaking of Nations*

Event	Scripture Reference	Est. Date
Fourth Beast Judged in Court of Heaven	Dan. 7:9-10,26; 2 Esd. 11:38-46; Rev 12:1-2; Ezek. 7:10; 28:1-19; Isa. 3:13-26; 10:1-4; 18:3-5; 31:4-5; 2 Bar. 29:4; 1 Enoch 93:10	9/23/2017
Man-From-The-Sea Begins Battle	2 Esd. 12:28; 13:29-32; Isa. 10:26-27; 19:4,11-17; 25:2-5; 41:2-3; 45:1-6,13-14; 46:11; 48:14-15; Hag. 1:12; 2:6-7; 2:21-23; 2 Esd. 13; 2 Bar. 83:7; Hab. 2:9-10	Q4 2017
Ekklesia Deports Principalities	1 Enoch 1:9; 10:12-13; 16:1; 90:19, 91:12; 2 Esd. 16:1-3; Isa. 27:1-2; Ezek. 29:3-5; Dan. 7:25; Mal. 4:3; Matt. 8:29; 11:12; 18:18; Luke 2:25,37; 2 Cor. 10:4; 2 Thess. 2:7	2024-2025
Fourth Beast and Whore (Babylon) Die	2 Esd. 13:12; 15:24-45; Isa. 2:14-17; 5-8-10; 8:9-10; 13:1-9,19-22; 14:22-27; 17:12-14; 19:1-3; 27:2; 41:25; 47:5-15; Ezek. 17:17-18; 27:27-36; Dan. 2:34-35,44; 7:11; Mark 9:42; Rev 17:4-7; 18:2-24	9/23/2024
Little Horn Dies	Isa. 5:18-21; 10:12-18; 29:13-16; 30:8-14; Ezek. 13:8-12; 14:23; 22:18-30; 34:4-10; 35; Dan. 11:44-45; Obad. 15-18; 1 Thess. 2:15; Rev. 3:9;	2024-2025
Jerusalem Destroyed	Isa. 6:11-13; Ezek. 21:14-15,27 Dan. 11:41	2024-2025
Wealth of Wicked Distributed	2 Bar. 29:4; Job 27:16-17; Prov. 6:31; 10:22; 13:22; 28:8; Isa. 13:14; 33:1-4,23; 45:3; Ezek. 7:10-11; 34:23-24; Matt. 24:48-49	2024-2025
Judean Shame Removed	Isa. 10:20-22; 11:10-16; 14:1-2; 27:6,12; 28:25-26; 29:22-24; 31:6-9; 41:8-10; 52:9; Ezek. 11:17-18; 28:24-26; 34:11-16; 36:8-37; 37:15-19,22; Obad. 19-21	2024-2026

SHAKING OF NATIONS (vertical side label)

Figure 6 shows a detailed sequence of events during the Shaking of Nations portion of the Stone Judgment. In the figure, I reference many scriptures across the Bible and "extra biblical" books for the convenience of readers. The scripture list is not comprehensive—almost daily I discover more promises related to the Stone Judgment. After you complete this book, go back and study each promise carefully! This figure includes the estimated dates or year ranges corresponding to the events. In Figure 6, I indicate by the dates shown that the Shaking of Nations indeed began in 2017.

Fourth Beast Judged in Court of Heaven

But the judgment shall be set [by the court of the Most High], and they shall take away his dominion to consume it [gradually] and to destroy it [suddenly] in the end (Dan. 7:26 AMPC).

The Stone Judgment kicks off with the judgment of the Fourth Beast in the Court of Heaven. Yeshua delivers the verdict to his face on behalf of YHWY (2 Esd. 11:38-46). In the Bible, the Leviathan and Behemoth represent the spiritual principalities over the Fourth Beast and Little Horn, respectively. The Bible calls Leviathan the dragon of the sea. Recall from Chapter 5 that the Fourth Beast comes from the sea. Behemoth represents a chaos-monster, paired with Leviathan (2 Bar. 29:4).

After Yeshua delivers judgment on the Fourth Beast, his power begins to wane and his ability to conceal himself falls apart. The Bible says, "And Behemoth shall be revealed from his place and Leviathan shall ascend from the sea" (2 Bar. 29:4). We see this playing out now on a worldwide scale. Platforms like *Telegram*, *Rumble*, *Gab* and others stream forth formerly classified documents exposing the corruption behind the Fourth Beast and the Little Horn. The Great

Awakening steams ahead. Even mainstream media now covers the corrupt system!

After the judgment of the Fourth Beast in the Court of Heaven, his demise begins gradually at first, then ends in a single day. Currently, we see the gradual exposure of the beast. However, the final battle consummates in a single day! As discussed in Chapter 6, I believe YHWY convened the Court of Heaven to judge the Fourth Beast on September 23, 2017, evidenced by a rare sign in the stars, prophesied in Revelation 12:1-2.

Man-From-The-Sea Executes Strategy

The days are coming when the Most High will deliver those who are on the earth. And bewilderment of mind shall come over those who inhabit the earth. They shall plan to make war against one another, city against city, place against place, people against people, and kingdom against kingdom. When these things take place and the signs occur that I showed you before, then my Son will be revealed, whom you saw as a man coming up from the sea (2 Esd.13:29-32 NRSV).

As covered extensively in *Blast of Fire*, YHWY raises up a special man, a man-from-the-sea, to redeem humanity from the grips of the deep state—right before the Fourth Beast *plans* to destroy humanity. I believe this man can only be President Donald Trump. When I first saw "Son" capitalized in the passage above, I confused the man-from-the-sea with

Yeshua. However, Yeshua would not be described as the "man from the sea." The sea in the Bible represents worldly evil, and is where the Whore of Babylon resides. To ascribe Yeshua to the sea would represent apostasy and a recanting of the Virgin Birth. In *Blast of Fire*, I analyzed the multitude of prophecies related to President Trump from respected prophets such as the late Kim Clement. I connected the dots on 17 prophecies in the Bible describing the man-from-the-sea to President Trump. While Trump already fulfilled many of them, more realizations will come. I also detailed in *Blast of Fire* how YHWY gifted President Trump with the anointing of both King Cyrus and King David.

Trump's mean tweets are in the Bible! YHWY also names the military operation, #STORM, in the Bible. The battle of the entire deep state apparatus against President Trump—also in the Bible. I used to stand in awe of Satan's plans. Now I stand in wonder and veneration at YHWY's plans. He told us *everything* that would happen. Saints, hold your heads high! Not only does YHWY win, but Satan never stood a chance. YHWY prophesied Satan's defeat in the Garden of Eden.

Many modern-day prophets compared President Trump with King Cyrus and King David. I first made the prophetic connection between the man-from-the-sea in 2 Esdras and President Trump. Moreover, I believe Trump carries the anointing of Zerubbabel. Zerubbabel led the remnant of the people of Israel back to Jerusalem after their captivity in Babylon and worked for two years, laying the foundation of the second Judean Temple. Zerubbabel held office as governor in Judah prior to this assignment.

Zerubbabel's name means "out of Babel." Trump came out of modern Babylon, out of the world. Zerubbabel held office as a governor, not a priest or soldier—just like Trump. However, the Bible says that Zerubbabel listened to and obeyed the voice of YHWY (Hag. 1:12). His obedience opened up the door for YHWY's blessing on His people. Zerubbabel's role in the Bible included building the foundation of the house of YHWY. Trump will also serve in this capacity once he and his military alliance defeat the Fourth Beast with the Lord's help.

In 2017, President Trump began his first term as President of the United States and immediately began to dismantle the deep state. He signed numerous executive orders authorizing him to raid the coffers of entities engaged in human trafficking. He began to build a private army of over 60,000 forces and engage other world leaders in the battle.[52] This ongoing battle persists. The Bible says YHWY gives us a natural "sword" to execute His judgment (2 Esd. 12:28). This sword represents Donald Trump and the military alliance around the world helping him. (We know the sword of the Spirit represents the Word of YHWY). The military squashes evil and protects the righteous. One major assignment for the military includes cutting off the insidious controllers of the United States and restoring her to a Constitutional Republic.

52   Arkin, William M. "Exclusive: Inside the Military's Secret Undercover Army." *Newsweek.* July 5, 2021. https://www.newsweek.com/exclusive-inside-militarys-secret-undercover-army-1591881

YHWY called President Trump for this time. We don't select our deliverer, just like Israel could not choose their redeemer from Babylon—King Cyrus. Be thankful for President Trump and YHWY's divine plan. President Trump simply answered the call and now the hosts of Heaven help him. As Christians, we must recognize and support YHWY's vessel! We must pray for President Trump and the military alliance *daily*. Soon we will discover that brave men and women in uniform systematically dismantled and dismembered the Fourth Beast system over many years. Get ready to watch the greatest documentary films ever produced!

Ekklesia Deports Principalities

And I saw till a great sword was given to the sheep, and the sheep proceeded against all the beasts of the field to slay them, and all the beasts and the birds of the heaven fled before their face (1 Enoch 90:19).

Prayer ushered in the prophecies regarding Yeshua's birth on Earth. YHWY revealed Messiah to Anna the prophetess. After her husband died, scripture says, "she chose to worship God in the temple continually. For the past eighty-four years she had been serving God with night-and-day prayer and fasting" (Luke 2:37 TPT). Another elderly man Simeon also believed he would one day witness the coming of Messiah (Luke 2:25). Both Anna and Simeon recognized the day of the Lord.

The Holy Spirit prepares the way for prophetic fulfillment. The Holy Spirit prepares the hearts of men and women in advance by imparting an unusual hunger we respond to through prayer, fasting, and declaration. We must hunger and thirst to bring the Kingdom of YHWY to Earth. We also must take our place as Soldier Saints in the Army of the Lord.

To some, it might seem small and meaningless for a couple of senescent prayer-warriors to answer the call to pray in the Temple and fast, looking for the coming of Messiah. However, this is YHWY's way. Listen to how Yeshua described the spiritual warfare at that time, "And from the days of John the Baptist until the present time, the kingdom of heaven has endured violent assault, and violent men seize it by force [as a precious prize—a share in the heavenly kingdom is sought with most ardent zeal and intense exertion]" (Matt. 11:12 AMPC). Yeshua spoke of prayer-warriors like Anna and Simeon!

The Lord showed me that we the Ekklesia must rise up in this hour to banish the Demon-gods and Evil Spirits from Earth. We must send them to the fifth and second heavens, respectively, to serve out their prison term. In the scripture in Enoch above, we see the sheep are given a great sword with which to slay the beasts and birds of heaven, symbolizing the Demon-gods and Evil Spirits, respectively. *Now* we must use the sword—the Word of YHWY. "For the weapons of our warfare are not of the flesh but have divine power to destroy strongholds" (2 Cor. 10:4 ESV).

The lease which authorizes Demon-gods and Evil Spirits to exercise dominion on Earth expires no later than 2027—the end of the age. However, Yeshua already judged the Fourth Beast and related principalities in the Court of Heaven in 2017. We now possess authority in the spirit realm to banish these unlawful agents of chaos and wickedness from Earth.

Enoch served as liaison between YHWY and the Watchers, a type and shadow of our role today. He pronounced the judgment from YHWY upon the Watchers. He prophesied the Watchers and their progeny (Evil Spirits) would be banished to the outer heavens at the end of the age. This promise represents the authority by which we speak to these evil principalities. We don't yet possess the authority to banish Satan or Unclean Spirits (fallen angels) from Earth. However, based on the book of Enoch, now is go-time to expel Demon-gods and Evil Spirits. (See 1 Enoch 10:12-13, 16:1).

We the Ekklesia must rise up and use our authority in this hour and usher in the Kingdom of YHWY. We recognize from scripture that Demon-gods and Evil Spirits are now illegal interlopers—their time to rule finished. YHWY expects His Ekklesia to take their place and demand the demons leave Earth. *This is YHWY's way!* Answer the call—dedicate time each day to banishing these principalities from Earth. In the Appendix, I include a Banishment of Principalities proclamation to get you started. Start in your local community, then shift to your city, and then your state. Already, positive testimonies stream in from around the world from prayer warriors, who with little effort, witness powerful results.

When you hear about a storm coming, rebuke the storm and deport the demon behind it to his prison cell off the earth. When you hear the mainstream media spout fear-porn, banish the Demon-god in charge of corrupt media from Earth. When you hear about President Trump listening to power-hungry evil advisors, expel the Demon-gods and Evil Spirits within Trump's circle from Earth, in Yeshua's Name. Yeshua already sentenced the Fourth Beast. The Most High already delivered a verdict on the Demon-gods and Evil Spirits. It's time for Soldier Saints to boldly enforce YHWY's injunction within the spirit realm, in Yeshua's name.

When Yeshua spoke to the Evil Spirits (demons) in Gadara, He sent them into pigs. At that time, Evil Spirits still had roughly 2,000 more years to rule. The Evil Spirits knew their days were numbered, for they asked Yeshua, "Have you come to torment us before the appointed time?" (Matt. 8:29b TPT). The appointed time for torment of Evil Spirits IS NOW! That evil era—their age to rule—ceases. Now we possess the authority to deport them to their bastille, where they are lawfully bound until the White Throne Judgment. The scripture promises all the beasts (Demon-gods) and the birds of the heaven (Evil Spirits) *flee* before our face (1 Enoch 90:19). Whatever we bind on Earth, is bound in Heaven (Matt. 18:18).

Fourth Beast and Whore (Babylon) Die

> I watched closely to see what would happen to this smaller horn because of the arrogant things it was saying. Then before my very eyes, the fourth beast was killed and its body destroyed by fire
> (Dan. 7:11 CEV).

While the destruction of the Fourth Beast begins slowly, his death occurs on a single day. YHWY destroyed Egypt's armies and conquered Ancient Babylon in a single day. The same fate awaits the Fourth Beast. Up until the time of his death, the Little Horn continues to speak arrogantly. The voice-box of the Little Horn represents the mainstream media. Note in the passage above that the Fourth Beast dies, but then "its body (is) destroyed by fire." While military forces kill the Fourth Beast by eliminating the top leadership structure, the Ekklesia banishes the principalities behind the Fourth Beast. YHWY finishes the work by burning up its body, the evil men that skirted justice, in the final phase—the Fire Judgment.

The Whore, Babylon, represents the Roman Catholic Church, allied and inextricably coupled with the Fourth Beast power structure. The Bible confirms this linkage:

> The woman was robed in purple and scarlet and was glittering with gold, precious stones, and pearls. She was holding in her hand a golden chalice brimming full with defiling obscenities and the filth of her lewdness. On her forehead was written these mysterious titles: "The great Babylon, mother of prostitutes and of the abominations of the earth."
>
> I saw the woman was drunk with the blood of God's holy believers—drunk on the blood of the loyal martyrs of Jesus. And when I saw her, I was utterly astonished! But the angel said to me, "Why are you so astonished? I will reveal to you the mystery of the woman, and **of the wild beast**

with seven heads and ten horns that carries her" (Rev 17:4–7 TPT, emphasis added).

Every description of the Rome-rooted Fourth Beast in the Bible discusses seven heads and ten horns. For centuries, the Roman church, the official religion of the state, squashed revival, hid Bibles, and waged war against Christians. The Catholic Church demonstrates a sordid history, rife with child abuse. In Pennsylvania alone, 300 Catholic priests were convicted of this heinous crime.[53] This false religion, which marries paganism with Christianity, falls at the same time as the Fourth Beast. As documented in *Blast of Fire*, the military already plundered the Vatican Bank of its ill-gotten gold.[54] Child predators within the walls of the Catholic Church continue to face justice.

The book of Revelation makes a connection between the judgment of the Whore of Babylon and the Stone Judgment:

Rejoice over her, O heaven You apostles and prophets and holy believers, rejoice! For on your behalf God pronounced the judgment against her that she wanted to bring upon you! Then a mighty angel **took up a stone,** like a huge millstone, and threw it into the sea, saying: "With this kind of sudden violence, the great city Babylon will be

[53] Graham, Ruth. "What the Latest Investigations Into Catholic Church Sex Abuse Mean." *The New York Times*, June 2, 2023. https://www.nytimes.com/2023/06/02/us/catholic-church-sex-abuse-investigations.html#:~:text=More%20than%20300%20priests%20were,and%20sorrow%E2%80%9D%20over%20the%20findings.
[54] Thomas, *Blast of Fire*, 154.

thrown down and exist no more" (Rev 18:20–21
TPT, emphasis added).

Notice in the scripture the judgment of the Whore of Babylon
comes swiftly with "sudden violence." The Bible compares
the judgment of Babylon with an angel throwing a mighty
stone into the sea, and uses the word millstone. Yeshua used
the world millstone when describing child abuse, "But if you
cause one of these little ones who trusts in me to fall into sin,
it would be better for you to be thrown into the sea with a
large millstone hung around your neck" (Mark 9:42 NLT). By
this proclamation, Yeshua forecasts the Stone Judgment in
the future dealt with child predators.

As mentioned in Chapter 7, not just the leaders of the
Catholic Church receive judgment. *All* elements of the
Ekklesia are judged during the Stone Judgment and *any*
organization, charity, trust or religious group linked to the
demonic agenda of the Fourth Beast faces utter elimination
—especially those involved with human trafficking and
abuse of children.

As discussed in Chapter 6, I believe the seven days
between the time of the judgment of the Fourth Beast and
the final victory represent seven years. If the heavenly signs
on September 23, 2017 represented the day that Yeshua
judged the Fourth Beast in the spirit realm, then this
indicates that by September 23, 2024, we should witness a
defeat of the Fourth Beast. When this happens, the man-
from-the-sea comes out of the mountain and declares peace

(2 Esd. 13:12). We will soon witness the death of the Whore of Babylon.

Little Horn Dies

For some of the Jews killed the prophets, and some even killed the Lord Jesus. Now they have persecuted us, too. They fail to please God and work against all humanity... (1 Thess. 2:15 NLT).

When studying scriptures on YHWY's judgment of the Little Horn, it became evident that the sins of the Little Horn in many ways mirrored those of the Whore, Babylon. Agents of the Fourth Beast often hid behind gowns of religion, mostly false Judaism (adherents to the Babylonian Talmud) or false Christianity (adherents to satanic elements of the Catholic religion). Jews served as treasurers of the Vatican for centuries.[55] Jews also made up the founding members of the Jesuits.[56] For all intents and purposes, they represent the same group—men and women using religion and pagan governments to achieve power; They both serve Satan.

Please do not misunderstand, there are God-fearing people who claim Judaism and Catholicism. However, the leadership at the top represents extensive compromise and evil.

The Shaking of Nations related to the Little Horn, the false Jews, already began. The ongoing battle between Russia and Ukraine represents a Biblically significant shaking. Modern Ukraine represents the birthplace of the Khazarians,

55   Saussy, F. Tupper. *Rulers of Evil* (n.p.: Ospray, 1999), 160-61.
56   Hughes, Bill. *The Secret Terrorists* (Truth Triumphant, 2002), 16-17.

who built a mighty maritime trading empire that peaked in AD 800. The Russians defeated Khazar in AD 1000, causing them to disperse into Western Europe, where they captured the banking system.[57] The book of Daniel outlines the *last battle* of the Little Horn before his reign of terror ends:

> But rumors from the east and from the north shall alarm *and* hasten him. And he shall go forth with great fury to destroy and utterly to sweep many away. And he shall pitch his palatial tents between the seas and the glorious holy Mount [Zion]; yet he shall come to his end with none to help him (Dan. 11:44-45 AMPC).

Directions such as east and north are always in relation to Jerusalem in the Bible. North and east of Jerusalem lie Ukraine and Russia, respectively. The Little Horn's beginning and ending are Khazaria—modern-day Ukraine. Note in the passage his end comes "with none to help him." Increasingly, Benjamin Netenyahu and Volodymyr Zelenskyy, who both identify as Jews, face increased isolation on the world stage —their end nears.

In Figure 6, I indicate an estimated range of 2024-2025 for the Little Horn to perish. His death may come as early as the Fourth Beast, who I expect to die by September 2024. What the military doesn't destroy by force, YHWY eliminates by a plague, disease, or fire.

---

57   Thomas, *Kingdom Age of the Saints*, 52-59.

Jerusalem Destroyed

> *A ruin, ruin, ruin I will make it. This also shall not be,*
> *until he comes, the one to whom judgment belongs,*
> *and I will give it to him (Ezek. 21:27 ESV).*

The above scripture states YHWY destroys Jerusalem three times. The first destruction came at the hands of Ancient Babylon, after they sacked Jerusalem in 586 BC. The Romans effected the second destruction in AD 70. Jerusalem likely endures destruction yet a third time. Afterward, YHWY ensures Jerusalem goes to its rightful heirs, the seed of Jacob —most of which already accepted Yeshua as their Messiah. However, I believe YHWY preserves the tomb and other sacred spots for when and if He destroys Jerusalem.

Prophecies related to the modern State of Israel exist in the Bible, but not in the manner currently taught in Sunday school. The prophet Daniel prophesied in Daniel 11:41 that the Little Horn, the Khazarian Jews, would enter the land of Israel and setup shop as false imposters casting the illusion they represent "God's chosen people." We should no longer swallow the deception. Today differs little from the time of Yeshua's ministry, when the false shepherds, the Pharisees, controlled Jerusalem. The King of Israel at that time, Herod, descended from an Edomite convert to Judaism, Antipater.[58]

In the most recent Covid-19 pandemic, the government of Israel imposed the deadly vaccine on nearly 80% of their inhabitants, the highest percentage of the populous in any

---

[58] J. Bigland. *A Compendious History of the Jews* (London: 1820), 179.

nation of the world.[59] Israel's government currently bans the teaching of the gospel of Yeshua, just like the Pharisees in the time of Yeshua. The State of Israel currently wages a murderous war on their neighbors in the Gaza Strip, justifying their genocidal acts towards children as a "holy war" while at the same time advertising new ocean-front property on freshly bombed ground. Something very evil surrounds the government of Israel. Don't be surprised if during the Stone Judgment, YHWY clears Jerusalem out. If that happens, many Christians, especially American Christians, likely will express shock and outrage. However, we should all love truth and recognize deception.

The table in Figure 6 indicates Jerusalem's estimated destruction occurs between 2024 and 2025, coinciding with the estimated date range of destruction of the Little Horn.

Wealth of Wicked Distributed

> *The nations retreat at the sound of your roaring voice. The nations scatter as you arise in your majesty. Their spoil will be harvested, carried away like locusts that strip a field bare. And like leaping locusts, men will leap upon the spoils (Isa. 33:3-4 TPT).*

The YHWY-ordained reparations coming to His people are unmatched. The entire modern industrial complex and advanced mining techniques, combined with the most sophisticated wealth-skimming techniques ever devised, created a vast hoard of wealth confined to a few hands.

---

59   Estrin, Daniel. "Highly Vaccinated Israel Is Seeing A Dramatic Surge In New COVID Cases. Here's Why." *NPR*, August 20, 2021.

Moreover, many of Earth's storehouses YHWY supernaturally concealed from the Fourth Beast—He always planned to give this wealth to us.

The concept of "scarcity" amounts to a carefully orchestrated lie, propagated by the Fourth Beast to invent value for otherwise unlimited resources, such as energy. Inspired men such as Nikola Tesla discovered free energy many decades ago. The Fourth Beast squelched many discoveries designed to bless humanity in order to preserve their profit motive. Perceived scarcity of goods invents value in the same way that perceived value of paper money contrives value—both project and maintain the power of the architects of evil.

Through His anointed Soldier Saints, YHWY strips *all* wealth from the architects of evil and gives it back to the people. The righteously-minded give praise and credit to YHWY for this divine reversal. The unrighteous fail to understand YHWY's goodness and the sheer scope of this pending miracle.

The wonder of plundering our enemies and freely distributing to their victims causes many to come to YHWY. Many, hopefully billions, recognize YHWY's goodness and want to follow Him. YHWY's generosity shatters the lie that it's more beneficial to follow Satan versus YHWY. The spectacle of wealth redistribution illustrates YHWY's goodness and diffuses false beliefs about Satan that he so scrupulously foisted on humanity for millennia.

For the Ekklesia, newfound prosperity will represent a tremendous test sadly many won't pass. Will you seek YHWY on what to do with the wealth, or simply focus on yourself? Decide to function as a distributor of YHWY's goodness. Listen to Yeshua's warning:

> But the evil servant says in his heart, 'My master delays his coming, and who knows when he will return?' *And because of the delay, the servant mistreats those in his master's household. Instead of caring for the ones he was appointed to serve*, he abuses the other servants and gives himself over to party with drunkards (Matt. 24:48-49 TPT).

Decide now who YHWY appointed you to serve. To prepare yourself, document whom you plan to bless in advance of the wealth transfer. YHWY will honor your faith. In Figure 6, I estimate that the wealth distribution occurs between 2024 and 2025.

Judean Shame Removed

> The Lord YAHWEH says this: I will gather you back from the peoples, and draw you together from the countries where you have been scattered and give you the land of Israel. When you return, you will purge the land of all its filthy idols and detestable practices. I will give you a new, undivided heart, and I will put a new spirit in you. I will remove your stubborn heart of stone and give you a tender heart that responds to me—a devoted heart (Ezek. 11:17-18).

YHWY never forgets His covenant. We might forget, but He doesn't. YHWY fully intends to give Jerusalem to the seed of Jacob, fulfilling the original promises to Abraham, Moses, Isaac, and Jacob. If you study the promises in Figure 6 pertaining to the return of the Judeans, YHWY performs the work to preserve the integrity of His own name and covenant He made with their ancestors. I don't know precisely how He plans to do it. However, when the seed of Jacob returns, they must purge the land of idols and practices that don't please Him. YHWY supernaturally imparts a pure heart to the Judeans, likely through revival. When the Judeans return, the rivalry between Judah and Israel disappears—unity exists in acceptance of Yeshua as Messiah. (See Isa. 11:10-16).

Because of the utterly satanic practices of the Khazarian Jews, those who hijacked Judaism and called themselves Jews, the name Jew carries severe stigma and shame. In YHWY's immaculate plan, He even thought of this in advance and promises to clear their name. Listen to the acknowledgment of the problem and the promise:

> This is what I, Lord YAHWEH, say: People say about you, "You devour people and have robbed your nation of its children." But you will devour people no longer nor make your nation childless again, says Lord YAHWEH. I will silence the insults of the nations. You will never again have to hear the mocking of the peoples, and you will never again cause your nation to stumble. I, Lord YAHWEH, have spoken (Ezek. 36:13-15).

YHWY addresses the fact that people associate "Jew" with vile practices of child sacrifice, cannibalism, and abortion based on the satanic Khazarian Jews. Many of these vile practices are codified in the Babylonian Talmud, the preeminent law for rabbinic Jews. Somehow, YHWY removes this stigma for the Judean people. Perhaps YHWY ensures that people around the world understand the Khazarians (Edomites) differ from true Judeans (seed of Jacob) and vice versa. Many of the fiercest defenders of humanity in the battle against the Fourth Beast and his satanic minions come from the seed of Jacob—some from Yeshua's bloodline Himself.

YHWY promised to place Jerusalem in the hands of the seed of Jacob, the rightful heirs to the land. YHWY repeats His promise many times in the Bible. You see, YHWY owns all the land on Earth. He places land in the hands of whomever He wills. He does not forget His promises, which include:

- A population explosion among all tribes (Ezek. 36:10).
- Others of YHWY's people will live with them, without fear that Judeans will sacrifice their children to strange gods (Ezek. 36:13).
- YHWY gives Judeans a new pure heart, totally cleansing their past (Ezek. 36:26).
- Complete unification between all the tribes of Israel (Ezek. 37:19).
- Ruined cities are rebuilt (Ezek. 36:33).
- A single king shall rule them (Ezek. 37:22).

In Figure 6, I estimate YHWY grants the land surrounding Jerusalem to the seed of Jacob between 2024 and 2026. The transfer happens before the end of the age in 2027.

Soldier Saints

In *KAS*, I introduced the concept of the Soldier Saint. Soldier Saints are obedient warriors for YHWY who fearlessly move out in their high calling, regardless of the cost to their reputation or safety. Soldier Saints call out tyranny, right wrongs, and know how to fight for the truth. Let's honor the very epitome of the Soldier Saint—those fighting on the front lines in the war against evil on our behalf.

Thousands of years ago, YHWY promised a victorious outcome of today's battle. Nonetheless, the kinetic battle costs numerous lives. Satan controlled our world for 6,000 years. He built a fiercely loyal death-cult of deceived followers who believe Satan wins—not YHWY. They fight to the death, because they know if and/or when they get caught, they die. The crimes against humanity committed by the wretched agents of the Fourth Beast represent the darkest evil the world ever witnessed.

Voices of abused and murdered children cry out for judgment. Earth cries out for judgment. Parents of children who lost lives in pointless wars to enrich bankers cry out for judgment. J6-ers and other political prisoners, left to rot in dank jail cells, cry out for judgment. Victims of communism, forced to eat their starved and dead children to survive in Russia and China cry out. YHWY hears these cries, and even as I write thousands of military personnel deliver YHWY's righteous vindication out of the barrel of an M4 rifle— battling in extremely dark places where horrific crimes occurred. These soldiers deserve our thanks, our support, and our prayers. They represent YHWY's army. They heed His command in Revelation 18:6 (NLT) to:

> Do to her as she has done to others.
> Double her penalty for all her evil deeds.
> She brewed a cup of terror for others,
> so brew twice as much for her.

We know our military fought on the wrong side for a long time, taking out enemies of the deep state. Most had no idea and many suffer from emotional and physical PTSD as a result. As evidence, over 17 U.S. veterans commit suicide every day, a travesty.[60] For each of these deaths YHWY holds the Fourth Beast accountable. But I assure you, now our military fights for freedom for all humanity. They fly off to demonic underground caverns and plant munitions. They lie to family members and loved ones about their missions to keep their families safe. I pray for protection for our fighting men and women in the military every day. I ask you to join me.

Soon, we celebrate the greatest modern-day heroes of our age and hear their stories. They fight the enemy of humanity, for the survival of humanity. They fight alongside

---

[60] "2023 National Veteran Suicide Prevention: Annual Report." U.S. Department of Veteran Affairs. November 2023. https://www.mentalhealth.va.gov/docs/data-sheets/2023/2023-National-Veteran-Suicide-Prevention-Annual-Report-FINAL-508.pdf

angelic beings of the heavenly realm. Furthermore, they fight YHWY's war against Satan—they will win.

10. Harvest Before Fire

I declare from the beginning how it will end and foretell from the start what has not yet happened. I decree that my purpose will stand and I will fulfill my every plan.

— Isa. 46:10 TPT

After the Shaking of Nations consummates, we enter a critical juncture. To many, it appears the battle won—peace on Earth. Some mimic Dorothy in *The Wizard of Oz*, singing "Ding, dong the witch is dead!"[61] Most people now possess resources never dreamed possible. However, to those who know and understand YHWY's plan, this time represents the calm before the super-storm of the ages—the Fire Judgment and the appearance of our Savior, Yeshua.

---

[61] *The Wizard of Oz*, dir. Victor Fleming, prod. Mervyn LeRoy, 1939.

During this peaceful hiatus, we must gather with great urgency as many lost as possible into YHWY's family of Believers. Why?

Because this is their last chance.

After the Fourth Beast dies, many things are set right. Millions of the worst-of-the-worst minions of the Fourth Beast—dead. The ultra-elite mega-satanists—gone. But YHWY's judgment is far from over. He plans to finish the job by removing every unbeliever from Earth in an awe-inspiring Fire Judgment. The righteous remain protected. But the wicked shriek with agonizing terror as they are thrust violently into Hell and torment.

Anyone who witnesses YHWY move mightily against Satan, sees YHWY's goodness, benefits from His deliverance, and yet still does not accept Yeshua as his or her Savior faces removal from Earth. The End Times Harvest brings many to the Lord. However, please—don't neglect to labor in the fields of the lost.

Start praying for friends, family members and neighbors _now_. YHWY honors your faith. YHWY promises our households receive salvation (Acts 16:31). Stand on this promise daily _from now on_. Once the Fire Judgment starts, it's too late.

End Times Harvest

Even before the Shaking of Nations finishes, a radical revival breaks out and many lost discover Yeshua. Many evangelists in the field already report an unprecedented hunger for YHWY. The ministering angel in the book of Revelation goes forth after the fall of Babylon, as the Word explains:

> I saw another angel. This one was flying across the sky and had the eternal good news to announce to the people of every race, tribe, language, and nation on earth. The angel shouted, "Worship and honor God! The time has come for him to judge everyone. Kneel down before the one who created heaven and earth, the oceans, and every stream."
>
> A second angel followed and said, "The great city of Babylon has fallen! This is the city that made all nations drunk and immoral. Now God is angry, and Babylon has fallen" (Rev 14:6-8 CEV).

The entire world experiences peace for the first time in thousands of years, including in the Middle East. YHWY especially blesses the righteous, enticing many lost into His Kingdom. In His mercy, YHWY gives the lost a few short years to choose Him. Hidden technology and other wonders are revealed to humanity. This phase remains critical for Believers to gather in the fields of the lost. After the End Times Harvest, severe judgment occurs and those who reject YHWY are removed from Earth. Figure 7 outlines the events during the End Times Harvest, providing scripture references and estimated year ranges. Again, the scripture list represents a sample of promises that will get you started as you study the Bible.

Figure 7: *End Times Harvest*

	Event	Scripture Reference	Est. Date
END TIMES HARVEST	Foundation of Kingdom Age Prepared	1 Chron. 3:17; Ezra 3:2-3,8,10-11; 4:21-22; Isa. 16:5; Hag. 1:10; 2:9, 18-19, 21, 23	2025-2026
	Righteous Extraordinarily Blessed	2 Bar. 29:4-5; Ps. 126:1-2; Isa. 25:6-7; 26:1-6; 30:23-24; 49:22-26; 51:14; 54:2-4; 54:11-17; Ezek. 34:26-31; Joel 2:26	2025-2033
	Peace, Revival, End Times Harvest	1 Enoch 50:1-5; 2 Bar. 74:1; Isa. 4:1; 17:7-8; 29:17-21; 30:22; 33:13; 34:1-2; 19:22-23; 21:16-17; Ezek. 33:6-9; Joel 2:1, 12-13; Matt. 24:14; Acts 10:38; Rev 14:15-16	
	Dew of Health & Other Wonders	2 Bar. 29:6-7; 73:2; 2 Esd. 13:49-50	

© GLORIAM MEDIA, 2024

Foundation of Kingdom Age Prepared

> *Tell Governor Zerubbabel of Judah that I am going to shake the heavens and the earth and wipe out kings and their kingdoms. I will overturn war chariots, and then cavalry troops will start slaughtering each other. But tell my servant Zerubbabel that I, the LORD All-Powerful, have chosen him, and he will rule in my name (Hag. 2:21 CEV).*

The man-from-the-sea in scripture, fulfilled by President Trump, finalizes a fierce battle against the forces of the deep state and then prepares the foundation for the Kingdom Age. The Bible identifies the deep state players as the Fourth Beast, the Little Horn and the Whore of Babylon. After their death, the world *completely* changes.

As explained in Chapter 9, President Trump also carries the anointing of Zerubbabel, the governor of Judah who led the remnant of Israel back to Jerusalem after their captivity in Babylon. Zerubbabel, the grandson of King Jehoiachin of Judah, descended from King David (1 Chron. 3:17). As soon as

Zerubbabel arrived in Jerusalem, he set about rebuilding the second Judean Temple along with Joshua, the high priest (Ezra 3:2-3, 8). It took Zerubbabel two years to lay the foundation of the house of YHWY. After a 17-year hiatus, the structure of the Judean Temple came together on top of the foundation laid by Zerubbabel (Ezra 4:21).

The book of Haggai contains many prophecies regarding Zerubbabel and the times. First, Haggai calls attention to the fact that YHWY's people focused on building their own houses, not His. As a result, scarcity abounded because "the heavens withhold the dew and the earth produces no crops" for YHWY's people (Hag. 1:10 NLT). Haggai went on to prophesy great things about the future. First, he prophesied about a great shaking of the nations and a return of Glory even greater than in Solomon's Temple (Hag. 2:9). Second, he prophesied that once the foundation of YHWY's house begins construction, YHWY would bless His people *from that day onward* (Hag. 2:18-19). Finally, Haggai prophesied that YHWY would dethrone royal thrones and evil powers and their armies and honor Zerubbabel as a royal signet from YHWY (Hag. 2:23).

None of these prophecies came to pass in Haggai's time. Always quick to judge, the modern-day church would erroneously equate Haggai to "a false prophet!" Haggai's prophecies about the next great shaking and the Lord raising up Zerubbabel as a mighty leader pertain to *our* time!

It took Zerubbabel two years to rebuild the foundation of YHWY's house. For this reason, I believe the two years following the death of the Fourth Beast involve foundation building for YHWY's Kingdom. In Figure 7, I estimate foundation building to include 2025 and 2026, the years leading up to the end of the old age. The foundation of the Kingdom Age includes the creation and implementation of new laws, new financial systems, and new governance to replace the Babylonian system erected by Satan's henchman under the Fourth Beast.

Righteous Extraordinarily Blessed

> *And Behemoth shall be revealed from his place, and Leviathan shall ascend from the sea, those two great monsters which I created on the fifth day of creation, and shall have kept until that time, and then they shall be food for all that are left (2 Bar. 29:4).*

As the Fourth Beast dies, YHWY's refreshing and abundance shower the earth. All will know YHWY delivered the righteous from the wicked. The world begins to witness and decipher YHWY's hand through the blessing of the righteous and the punishment of the wicked leaders of the Fourth Beast. The world feeds on the now plundered Fourth Beast, referenced by the names of the Demon-gods in the passage above, Leviathan and Behemoth. These are the two evil principalities which controlled the Fourth Beast and Little Horn, respectively.

YHWY then commands the earth to produce supernatural abundance, another miracle. Massive harvests come forth for farmers, demonstrating the absolute goodness of YHWY:

The earth also shall yield its fruit ten-thousandfold and on each vine there shall be a thousand branches, and each branch shall produce a thousand clusters, and each cluster produce a thousand grapes, and each grape produces a cor of wine (2 Bar. 29:5).

Scarcity vaporizes across Earth as its crops yields bountifully. All effort put forth by the Fourth Beast to control and contaminate the food supply vanishes as YHWY commands blessing upon Earth. As the Kingdom of YHWY begins to establish on Earth, we richly feast on His blessings:

The Lord YAHWEH, Commander of Angel Armies, will host a rich feast on this mountain for all peoples—a feast with plenty of meat and well-aged wine, with an abundance of food and the finest of wine. And on this mountain, he will destroy the shroud wrapped around all the people, the veil spread over all nations (Isa. 25:6 TPT).

YHWY's people celebrate in great joy. We give praises to Him for His mighty deliverance. The revival and Glory pierce through the veil of deception over all peoples and nations. Seeds sown in the past by YHWY's people begin to spring up supernaturally—the earth begins to produce for YHWY's people uniquely. Wine, mentioned twice in the passage, represents YHWY's abundant blessings but also great spiritual enlightenment and revival. YHWY draws a sharp line of distinction between the blessings of the righteous and the wicked. In the past, the wicked prospered and the righteous suffered. The reversal begins and the righteous prosper while the wicked suffer. The Lord shows the world the benefits of following Him, and He hosts a feast for "all peoples" to draw them to Him.

In Figure 7, I estimate the righteous enjoy extraordinarily blessing beginning in 2025 and continuing up until the Fire Judgment, which I believe occurs no later than 2033.

Peace, Revival, End Times Harvest

Sound the trumpet on Zion, the Lord's sacred hill. Warn everyone to tremble! The judgment day of the Lord is coming soon. The Lord said: It isn't too late. You can still return to me with all your heart. Start crying and mourning! Go without eating... I am merciful, kind, and caring. I don't easily lose my temper, and I don't like to punish (Joel 2:1, 12, 13b).

The entire world recognizes the miracle of YHWY's defeat of the Fourth Beast and the blessings of the righteous. The most powerful revival the world witnessed since Yeshua's earthly ministry breaks out as the veil of darkness lifts. Miracles abound as YHWY's people, emboldened and empowered by YHWY's goodness, spread the Gospel throughout the entire earth. We spread the true Gospel message that Peter first preached to the lost in Acts:

Jesus of Nazareth was anointed by God with the Holy Spirit and with great power. He did wonderful things for others and divinely healed all **who were under the tyranny of the devil**, for God had anointed him (Acts 11:38, emphasis added).

You see, Yeshua delivers *all humanity* from Satan's grips, not just His followers. Our simple message to the lost: "Yeshua just delivered you from Satan's tyranny—He's that good— won't you receive Him as Lord?" This message, accompanied by mighty miracles of healing and deliverance, draws hundreds of millions or more to Yeshua. The prophet Enoch describes this time succinctly:

> And in those days a change shall take place for the holy and elect, And the light of days shall abide upon them, And glory and honour shall turn to the holy, On the day of affliction on which evil shall have been treasured up against the sinners.
>
> And the righteous shall be victorious in the name of the Lord of Spirits: **And He will cause the others to witness (this), That they may repent and forgo the works of their hands**.
>
> They shall have no honour through the name of the Lord of Spirits, yet through His name shall they be saved, And the Lord of Spirits will have compassion on them, For His compassion is great (1 Enoch 50:1-3, emphasis added).

Enoch refers to this unique time as one of great compassion by the Lord. YHWY shows the world the benefits of serving

Him, while at the same time giving them a final chance to repent before the Fire Judgment. Again, we see a dividing line between YHWY's followers and the lost—His children receive more blessing than the lost. Many are attracted to YHWY's goodness, and billions receive Yeshua during the End Times Harvest. However, the End Times Harvest only lasts a few years before the Fire Judgment occurs.

In the next verse, Enoch describes the Fire Judgment that follows the End Times Harvest:

> And He is righteous also in His judgement, And in the presence of His glory unrighteousness also shall not maintain itself: at His judgement the unrepentant shall perish before Him. And from **henceforth I will have no mercy on them**, saith the Lord of Spirits (1 Enoch 50:4-5, emphasis added).

The End Times Harvest and revival represents the *absolute last chance* for the wicked to repent and turn to YHWY. I outline in Figure 7 that I expect the End Times Harvest to last a few years, between 2025 and 2033. If you recall from Chapter 9, the current age ends by 2027 and the third day of the Ekklesia, the third biblical millennia begins as early as 2027 or as late as 2033, based on best information available for dating Yeshua's resurrection from the dead.

Put another way, the End Times Harvest may last only two or three years, or it could last as long as eight years. We must maintain a sense of urgency to gather the lost into YHWY's Kingdom. Only because of YHWY's extreme compassion does He make this final opportunity available to the lost.

Dew of Health & Other Wonders

And those who have hungered shall rejoice: moreover, also, they shall behold marvels every day. For winds shall go forth from before Me to bring every morning the fragrance of aromatic fruits, and at the close of the day clouds distilling the dew of health (2 Bar. 29:6-7).

During the End Times Harvest, we witness mighty wonders *daily*. An aroma from the Lord begins to blow over the land. Clouds containing the dew of health begin to fall on humanity. YHWY orchestrates a divine reversal of the damage done by the Fourth Beast over many decades as they poisoned our food, water, and air. Supernatural healing also comes to billions who received at least one injection of the Covid-19 vaccine, and are now suffering from an explosion of spike proteins in their bodies.

In YHWY's mercy, He begins to shower the earth with healing dew, reversing the damage inflicted upon humanity by the Fourth Beast. The "dew of health" also reverses the aging process for YHWY's righteous—we feel and look younger daily.

Other "wonders" include the release of hidden technologies that bless humanity and raise the standard of living. These include free energy, based on converting aether in the atmosphere and splitting water molecules. Wonders include anti-gravitational craft, quickening transport. When the man-from-the-sea finalizes the destruction of the Fourth Beast, the Bible says, "Therefore when he destroys the multitude of the nations that are gathered together, he will defend the people who remain. And then he will show them very many wonders" (2 Esd. 13:49-50 NRSV).

Merriam-Webster defines wonder as a cause of astonishment or admiration: MARVEL. It also refers to wonder as a miracle. Humanity witnesses many miracles at the hands of Believers. The dew of Heaven grows back missing limbs lost in wars fought for the Fourth Beast. Autistic children speak for the first time. The End Times Harvest represents a time of great revival, before the Fire Judgment.

In Figure 7, I estimate YHWY's incredible, miraculous wonders start in 2025 and continue up until the Fire Judgment, occurring no later than 2033.

Fire Judgment

The Fire Judgment encompasses all humanity, Earth, and its heavens and occurs over one actual week. It represents the largest judgment and most substantial event in human history ever. It combines elements of all past judgments including the Great Flood, the Egyptian plagues, the earth swallowing the rebellious of Korah, fire consuming Sodom and Gomorrah, and the destruction of Pharaoh's army in the Red Sea. YHWY rocks the world with undeniable signs, visible across the entire earth including; blood rain, thunder, smoke, fire, the stench of sulfur, a mighty worldwide earthquake, and total darkness.

In the grand finale of the Fire Judgment, Yeshua appears in Glory in the sky. His appearing terrifies the wicked, and they hide in caves. The Lord removes every wicked person on Earth. In contrast, YHWY raises every righteous person from Adam to the present day from the dead. After the righteous dead rise, all of the righteous remnant who never physically died receive a glorified body. The curse pronounced over man after he fell in the Garden of Eden breaks, and we experience true peace. YHWY then refreshes the earth. However, Yeshua still dwells on His throne in Heaven awaiting the perfection of His Bride.

Figure 8 describes the events during the Fire Judgment, as well as provides a corresponding partial list of scripture references. Believers are safe during the Fire Judgment, and should not fear. YHWY reserves this judgment for the wicked, not the righteous (1 Thess. 5:9). I estimate the Fire Judgment occurs between 2027 and 2033, corresponding to the end of the age and the third millennial day of the Ekklesia after the resurrection of Yeshua. I estimate the events outlined in Figure 8 occur over one actual week, beginning anytime between 2027 and 2033.

Figure 8: *Fire Judgment*

Event	Scripture Reference
Remnant Protected During Judgment	1 Enoch 1:7-8; 2 Baruch 21:17; Ex. 12:14-17, 21-22; Ps. 91:7-8; Isa. 24:14-16; 26:20-21; 32:18-20; 33:22; Dan. 7:25; Matt. 24:37-39; Luke 21:34-36; 1 Thess. 5:2-3, 9
Day 1: Blood Rain	Joel 2:30; Rev 6:12
Day 2: Thunder, Smoke and Fire	1 Enoch 91:9; 2 Esd. 15:38; 16:10; Ps. 50:3; Isa. 28:17-19; 29:6; 30:27; 30:30; 33:10-12; Jer. 30:23-24; Joel 2:3, 30; Nah. 1:3; Mal 4:1
Day 3: Stench of Sulfur	Ps. 11:6; Isa. 30:33; 34:9; Rev 6:14
Day 4: Earthquake	2 Esd. 16:12; Isa. 2:18; 13:13; 24:19-20; 29:6; 30:25; Joel 2:10; Rev 6:14;
Day 5: Darkness	Isa. 13:10; 24:17-18; 28:19-22; Joel 2:2, 10, 31; Rev 6:12
Day 6: Appearance of Yeshua and Angels	1 Enoch 69:29; 2 Bar. 30:1; Isa. 30:30; 34:5-7; 41:20; 45:8; 53:12; Dan. 7:13; Joel 2:31-32; 14:14; 22:12; Matt. 24:23, 27, 29-30; 26:64; Mark 14:62; Luke 18:8; 21:27; Acts 1:9-11; 3:19-21; 1 Thess. 4:16; 5:23; Titus 2:13; Rev 6:16
Signs in the Heavens, Wicked Hide	Isa. 2:10,19-21; 33:14; Jer. 25:30-31; Mark 14:62; 24:36; Luke 21:25; Rev 1:7; 6:15
Resurrection of Righteous Dead	1 Enoch 62:15; 91:10; 92:3; 2 Bar. 30:2; 50:2-4; 51:3-6; 2 Esd. 2:31; Ps. 21:4; Isa. 26:19; 43:7; 49:19-21; Ezek. 37:1-12; Dan. 12:1-2,13; Matt. 24:30-31; Mark 13:26-27; John 6:39-40; 1 Cor. 15:22-23, 26, 38, 51-57; 1 Thess. 4:16; 2 Thess. 2:1; Heb. 9:28
Living Righteous Glorified	1 Enoch 62:15-16; 2 Bar. 30:2; Matt. 24:31; Mark 13:26-27; John 6:39-40; 1 Cor. 15:22-23, 26, 38, 51-57; 1 Thess. 4:17-18; Heb. 9:28
Day 7: Battle in the Heavens	1 Enoch 1:1,4-7; Ezek. 31-33; Joel 2:2-10
Wicked Men Removed	1 Enoch 1:5-7; 69:27-29; 91:7-9,11; 94:1; 2 Bar. 30:4-5; Ps. 21:9-12; 2 Esd. 15:40; Isa. 2:11; 13:11; 24:6; 26:14; 28:18; 29:5; 7; 34:3; 41:11-12; 51:12; Ezek. 7:12-14; Matt. 24:40-42; Luke 17:28-30; 1 Cor. 15:24; Rev 14:17-20;
Remaining Evil Principalities Removed	1 Enoch 1:5-7; 16:1; 69:27-29; 91:8; Isa. 2:13; 14:12-21; 24:21-23; 34:4; 34:10-15; Joel 2:11; 1 Cor. 15:24; Eph. 6:12; Rev 6:13
Day 8: Peace After Saints Return	1 Enoch 10:17; 25:4-6; 62:13-16; 91:12; 96:2-3; Ps. 126:1-3; Isa. 2:2-5; 4:2-6; 6:1-7; 13:12; 25:6-9; 28:15, 18; 30:25-26; 32:1-8; 35:1-2, 7; 36:18-10; 43:18-21; 44:3-5; 51:3, 11; 65:17-24; Ezek. 34:25; 43:12; Dan. 2:35; 7:18, 22, 27; 12:3; Joel 2:21-22, 28-29; Hag. 2:9; Mal. 4:2-3; Col. 3:4; 2 Tim. 4:8; 2 Pet. 3:10; 1 John 3:2

Sidebar: FIRE JUDGMENT

Remnant Protected During Judgment

Go, my people, into your inner chambers and close the doors behind you. Hide for a little while, until his indignation is over. For the Lord is coming out from

his heavenly place to punish people for their sins (Isa.
26:20-21a TPT).

YHWY's people should not fear during the Fire Judgment. Our Father promises complete protection. We rejoice and stay in peace, safe in our homes. We praise and worship YHWY during this time. The Fire Judgment lands on the wicked, not the righteous.

Note the scripture commands us to go into our homes and shut the door. If you recall from Exodus, the Lord told Israel to stay inside when the death angel passed over Egypt. YHWY also commanded them to apply the blood of the lamb to their doorposts:

> Each family is to pick out a sheep and kill it for Passover. Make a brush from a few small branches of a hyssop plant and dip the brush in the bowl that has the blood of the animal in it. Then brush some of the blood above the door and on the posts at each side of the door of your house. After this, everyone is to stay inside... (Ex. 12:21b-22 CEV).

Under the New Covenant, we apply the Blood of Yeshua to our lives, family, and possessions for protection. In the Appendix, I include a Prayer of Protection for you to pray over your family.

The Apocalypse of Thomas

Many passages describe the Fire Judgment in the Bible, including scriptures in the book of Revelation. The opening of the sixth seal in Revelation describes the Fire Judgment:

> And behold! I saw the Lamb break open the sixth seal, which released a powerful earthquake. I saw the sun become pitch black and the full moon become bloodred. The stars fell from heaven to the earth, as a fig tree shaken by a stormy wind sheds its unripe figs. The sky receded with a snap—as a scroll rolls itself up. And every mountain and island was moved from its place.
>
> Then the kings of the earth and its great princes and generals, the rich and powerful, and everyone, whether they were slave or free, ran for cover and hid in the caves and among the mountain boulders. They called out to the mountains and the boulders, saying, "Fall on us at once! Hide us quickly from the glorious face of the one seated on the throne and from the wrath of the Lamb, **for the great day of their wrath has come**, and who is able to stand?" (Rev 6:12-17 TPT, emphasis added).

During the Fire Judgment, the kings of the earth cry out when they see Heaven, Yeshua and His angels! The sixth seal releases red skies, darkness, storms, falling stars, and a mighty earthquake. I referenced the sixth seal in my prior books as an event occurring during the Stone Judgment. The book of Isaiah lists the same heavenly signs in connection with a mighty judgment of the Lord, confirming that the sixth seal in Revelation represents the Stone Judgment. (See Figure 8 for scripture references). However, the *sequence and timing* of events during the sixth seal remains unclear when relying solely on the book of Revelation.

One ancient apocalyptic text provides the detailed *sequence* of events during the Fire Judgment—the *Apocalypse of Thomas*. According to scholars, this ancient text dates to between AD 100 and AD 300, and remained widespread in popularity over most of Europe for centuries. William Shakespeare's writings were likely influenced by the *Apocalypse of Thomas*. Most believe Gelasius of Cyzicus, a fifth century Roman priest, struck the *Apocalypse of Thomas* from church canon in the fifth century, although the book remained canonical "in certain parts of the Western Christendom in the 9th and 10th centuries."[62]

The *Apocalypse of Thomas* defines the Fire Judgment as a one-week event, beginning on a Sunday. YHWY commanded Israel to remember Passover for a week. In those seven days He commanded them to eat unleavened bread and perform no work, other than preparing bread (Ex. 12:14-17). Given the specific instructions regarding the seven-day Passover celebration, it's likely that YHWY's Fire Judgment also lasts seven days, as the Fire Judgment equates to a "second Passover."

Some confuse the judgment in the *Apocalypse of Thomas* with the Battle of Armageddon, since the text twice

[62] James, M.R. "The Apocalypse of Thomas." Introduction. In *The Grand Bible*, 4th ed., 2001–2. England: Guildford Scientific Press, 2022.

states the events occur, "when Antichrist draweth near." The Fourth Beast attempts to change "God's Law and the sacred seasons" (Dan. 7:25 CEV). The Fourth Beast attempts to draw in the anti-Christ before his time. So while the arrival of the anti-Christ draws *near*, he's not yet here during the Fire Judgment. Also remember that the anti-Christ appears during the *seventh* seal in the book of Revelation, which occurs *after* the sixth seal opens. The anti-Christ appears after the Ekklesia translates to Heaven to marry Yeshua as His Bride. This event occurs approximately 1,000 years after the Fire Judgment on Earth, when our Lord sets things right. After the Fire Judgment, we leap closer to qualifying as the Ekklesia worthy to marry our Lord.

Day 1: Blood Rain

> On the first day of the judgement will be a great
> marvel (or, the beginning shall be). At the third hour of
> the day shall be a great and mighty voice in the
> firmament of the heaven, and a great cloud of blood
> coming down out of the north, and great thunderings
> and mighty lightnings shall follow that cloud, and
> there shall be a rain of blood upon all the earth. These
> are the signs of the first day (Apoc. Thomas).

Blood-rain falls worldwide on the first day of the Fire Judgment. We assume the first day starts on the first day of the week—Sunday according to the Hebrew calendar (Monday on the Anglo-Saxon calendar).

Cases of blood-rain are recorded as far back as Homer's *Iliad*, composed around the eighth century BC. Recorded instances usually covered only small areas. Scientists believe that rain assumed a blood-red color from the dust of red clay or the presence of microorganisms in these instances. Most consider blood-rain a bad omen.[63]

Day 2: Thunder, Smoke, and Fire

> *And on the second day there shall be a great voice in the firmament of the heaven, and the earth shall be moved out of its place: and the gates of heaven shall be opened in the firmament of heaven toward the east, and a great power shall be sent (belched) forth by the gates of heaven and shall cover all the heaven even until evening (al. and there shall be fears and tremblings in the world). These are the signs of the second day (Apoc. Thomas).*

For the second day, some versions of this passage say smoke and fire shall proceed from Heaven. Passages from Isaiah and Joel also mention smoke and fire. Of course, the smoke and fire may signify the Glory of YHWY! It causes great fear and trembling across the earth.

Day 3: Stench of Sulfur

> *And on the third day, about the second hour, shall be a voice in heaven, and the abysses of the earth shall utter their voice from the four corners of the world.*

---

[63] Wikipedia. 2024. "Blood rain." *Wikimedia Foundation*. Last modified May 27, 2024. https://en.wikipedia.org/wiki/Blood_rain.

The first heaven shall be rolled up like a book and shall straightway vanish. And because of the smoke and stench of the brimstone of the abyss the days shall be darkened unto the tenth hour. Then shall all men say: I think that the end draweth near, that we shall perish. These are the signs of the third day (Apoc. Thomas).

The passage indicates that our sky disappears and Hell opens, releasing a violent stench of sulfur and death. Apparently, this dramatic sign strikes fear in the hearts of men, as "all men" say they believe the end of the earth nears. This might explain why the Lord commanded Believers to stay inside their homes! Perhaps we are not supposed to look.

When our blue sky disappears, we will look directly into space. We now see beyond Earth's firmament. It likely looks very different than NASA photos and Hollywood movies!

Upon visiting spiritually dark places, such as the French Quarter in New Orleans, I recall smelling a foul sulfur-like odor, indicating spiritual oppression. The signs of the third day are a multiplied factor worse—worldwide in scope. The abyss of Hell will open, and we will smell the stench of spiritual depravity across the earth.

In the book of Revelation, it describes the same phenomena occurring with the sky, "The sky receded with a snap—as a scroll rolls itself up. And every mountain and island was moved from its place" (Rev 6:14 TPT). The mountains being moved in Revelation may describe the extinction of the corrupt seven mountains of cultural influence in the earth today. It may also describe the final removal of corrupt governments—every institution standing on shakable foundation will lay in ruin.

Day 4: Earthquake

And on the fourth day at the first hour, from the land of the east the abyss shall melt (so) and roar. Then shall all the earth be shaken by the might of an earthquake. In that day shall the ornaments of the heathen fall, and all the buildings of the earth, before the might of the earthquake. These are the signs of the fourth day (Apoc. Thomas).

The earthquake on day four impacts the entire earth. It functions to remove the "ornaments of the heathen" and "all the buildings." All satanic statues, temples, shrines, etc. of the wicked fall during this worldwide earthquake. I believe the military alliance takes out quite a few of these beforehand in the Shaking of Nations. However, whatever remains of the wickeds' ungodly structures, this earthquake destroys.

The earthquake in the Fire Judgment does not impact the homes of the righteous, as the Lord instructed us to stay in our homes. However, it's imperative that we apply the blood of Yeshua over our homes and property! Scriptures within Isaiah and Revelation also mention the earthquake occurring during the Fire Judgment. (See Figure 8).

Day 5: Darkness

> *And on the fifth day, at the sixth hour, there shall be great thunderings suddenly in the heaven, and the powers of light and the wheel of the sun shall be caught away, and there shall be great darkness over the world until evening, and the stars shall be turned away from their ministry. In that day all nations shall hate the world and despise the life of this world. These are the signs of the fifth day (Apoc. Thomas).*

The fifth day of the Fire Judgment brings total darkness for a day. Note the darkness starts in the sixth hour, when the Sun normally shines brightly (around noon). There is something unique about this darkness, as it causes men to hate the world and despise the life of this world. I believe that in the darkness, YHWY shows the wicked a picture of themselves—causing them to see their own wretchedness. The Bible mentions darkness as a sign of the Fire Judgment in Isaiah, Joel and Revelation. I included these references in Figure 8.

Day 6: Appearance of Yeshua and Angels

> *And on the sixth day at the fourth hour there shall be a great voice in heaven, and the firmament of the heaven shall be cloven from the east unto the west, and the angels of the heavens shall be looking forth upon the earth by the openings of the heavens, and all these that are on the earth shall behold the host of the angels looking forth out of heaven. Then shall all men flee unto the monuments (mountains?) and hide*

themselves from the face of the righteous angels, and say: Would that the earth would open and swallow us up! And such things shall come to pass as never were since this world was created.

Then shall they behold me coming from above in the light of my Father with the power and honour of the holy angels. Then at my coming shall the fence of fire of paradise be done away—because paradise is girt round about with fire. And this shall be that perpetual fire that shall consume the earth and all the elements of the world (Apoc. Thomas).

On the sixth day of the Fire Judgment, Yeshua our Lord appears in the sky—the angels of Heaven also visible. Heaven, where YHWY lives, now remains visible from Earth with the naked eye. YHWY removes the firmament from Earth and the fire surrounding Heaven *because He wants the wicked to watch what happens next*. Recall that on day three of the Fire Judgment, Hell opens up. So when the mighty miracles occur on the sixth day of the Fire Judgment, all creation watch, including those in Hell.

For the righteous, the appearance of Yeshua in the sky represents an incredibly glorious moment. For the wicked—a moment of sheer terror. The wicked then try to hide in the rocks of the mountains, consistent with the sixth seal in Revelation chapter 6 as we read earlier.

In the passage, notice that the heavens are split (cloven) east to west. Yeshua confirmed His appearance in Matthew 24:

> The coming of the Son of Man will be like lightning that can be seen from east to west…
>
> Right after those days of suffering, "The sun will become dark, and the moon will no longer shine. The stars will fall, and the powers in the sky will be shaken."
>
> Then a sign will appear in the sky. And there will be the Son of Man. All nations on earth will weep when they see the Son of Man coming on the clouds of heaven with power and great glory (Matt. 24:27, 29-30 CEV).

Yeshua's description (in Matthew 24) of His appearance also mentions the tremendous signs in the heavens, as well as the stripping of stars and powers in the sky. The passage lines up with the *Apocalypse of Thomas*, where the coming of the Son of Man "will be like lightning that can be seen from east to west." Yeshua also warns in Matthew 24:23 for us to not be fooled by false Messiahs. In the near future, some may even attempt to project an image of Yeshua in the sky using Bluebeam technology already in use on billboards in New York City. Curiously, the Vatican recently released guidance on investigating "supernatural phenomena," warning followers to wait for *their* interpretation of upcoming events.[64] Based on what we just read about the days leading

---

[64] Nerozzi, Timothy H.J. "Vatican releases guidance on investigating 'supernatural phenomena.'" *Fox News.* May 18, 2024.

up to the Fire Judgment, we discern the real event based on the preceding blood rain, earthquakes, and darkness, etc. The entire world will see Yeshua. Soldier Saints should easily discern between any "fake signs" and the real thing.

Yeshua's appearing triggers breathtaking promises fulfilled on the sixth day of the Fire Judgment:

Signs in the Heavens, Wicked Hide

*Soon you will see the Son of Man
sitting at the right side of God All-Powerful, and
coming with the clouds of heaven (Mark 14:62b CEV).*

*People will hide in caves and holes in the ground from
the dreadful presence of YAHWEH and from his
majestic glory when he rises to mightily shake the
earth (Isa. 2:10 TPT).*

When Yeshua appears in the now open sky in His full Glory, the wicked seize in horror. In futility, they attempt to hide in rocks and caves. In contrast, the righteous rejoice.

According to the *Apocalypse of Thomas,* Yeshua appears on the sixth day of the Fire Judgment, at the fourth hour. This equates to four hours after sunrise on a Friday. Yeshua said, "No one knows the day or hour. The angels in heaven don't know, and the Son himself doesn't know. Only the Father knows" (Matt. 24:36 CEV). We don't know precisely when the Fire Judgment begins. However, once it does begin, we are given guidance on the sequence of events. In the next

https://www.foxnews.com/faith-values/vatican-releases-guidance-investigating-supernatural-phenomena.

chapter, I discuss more clues related to the signs of His appearing and how Christians should discern the times.

Resurrection of Righteous Dead

For the Lord himself will appear with the declaration of victory, the shout of an archangel, and the trumpet blast of God. He will descend from the heavenly realm and command those who are dead in Christ to rise first (1 Thess. 4:16 TPT).

The resurrection of the "dead in Christ" mentioned in the passage above represents the mightiest display of power by YHWY in the history of the world. Bodies literally reassemble from the ground and join their spirits in the air! The *Apocalypse of Thomas* provides a detailed description:

> Then shall the spirits and souls of all men come forth from paradise and shall come upon all the earth: and every one of them shall go unto his own body, where it is laid up, and every one of them shall say: Here lieth my body. And when the great voice of those spirits shall be heard, then shall there be a great earthquake over all the world, and by the might thereof the mountains shall be cloven from above and the rocks from beneath. Then shall every spirit return into his own vessel and the bodies of the saints which have fallen asleep shall arise.
>
> Then shall their bodies be changed into the image and likeness and the honour of the holy

angels, and into the power of the image of mine holy Father. Then shall they be clothed with the vesture of life eternal, out of the cloud of light which hath never been seen in this world; for that cloud cometh down out of the highest realm of the heaven from the power of my Father.

In this passage, we learn that the saints in paradise (Heaven) come to Earth. We learn that their spirits are reunited with their bodies from the earth. Their old bodies are now clothed with Glory. Finally, we learn that the glorified saints are then transported "unto heaven" and continue in the Glory of the Father. Paul clarifies in 1 Thessalonians 4:17 that the "heaven" in *Apocalypse of Thomas* refers to the sky.

Words can only marginally portray the sheer scope of this miracle. YHWY literally reassembles corpses from the earth buried for thousands of years—now reduced to dust. In a vision, the prophet Ezekiel sees YHWY restore life to a valley of bones. YHWY told him what to say, "I, the LORD God, will put breath in you, and once again you will live. I will wrap you with muscles and skin and breathe life into you. Then you will know that I am the LORD" (Ezek. 37:5-6 CEV). YHWY places His power on full display, as He performs an inimitable sign for all in Heaven, Earth, and Hell to see. YHWY explains this to Baruch:

For the earth shall then assuredly restore the dead, [Which it now receives, in order to preserve them]. It shall make no change in their form, But as it has received, so shall it restore them, and as I delivered them unto it, so also shall it raise them.

For then it will be necessary to show the living that the dead have come to life again, and that those who had departed have returned (again). And it shall come to pass, when they have severally recognized those whom they now know, then judgement shall grow strong, and those things which before were spoken of shall come (2 Bar. 50:2-4).

Scripture clarifies that initially, the dead come to life in the same state as the person left. For instance, if a person died at 80 years old, then he or she comes back in the same 80-year-old body. The Lord does this so that the unrighteous recognize the people they persecuted for their faith. The unrighteous will see the miracle of the dead coming to life prior to enduring their own dreadful fate—for the next day, they sink into the abyss of Hell.

Imagine all the saints we read about coming back to Earth; Adam, Eve, Abraham, Noah, Moses, Daniel, Peter, Paul, James, and John, etc. Now envision all the aborted children and all the miscarried children returning. Further, consider all the righteous dead that served in wars. *Billions* of people will resurrect on Earth. Aborted and miscarried children will likely revive as infants, as we discuss in the next chapter.

In Chapter 2, I discussed YHWY's promise to redeem unfulfilled destinies and callings for His people—now we see how He does this. Whatever dreams YHWY gave a righteous person that seemed truncated in their prior presence on Earth, now fulfill in the Kingdom Age. Glory to YHWY!

The Lord shows the wicked the restored state of the previously dead righteous in their departed form only briefly. For then YHWY shows them the transformation of the old bodies into a new, glorified body. Baruch elaborates:

> Also (as for) the glory of those who have now been justified in My law, who have had understanding in their life, and who have planted in their heart the root of wisdom, then their splendor shall be glorified in changes, and the form of their face shall be turned into the light of their beauty, that they may be able to acquire and receive the world which does not die, which is then promised to them.
>
> For over this above all shall those who come then lament, that they rejected My law, and stopped their ears that they might not hear wisdom or receive understanding.
>
> When therefore they see those, over whom they are now exalted, (but) who shall then be exalted and glorified more than they, they shall respectively be transformed, the latter into the splendour of angels, and the former shall yet more waste away in wonder at the visions and in the beholding of the forms.
>
> For they shall first behold and afterwards depart to be tormented (2 Bar. 51:3-6).

The bodies of righteous dead, now alive, will transform into magnificently beautiful men and women, shining in Glory. The scripture describes this state as the "splendour of angels." In contrast, the wicked morph into grotesque monsters just before their departure from Earth.

Living Righteous Glorified

Then we who are alive will join them, transported together in clouds to have an encounter with the Lord in the air, and we will be forever joined with the Lord. So encourage one another with these truths (1 Thess. 4:17-18 TPT).

The righteous generation that lives on Earth to see the onset of the Fire Judgment represents a unique group—we never taste bodily death (the Second Death). After the righteous dead come back to life, we meet them in the air, for a divine encounter with Yeshua. In the passage, it mentions we are forever "joined with the Lord." This passage refers to the Glory of YHWY coming upon us—we receive our glorified bodies! A trumpet blast lets us know to leave our homes and meet our Lord:

It will happen in an instant—in the twinkling of his eye. For when the last trumpet is sounded, the dead will come back to life. We will be indestructible and we will be transformed.

For we will discard our mortal "clothes" and slip into a body that is imperishable. What is mortal now will be exchanged for immortality.

And when that which is mortal puts on immortality, and what now decays is exchanged for what will never decay, then the Scripture will be fulfilled that says:

Death is swallowed up by a triumphant victory! So death, tell me, where is your victory? Tell me death, where is your sting? (1 Cor 15:52-55 TPT).

The *Apocalypse of Thomas* also describes the transformation:

And that cloud shall compass about with the beauty thereof all the spirits that have believed in me.

Then shall they be clothed, and shall be borne by the hand of the holy angels like as I have told you aforetime. Then also shall they be lifted up into the air upon a cloud of light, and shall go with me rejoicing unto heaven, and then shall they continue in the light and honour of my Father. Then shall there be unto them great gladness with my Father and before the holy angels. These are the signs of the sixth day.

Recall from earlier, that the *Apocalypse of Thomas* uses "paradise" to describe Heaven and "heaven" to depict the earth's atmosphere, or clouds. Saints, do you comprehend the amazing promises reserved for YHWY's people? In just a few years, we will bask in the Glory of YHWY and receive new bodies! We enjoy a "family reunion," put on by Yeshua!

Hallelujah! In the next chapter, I go into detail about our encounter with Yeshua.

Day 7: Battle in the Heavens

*And on the seventh day at the eighth hour there shall
be voices in the four corners of the heaven. And all the
air shall be shaken, and filled with holy angels, and
they shall make war among them all the day long. And
in that day shall mine elect be sought out by the holy
angels from the destruction of the world. Then shall
all men see that the hour of their destruction draweth
near. These are the signs of the seventh day
(Apoc. Thomas).*

On the final day of the Fire Judgment, an extreme battle in the heavenly realm takes place. On this day wicked men are removed and Earth thoroughly purged of any remaining Demon-gods and Evil Spirits. Again, scripture makes it clear that the righteous are protected during this time. The prophet Enoch discusses this moment:

> And the eternal God will tread upon the earth,
> (even) on Mount Sinai, [And appear from His
> camp] and appear in the strength of His might
> from the heaven of heavens. And all shall be
> smitten with fear, and **the Watchers shall
> quake**, and great fear and trembling shall seize
> them unto the ends of the earth. And the high
> mountains shall be shaken. And the high hills
> shall be made low, and shall melt like wax before

the flame and the earth shall be wholly rent in sunder, and all that is upon the earth shall perish, and **there shall be a judgement upon all (men)** (1 Enoch 1:4–7, emphasis added).

In Chapter 9, I exhorted the Ekklesia to take our place of authority and banish the Demon-gods and Evil Spirits. By day seven of the Fire Judgment, I believe most principalities exiled. Any remaining will be here by permission of the wicked who refused to give them up. After the wicked are removed on day seven of the Fire Judgment, any remaining Demon-gods and Evil Spirits have no host and thus are deported to their prison in the outer heavens.

The book of Enoch resurfaced within the Ekklesia only recently. The very first verse in the book of Enoch indicates that Enoch's message pertains to today's time. "The words of the blessing of Enoch, wherewith he blessed the elect and righteous, who will be living in the day of tribulation, when all the wicked and godless are to be removed" (1 Enoch 1:1). As I have said numerous times, I believe our generation represents the most blessed generation to ever live! We will witness the end of the old age, and the beginning of an entirely new era! On the very last day of the old age, wicked men and women, along with remaining Demon-gods and Evil Spirits leave Earth permanently:

Wicked Men and Women Removed

When Lot lived, people were also eating and drinking. They were buying, selling, planting, and building. But

on the very day Lot left Sodom, fiery flames poured
down from the sky and killed everyone. The same will
happen on the day when the Son of Man appears
(Luke 17:28 CEV).

At that time, two men will be working on the farm; one
will be taken away in judgment, the other left. Two
women will be grinding grain; one will be taken away
in judgment, the other left. This is why you must stay
alert: because no one knows the day your Lord will
come (Matt. 24:40-42 TPT).

YHWY forces the wicked men on Earth and in Hell to watch *everything* during the Fire Judgment. They see Yeshua appear, they see the righteous dead rise, they see the Glory of YHWY encompass the righteous, and now their final day on Earth ends—they die and are confined to Hell. They, along with any remaining Demon-gods and Evil Spirits, await their final judgment during the White Throne Judgment.

However, the evangelical church currently teaches that in the Rapture, the righteous are removed. This teaching actually opposes the Bible—for *the wicked* are removed unto judgment, not the righteous. All the wicked are consumed with fire after Yeshua appears during the final day of the Fire Judgment.

Earlier in the *Apocalypse of Thomas* we read, "And this shall be that perpetual fire that shall consume the earth and all the elements of the world." The Glory—the Fire of YHWY —will consume the earth and all the elements of the world. I believe this statement applies to all the wicked elements. Fire consumes every plant, animal, or man that rebelled against YHWY in the old age. Any genetically-modified plants, against YHWY's design, burn up. Rebellious animals will perish. All wicked and rebellious men, all those that refuse to honor YHWY and accept His Son Yeshua, will also be consumed by fire. The prophet Enoch describes this event as a "judgment of fire":

> And when sin and unrighteousness and blasphemy and violence in all kinds of deeds increase, and apostasy and transgression and uncleanness increase, a great chastisement shall come from heaven upon all these,
>
> And the holy Lord will come forth with wrath and chastisement to execute judgement on earth. In those days violence shall be cut off from its roots, And the roots of unrighteousness together with deceit, And they shall be destroyed from under heaven. And all the idols of the heathen shall be abandoned,
>
> And the temples burned with fire, And they shall remove them from the whole earth, And they (i.e. the heathen) shall be cast into the **judgement of fire**, And shall perish in wrath and in grievous judgement for ever (1 Enoch 91:7-9, emphasis added).

In Enoch's account, all wicked temples are burned with fire and removed from Earth. Earlier we read that an earthquake knocks down wicked monuments and buildings. Based on Enoch's account, fire takes care of any remains!

Remaining Evil Principalities Removed

From the days of the slaughter and destruction and death of the giants, from the souls whose flesh the spirits, having gone forth, shall destroy without incurring judgment—thus shall they destroy until the day of the consummation, the great judgment in which the age shall be consummated, over the Watchers and the godless, shall be wholly consummated
(1 Enoch 16:1).

As discussed, certain principalities are permanently banished from Earth after the Fire Judgment, awaiting their final judgment in the White Throne Judgment. The Watchers, fallen "sons of God," rebelled against YHWY and laid with women to produce Nephilim, the Giants. While the bodies of the Nephilim died in the Great Flood, their spirits remained. The Bible calls these spirits Evil Spirits and the Watchers, Demon-gods. In the pecking order of the spirit realm, Satan rules over both. Soldier Saints within the Ekklesia banish most of the Demon-gods and Evil Spirits before the final day of the Fire Judgment. Some remain, however, hosted by wicked men and women. When these wicked men and women are removed, any that remain of these two classes of wicked principalities also must go. The prophet Enoch calls this day, the "day of consummation." On the final day of the old age, any remaining principalities are sent to prison in the outer heavens.

Recall Paul's instruction to the church of Ephesus, when he educated the Ekklesia on the power of the Demon-gods and Evil Spirits:

> Your hand-to-hand combat is not with human beings, but with the **highest principalities and authorities** operating in rebellion under the heavenly realms. For they are a powerful class of **demon-gods and evil spirits** that hold this dark world in bondage (Eph. 6:12 TPT, emphasis added).

The "highest principalities and authorities" operating in rebellion on Earth are now removed—Glory to YHWY! These are Satan's A-team, and B-team, respectively. For the first chapter of the next age, Satan is left with only his C-team of Unclean Spirits—fallen angels. When the saints return from our encounter with Yeshua, we find our world a very different place, in part because spiritual oppressors left.

Day 8: Peace After Saints Return

And when the seven days are passed by, on the eighth day at the sixth hour there shall be a sweet and tender voice in heaven from the east. Then shall that angel be revealed which hath power over the holy angels: and all the angels shall go forth with him, sitting upon chariots of the clouds of mine holy Father (so) rejoicing and running upon the air beneath the heaven

to deliver the elect that have believed in me. And they
shall rejoice that the destruction of this world [age]
hath come (Apoc. Thomas).

We don't move to Heaven after our encounter with Yeshua in the sky. Rather, we return to a *very* different Earth. An earth purged of evil and wickedness. An earth devoid of idols and satanic buildings. An earth emptied of Demon-gods and Evil Spirits. According to the *Apocalypse of Thomas*, we return to Earth a couple of days after our encounter with Yeshua in the clouds, on the eighth day. Our encounter begins on Friday, and ends on Sunday!

In the Bible, the number eight represents a new beginning, meaning a new order or creation, and points to man's "full salvation" event when he is resurrected from the dead into eternal life.[65] After the seven weeks of the spring harvest, the next day, the 50th day, is Pentecost—the eighth day of the seventh week. This eight and 50 day combination also points to the resurrection of the dead. After the seven days of the Feast of Tabernacles, an eighth and final Feast day occurs, the "Last Great Day." This fall period represents the most joyous of all of YHWY's yearly days to worship Him. It's no coincidence the eighth day of the Fire Judgment starts the next era for YHWY's people. Glory to YHWY!

Figure 8 provides many other scripture references regarding Day 8 of the Fire Judgment. Study these scriptures and get them down in your heart! Anticipate all YHWY plans for His Ekklesia in the next age.

---

[65] "Meaning of Numbers in the Bible: The Number 8." *Biblestudy.org*, accessed May 28, 2024, www.biblestudy.org/bibleref/meaning-of-numbers-in-bible/8.html.

The Judgment Movie

After studying the Fire Judgment, I discovered much regarding YHWY's justice and vengeance. For 6,000 years, Satan influenced men to commit vile acts against YHWY's servants and innocent kids. Wicked men lied about them, stole from them, persecuted them, and abused or murdered their bodies. The Fire Judgment indelibly sears into the mind of evil men the gravity of their wickedness and the justice of YHWY. The Father accomplishes this with a live feature tailored specifically for each being. YHWY's skills in filmmaking far exceed Hollywoods'—He invented movies.

When we go to a play, the curtains open to reveal the scenes. In day three of the Fire Judgment, YHWY opens up Hell so its inhabitants can witness the unfolding movie. He opens up Hell for those on Earth to see that Hell exists. YHWY then removes Earth's firmament so all wicked on Earth and in Hell can see the action with their own eyes. YHWY even turns out all the lights on day five, just before the main story begins on day six.

In the first scene, YHWY removes the fire barrier surrounding Heaven, so *all* can see Heaven, Yeshua, and the angels. I can just imagine all atheists on Earth screaming, "Oh no! Jesus is real! Heaven is real!" Their moment of realization causes them to scream in agony, as they realize they believed and placed their faith on a lie. Of course, those in Hell already know—although they likely will see the gates of Heaven for the first time. The next scenes in YHWY's live feature are idiomatic—they vividly portray every righteous victims' fate to their malefactor. I will use fictitious character names to provide additional context.

Salome lived as a prestigious religious leader among the Jews. His invaluable contribution to the order was his powerful rolodex among Roman authorities. Salome personally arranged for midnight arrests and the murder of hundreds of pesky Christians who threatened their power. During Salome's movie, He sees each Christian return from the dead in perfect health, shining even brighter than those around them. Their future shines bright—though he continues his torment in Hell. Salome's movie in the sky seemed to last about 10 years to him—he could not look away. Now Salome lives with the bright, happy faces of his victims forever imprinted upon his memory bank. Salome also realizes all his work on Earth accomplished absolutely nothing.

Whereas George is still alive. He's an unrepentant abortion doctor who performed thousands of abortions. George believes he did the world a favor by conserving resources and sparing these children a dim future. In George's movie, he sees each child raised from death and placed in a loving home as he or she glows with a strange aura of light. He knows each child will now develop in a world full of light where destructive secular education won't exist. YHWY shows George how they plan to beget many more children, further populating this new "light world." After George's movie, which seemed to go on for 50 years, George realizes that all his work during his time on Earth accomplished zero. He realizes he listened to Satan, a total loser. Suddenly, George's wife Ellie grabs his arm. George finally looks at her and is shocked that her face has distorted and disfigured nearly beyond recognition. Ellie worked as a nurse alongside him for twenty years at the clinic. She points out the window in horror. A raging inferno of fire heads straight towards their home.

Billions of scenes similar to these play for each wicked person over the last two days of the Fire Judgment. However, each person's unique film might appear to go on for years. Different scenes with a similar outcome play for Satan's entire team. YHWY shows them that they accomplished zero and gained nothing. Every person they hurt, YHWY richly rewards for the hurt they suffered in His name. To a being, everyone on Satan's team realizes he or she played on a losing team, with nothing to show for it except an eternity of torment, agony, and regret.

The Next Age

After the 12,000 year age ends (including the last 6,000 years of humanity), a new age begins. The first chapter of the next age begins with the Kingdom Age of the Saints. In this chapter of the age, the saints rule the nations with a rod of iron. We learn how to function as the Ekklesia by leading the seven mountains of cultural influence. The seven Spirits of YHWY assist Soldier Saints as He shows us how to lead.[66] Each mountain corresponds to a different spirit of YHWY, who now descends to Earth for the next age (Rev. 5:6). The Ekklesia must learn how to lead again. The early Ekklesia in

---

[66] Enlow, Johnny. The Seven Mountain Prophecy: Unveiling the Coming Elijah Revolution. (Lake Mary, FL: Creation House, 2018), 187.

the book of Acts demonstrated our last great example of Christian leadership, before Rome scattered them.

In about 1,000 years, at the end of the Kingdom Age of the Saints, Believers are taken to Heaven to marry our Lord in the Marriage Supper of the Lamb (Rev 19:9). While we are enjoying the marriage ceremony, those that remain on the earth that refused to accept the Lord, will coalesce along with many Unclean Spirits around the anti-Christ, who will rule for a very short time—a few years.

At the end of the Marriage Supper of the Lamb, Yeshua returns on a white horse with His saints to destroy the anti-Christ and his armies. Yeshua raises up the dead beheaded at the hands of the anti-Christ (Rev. 20:4). Satan and Unclean Spirits are bound. Yeshua then rules the nations Himself for a 1,000 years.

11. Back in the Garden

*He will descend from the heavenly realm and
command those who are dead in Christ to rise first.
Then we who are alive will join them, transported
together in clouds to have an encounter with the Lord
in the air, and we will be forever joined with the Lord.*

— 1 Thess. 4:16b-17 TPT

After our encounter with Yeshua in the clouds of Glory, life
on Earth only faintly resembles the former age. For one, the
Saints now beam with the Glory of YHWY. Our robe of
righteousness covers our nakedness—we no longer need to
shop at the outlet mall to buy clothing! We experience full
salvation.

Second, we comprehend our full purpose. During our encounter with Yeshua, I believe He will give us specific instructions to carry out in the Kingdom Age of the Saints. We then carry out any unfulfilled dreams and destinies. We rule Earth's kingdoms the way Adam and Eve ruled in the Garden of Eden.

Finally, we will have work to do. We must fulfill our complete purpose on Earth, and come into the perfection to which YHWY called us. The Ekklesia will learn to lead nations as well as the the seven mountains of cultural influence as YHWY's leaders. We will master functioning in complete unity as His Ekklesia. We discover how to operate in the fullness of the Spirit of YHWY. We will truly serve the Master as His Body, fully functioning in the way YHWY designed the Ekklesia to function.

Resurrection Encounter with Yeshua

... watch ye, then, in every season, praying that ye may be accounted worthy to escape all these things that are about to come to pass, and to stand before the Son of Man (Luke 21:36 YLT).

Once one stands face-to-face with Yeshua, he or she changes forever. I recently watched the documentary *After Death*.[67] The film outlined many near-death experiences from people whose heart stopped—they later came back from the dead after witnessing the afterlife. Howard Storm, a former atheist featured in the film, described demons dragging him into

---

[67] *After Death*, dir. Stephen Gray, Chris Radtke, prod. Stephen Gray, 2023.

Hell. After crying out to God, his direction reversed towards Heaven and he met Yeshua. Yeshua and the angels played a life-reel for Howard of his entire life. Howard realized the many mistakes he made during his time on Earth. After the movie, he asked Yeshua questions for what seemed like years, and He patiently answered each one. At the end, Yeshua gave him a set of instructions for when he returned to Earth. His assignment included telling people his testimony of God's mercy and walking in complete love and forgiveness. I picture our encounter with Yeshua as similar to Howard's story. However, after our encounter with Yeshua, we receive our glorified body and return to a very, very different Earth!

According to the *Apocalypse of Thomas*, we leave the surface of Earth to meet Yeshua in the clouds on a Friday (the sixth day) after the fourth hour (mid-morning), and return to Earth on a Sunday afternoon around midday. During this time, we each meet Yeshua for a personal encounter. "Then we who are alive will join them, transported together in clouds **to have an encounter with the Lord in the air**, and we will be forever joined with the Lord" (1 Thess. 4:17 TPT, emphasis added).

The Greek word for encounter, *apantēsis*, is not a verb (go to meet) but a feminine noun (to meet or have an encounter). Rarely used in the New Testament, we see the use of the word also in the parable about the ten virgins who went to meet the bridegroom in Matthew 25:1-13. Although all virgins, only five of the ten kept their oil in their lamp full. This parable represents a dual-prophecy, both for the appearing of the Lord and for the Marriage Supper of the

Lamb. In both cases, we must stay ready and full of the Holy Spirit.

We will encounter Yeshua one-on-one. The encounter prepares us for the Kingdom Age. In the encounter we receive our assignments and any needed exhortation. The place of quiet that the Lord calls us to right now affords preparation time for our coming encounter with Yeshua. So many Believers are now called into a deep study of the Bible —purging petty sins and cares. Careers aren't working out, and businesses are failing, as YHWY slowly eliminates unnecessary distractions from our lives. He wants us ready for our encounter with Him. This should be our focus right now.

The Lord showed me several types of encounters with Yeshua. For some, the encounter represents pure delight and celebration. For others, the encounter amounts to receiving a slice of "humble pie" followed by a painful exhortation. Now is an important time to carefully study Yeshua's warnings to the seven churches in the first, second, and third chapters of Revelation and conduct an honest self-assessment—you don't have much time before your encounter with Yeshua. *Today*, repent and purge any compromise from your heart and life.

Finally, many in "church leadership" risk missing the encounter altogether unless they repent. Every person who misses the encounter with Yeshua spends eternity in the darkness of Hell and ultimately, the lake of fire.

The "Well Done" Encounter

*The master answered, 'You did well. You are a good
and loyal servant. Because you were loyal with small
things, I will let you care for much greater things.
Come and share my joy with me' (Matt. 25:21 NCV).*

For His obedient servants, the encounter with Yeshua amounts to sheer bliss—a promotion event. The passage describes Soldier Saints who know YHWY's voice and follow through on His instructions. They don't compromise. They are humble and grateful to stand before their Master.

Brand new Believers who consistently followed YHWY's simple instructions to help a homeless person, or tithe their income are in great shape. Believers obedient *to what they know to do*, YHWY promotes. Lifelong Believers who consistently practiced obedience, regardless of earthly consequences, enter into bliss.

Our obedience, even in the smallest detail, determines our reward in the Kingdom Age. Yeshua promotes many to rule over nations because they don't ignore His instruction. He promotes quiet intercessors who faithfully rise in the wee hours to pray as advisors to kings. He promotes the humble, the meek, and the grateful.

The "Humble Pie" Encounter

*I know all the things you do, and that you have a
reputation for being alive—but you are dead. Wake up
(Rev 3:1b-2a NLT)!*

> *I know all the things you do, that you are neither hot*
> *nor cold. I wish that you were one or the other! But*
> *since you are like lukewarm water, neither hot nor*
> *cold, I will spit you out of my mouth! You say, 'I am*
> *rich. I have everything I want. I don't need a thing!' And*
> *you don't realize that you are wretched and miserable*
> *and poor and blind and naked (Rev 3:15-17).*

Unfortunately, many Christians believe in Yeshua but remain distracted by the world. They don't seek YHWY's will on decisions. They don't hunger for YHWY. They may attend church but ignore the promptings of the Holy Spirit. Some describe these Christians as "social Christians"—they look at church as yet another business networking event or a social club, but their faith never moved forward after believing on Yeshua.

Many trust in their bank accounts more than they trust the Lord. When faced with difficult truths, they get offended. Others refuse to let go of offenses from years ago, and thus remain frozen in their walk with Yeshua.

Go back to the *last thing* YHWY led or asked you to do and DO IT. Perhaps you need to call your mother or father and forgive them. Maybe you accepted the Lord years ago but don't read the Bible or pray—get back to YHWY. Others accepted Yeshua but treat those around them hatefully— repent now and make it right; Change the way you treat others! Arrogant and proud people, who look down on others need to repent now.

If you make it to your encounter, expect Yeshua to dress you down like a U.S. Marine drill sergeant. Your encounter with Yeshua won't be a pleasant situation. Either repent now or prepare to bow before Him and eat humble pie.

Repent Now or <u>You Won't Make It</u>

And a servant who knows what the master wants, but isn't prepared and doesn't carry out those instructions, will be severely punished. But someone who does not know, and then does something wrong, will be punished only lightly. When someone has been given much, much will be required in return; and when someone has been entrusted with much, even more will be required (Luke 12:47-48).

Yeshua provides examples of His granting mercy to those who demonstrate awareness of their sin, express shame for their faults, and earnestly try to do better. Yeshua contrasts the humble tax collector in the Temple with the self-righteous Pharisee who bragged about his accomplishments to the Lord. Yeshua said, "I tell you, this sinner, not the Pharisee, returned home justified before God. For those who exalt themselves will be humbled, and those who humble themselves will be exalted" (Luke 18:14).

Self-righteous "church leaders" who keep the rules but repeatedly judge others risk missing their encounter with Yeshua altogether. Yeshua holds us accountable for what we know. If you are a "veteran" Christian who studies the Bible and yet fails to look in the mirror and allow YHWY's Word to convict you of your own faults, you risk missing out on the encounter.

If you are a church leader and mock the things of YHWY, the gifts of the Holy Spirit: speaking in tongues, healing, miracles, as well as prophetic gifts, etc.—repent and stop immediately. Listen to the words of Yeshua as He addressed "church leaders" who accused *Him* of demon-possession because He cast out demons: "I tell you the truth, all sin and blasphemy can be forgiven, but anyone who blasphemes the Holy Spirit will never be forgiven. This is a sin with eternal consequences" (Mark 3:28-29). Whole denominations exist today who know *nothing* of the gifts of the Holy Spirit but erroneously believe YHWY appointed *them* to judge Charismatics. Fall on your face and repent now.

However, *many* in so-called Charismatic circles also won't make it. "On judgment day many will say to me, 'Lord! Lord! We prophesied in your name and cast out demons in your name and performed many miracles in your name.' But I will reply, 'I never knew you. Get away from me, you who break God's laws.'" (Matt. 7:22-23). How can someone used in YHWY's mighty gifts not make it you might ask?

Recall from the section scripture above in Luke 12, "When someone has been given much, much will be required in return." YHWY requires more from leaders who know better. He requires obedience, not sacrifice (1 Sam. 15:22b).

More and more, I recognize a nasty, vicious religious spirit among Christians. Many smugly and with an air of false humility label others of YHWY's servants, "false prophets." When Yeshua told us to beware of false prophets, He said they come "disguised as harmless sheep but are really vicious wolves" (Matt. 7:15). Pride induces ministers to attack other ministers. Perhaps someone else's ministry grew faster, or YHWY gave another servant more revelation on a topic in the Bible. Pride stops people from receiving and blocks their ability to see their own errors (Matt. 7:3-5). All of us deal with pride—a remnant of our fallen nature. However, operating with a heart hardened by pride disqualifies us from the Kingdom (Prov. 8:12, 16:5; Rom. 12:3). In the Appendix, I include a Pride Self-Assessment. I encourage you seriously consider it. *Everyone* struggles with pride from time-to-time!

Remember King David? He refused to touch a hair on Saul's head—he let YHWY take care of Saul's disobedience. David ignored the fact that Saul tried to murder him on *multiple* occasions. The highest prophet in the land already anointed David as king of Israel—while Saul lost YHWY's anointing. Yet David honored YHWY's command, "Do not touch my anointed ones; do my prophets no harm" (Ps. 105:15 NRSV). Today, Christians routinely attempt to harm others in the public square—it's the same sin, Internet or not.

If you are guilty of any sin discussed in this section, stop reading, call the person (or persons) you judged based on your own pride, and ask for forgiveness. Publicly repent to your flock for prideful accusations and judgments. Fall on your face before Yeshua and beg for forgiveness from Him for operating in pride. Ask Him to expose your prideful ways and begin to walk in humility—you don't have much time.

Kingdom Age of the Saints

After Yeshua appears, He gives the kingdoms of the world to His Soldier Saints to rule. If you recall, Satan offered Yeshua the kingdoms of the world before the Crucifixion, and Yeshua turned him down:

> And the devil took him up and showed him all the kingdoms of the world in a moment of time, and said to him, "To you I will give all this authority and their glory, for it has been delivered to me, and I give it to whom I will. If you, then, will worship me, it will all be yours."
>
> And Jesus answered him, "It is written, You shall worship the Lord your God, and him only shall you serve" (Luke 4:5-8 ESV).

Did Satan lie when He claimed all the kingdoms of the world belonged to him? No, otherwise the offer would fail to tempt Yeshua. In this instance, Satan told the truth. Who gave Satan the kingdoms, the dominion, the reign, and rule of the world? Adam gave them to Satan when he disobeyed YHWY and gave his God-given authority to Satan.

At this moment, the temptation of Yeshua became very personal. Yeshua at one point would reclaim the kingdoms of the world from Satan, but not for 2,000 more years. At the time of Yeshua's temptation, Ancient Rome served as Satan's appointed control center for the world. Roman hands would martyr the majority of Yeshua's disciples. His Body, the Ekklesia would suffer searing persecution for two millennia. Satan offered Yeshua an alternative way—a shortcut. Satan tempted Yeshua to avoid the cross, but also to save His Ekklesia from the extreme persecution and genocide that would follow—Yeshua already knew Satan would put them through "hell on earth."

Yeshua passed the test. He knew YHWY's perfect plan needed to happen YHWY's way, and He told Satan to get lost. Yeshua knew better than to rush YHWY's plan. But now that Satan's lease to rule Earth ends, Yeshua takes the kingdoms of the world back from Satan and gives them to His people, restoring their authority lost after the Fall. The prophet Daniel spoke about this dominion transfer to the saints:

> As I watched, that horn fought against the holy ones and was defeating them until the Everlasting One came on the scene. He handed judgment over to the saints of the Most High, and dominion was given to the holy ones of the Most High. Then the time came when the holy ones took possession of the kingdom (Dan. 7:21-22 TPT).

Yeshua also spoke to John the Revelator about the day of dominion transfer, and linked the dominion transfer to His appearing:

> Cling tightly to all that you have until I appear. To everyone who is victorious and continues to do my works to the very end I will give you authority over the nations to shepherd them with a royal

scepter. And *the rebellious will* be shattered as clay pots—even as I also received authority from the presence of my Father. I will give the morning star to the one who experiences victory (Rev. 2:25-28).

You see, Yeshua's divine plan all along included giving His saints the kingdoms of the world for us to rule the nations. When Yeshua came to Earth, He fulfilled Isaiah 61:1-2a. (See Luke 4:18-21). Now He fulfills the rest of Isaiah 61. Soon we will experience the reality of coming into our destiny as Yeshua moves His Ekklesia into the next age.

So what will the Kingdom Age of the Saints look like? For one, we will dine with the great prophets and patriarchs of old, as they all live on Earth after the resurrection. I personally plan to invite over the prophet Daniel and King David! To enjoy the great cloud of witnesses with us in our glorified bodies, free from any sickness, disease, or decay represents a thrilling proposition. When Yeshua transfigured on the mountain, He communed with Moses and Elijah, symbolizing the future Kingdom Age when Believers also fellowship with the patriarchs of our faith (Matt. 17:3)!

I can't wait to see my older brother, sister and dad. My older brother and sister perished from disease before their time and my dad died very young as well. After years of estrangement, our unfettered fellowship at the end of my dad's life proved too brief. YHWY designed the Kingdom Age of the Saints as a glorious time of rest and reward for His people.

Marriage and Children

After the resurrection of the saints, Yeshua states clearly that marriage ends:

> Jesus said to them, "Those who belong to **this age** marry and are given in marriage; but those who are considered worthy of a place in **that age and in the resurrection from the dead** neither marry nor are given in marriage. Indeed they cannot die anymore, because they are like angels and are children of God, being children of the resurrection" (Luke 20:34-36 NRSV). (See also Matthew 22:30).

The curse pronounced on Eve after the Fall included a multiplication of hardship and extreme pain in childbirth. The curse also caused Eve to desire to control her husband, however, her husband would rule over her. (See Gen. 3:16). These curses are broken after the resurrection of the saints. YHWY replaces the institution of marriage with something different *and better.*

Marriage in the present yet vanishing age constitutes men and women coming together into covenant with each other, under God. In the next age, our intimacy with YHWY elevates, and we receive a glorified body. If a daughter of YHWY desires to have a baby, then the Lord fulfills this desire differently than now. Listen to the passage in Romans, "God knew his people in advance, and he chose them to become like his Son, so that his Son would be the firstborn among many brothers and sisters" (v. 8:29 NLT). Mary gave birth to Yeshua without an earthly father—YHWY implanted a pure seed into Mary. Maybe the same thing happens for new babies born in the Kingdom Age!

In *The Message* translation, Matthew 22:30 reads, "At the resurrection we're beyond marriage. As with the angels, all our ecstasies and intimacies then will be with God." This particular translation calls attention to the intimate relationship between righteous men (and women) and their Creator in the next age. Our personal relationship with YHWY remains the highest priority—not infringed upon by any controlling desires of a spouse.

Recall from Genesis, "Then the LORD God said, 'It is not good for the man to be alone. I will make a helper who is just right for him'" (v. 2:18 NLT). YHWY gave Eve to Adam to help him. Clearly, YHWY only gave Adam one helper—under no circumstance did our Father ever condone polygamy. Adam and Eve complemented one another according to YHWY's original plan. After the Fall, YHWY instituted marriage. Based on Yeshua's words, marriage as an institution falls away during the Kingdom Age.

A friend of the family lost two prior husbands. She remarried and refers to her current husband as her friend. They sleep in separate bedrooms, and enjoy meals together. They keep each other company! Could this represent the model going forward? Soon we find out. Nothing gets in the way of our relationship with Yeshua in the Kingdom Age. At the end of the first chapter of the Kingdom Age, the Ekklesia presents itself to the Lord as His Bride.

Based on other passages, children *are* born in the Kingdom Age. The Lord told Baruch, "And women shall no longer then have pain when they bear, Nor shall they suffer torment when they yield the fruit of the womb" (2 Bar. 73:7). Other promises speak of thousands of children born during the Kingdom Age, gestation shortening, and toddlers learning to speak as young as one year old:

> And then shall all the righteous escape, and shall live till they beget thousands of children, And all the days of their youth and their old age shall they complete in peace (1 Enoch 10:17).
>
> And the children of a year old shall speak with their voices, the women with child shall bring forth untimely children of three or four months old, and they shall live, and be raised up (2 Esd. 6:21 NRSV).

How are children born if men and women no longer marry? Soon, the Lord will show us.

After the resurrection, billions of kids require foster homes. In prior books, I quoted one source estimating 1 billion babies perished since 1920 from abortion.[68] A billion murders shocks the human conscience. However, a recent *ChatGPT4* search came back with a much higher figure, estimating between *3.65 to 4.35 billion* abortions worldwide between 1920 and 2023. The artificial intelligence (AI) based search sourced the best available data from the Guttmacher Institute and the World Health Organization, and then made

---

68   W. Robert Johnston and Thomas Jacobsen. "Abortion Worldwide Report: 100 Nations, 1 Century, 1 Billion Babies." (Colorado Springs, CO: GLC, 2017).

assumptions for earlier years. Of course, these figures do not include babies in earlier history sacrificed to Baal, Moloch or other satanic Demon-gods. *ChatGPT4* also estimated that if the abortions didn't occur, the current world population would amount to *10-12 billion* additional people than the current world population!

Abortions don't stop YHWY's destiny for children—His gifts and calling are irrevocable regardless of a mother's actions. All of these babies come back in the resurrection. They ultimately choose whether to live out their YHWY-given destiny on Earth. Every human comes to a point after they lose innocence when they must *select* YHWY of their own free will (Heb. 9:27, Rom. 7:9). Remember, the loss of childlike innocence represents the First Death.

After our encounter with Yeshua at the end of the Fire Judgment, we may find youngsters in our homes to raise as part of our assignment! Consider this passage in Isaiah:

> You thought you had lost the children, but you will hear them say, "This place is too cramped for me. Make more room for me to live in." And you will say to yourself, "Where in the world did all these children come from? Who birthed these for me? I thought I was bereaved and barren. I thought I was all alone, forgotten in exile—so how did they all get here?" (Isa. 49:20-21 TPT).

Every righteous but barren mother who desires children receives an opportunity to raise many! YHWY promises in the Kingdom Age, "The number of thy children, whom thou longedst for, is fulfilled" (2 Esd. 2:41a NRSV). YHWY provides righteous women who lost one or more toddlers at a young age to disease or vaccine injuries an opportunity to raise them in the Kingdom Age. In YHWY's mercy, if a mom received an abortion and later repented, I believe she'll have a second chance. Mommies will raise children without the slightest concern over finances. In addition, because the Lord glorifies our bodies in the resurrection, we maintain perfect health—the days of our prime restored.

I spoke to my 80-plus-year-old mother about how she would raise my oldest sister Holly in the Kingdom Age. Holly died prematurely from disease at four years old. My mother responded, "But she's been in Heaven for 60 years!" Most people don't remember events that occur before a certain age. Holly never died the First Death—she never actively chose to serve YHWY. When Holly comes back, she must grow up in the things of YHWY and elect to serve Him. My mother got very excited! You see, YHWY redeems *everything* lost or stolen.

What about miscarried children? Do we receive the opportunity to raise raise them as well? YHWY told Enoch:

> And I swear to you, yea, yea, that there has been no man in his mother's womb, but that already before, even to each one there is a place prepared for the repose of that soul, and a measure fixed how much it is intended that a man be tried in this world (2 Enoch 49:4).

This remarkable passage discusses a mystery of YHWY—a man's spirit enters the womb to then "be tried in this world." If a woman miscarries her baby, that baby never got the chance "to be tried." In 1 Enoch 69:12, we learn that a Demon-god named Kasdeja showed men how to conduct abortions and the "smitings of the embryo in the womb, that it might pass away." Thankfully, Demon-gods are exiled from Earth during the Kingdom Age—miscarriage becomes a thing of the past!

In my own family, we experienced numerous miscarriages. I witnessed firsthand the emotional trauma and sense of loss associated with a miscarriage. YHWY also redeems this loss in the Kingdom Age, and the miscarried infants await us when we arrive back from our encounter with Yeshua. I sense that aborted and miscarried infants return at about three months of age, but I don't (yet) see their age revealed in scripture.

The Tree of Life

Scripture indicates that after the resurrection, the righteous are granted access to the Tree of Life—the key to immortality. Recall from Genesis that eating of the Tree of Life causes humans to live forever (Gen. 3:22). In the book of Revelation, Yeshua gives us a promise to once again eat of the Tree of Life, "To the one who overcomes I will give access to feast on the fruit of the Tree of Life that is found in the paradise of God" (Rev 2:7b TPT). Later in the same chapter, Yeshua promises, "The one who conquers will not be harmed by the second death" (v. 11b). As discussed, the Second Death refers to physical death, while the First Death describes reaching the age of accountability, where every human makes a choice whether or not to serve YHWY. So what does Yeshua mean, when He says conquer?

When Yeshua addressed the various churches through John in the book of Revelation, the young Ekklesia would endure another couple thousand years of brutal persecution before the end of the age. Persecution for our faith and resisting Satan's demons constitutes biblical suffering (2 Tim. 3:12, 1 Pet. 5:9). Even Yeshua endured the same as the pioneer of our faith:

> For now he towers above all creation, for all things exist through him and for him. And that God made him, pioneer of our salvation, perfect through his sufferings, for this is how he brings many sons and daughters to **share in his glory**. Jesus, the Holy One, makes us holy (Heb. 2:10-11 TPT, emphasis added).

Every character in the Bible endured biblical suffering. In addition, everyone I know that faithfully serves Yeshua suffered hardships. Yes, sometimes these hardships constitute self-inflicted wounds—moments of weakness in the flesh allows avoidable demonic pressure. However, I see in the Word these sufferings are part of YHWY's plan—His refinement to prepare us for the Glory:

> Stay alert! Watch out for your great enemy, the devil. He prowls around like a roaring lion, looking for someone to devour.

Stand firm against him, and be strong in your faith. Remember that your family of believers all over the world is going through the **same kind of suffering** you are.

In his kindness God called you **to share in his eternal glory** by means of Christ Jesus. So after you have suffered a little while, he will restore, support, and strengthen you, and he will place you on a firm foundation (1 Pet. 5:8–10 NLT, emphasis added).

The sufferings we endured prepared us, like fine gold in the furnace, for YHWY's Glory! We, as well as many saints before us, endured the suffering of the age when Satan ruled, as preparation for the Glory set before us. Not one drop of blood spilled in the name of the Lord is ever wasted—He redeems all. "Precious in the sight of the LORD is the death of his saints" (Ps. 116:15 ESV). YHWY rewards His faithful. Promises include:

- God blesses those who patiently endure testing and temptation. Afterward they will receive the crown of life that God has promised to those who love him. (Jam. 1:12 NLT).
- All who are victorious will be clothed in white (Rev 3:5a).
- If we endure hardship, we will reign with him (2 Tim. 2:12a).

- You have been faithful with the little I entrusted to you, so you will be governor of ten cities as your reward (Luke 19:17b).
- God blesses those who are humble, for they will inherit the whole earth (Matt. 5:5).
- Remain faithful to the day you die and I will give you the victor's crown of life (Rev 2:10b TPT).

Summarizing the verses above, faithful victors over the satanic temptations, pressures, and persecutions receive the crown of immortal life, are clothed in Glory, and inherit the earth. However, saints *who also used their gifts* during their time on Earth rule cities! YHWY remains faithful—He promises to reward the righteous. After our encounter with Yeshua, we return to Earth and access the Tree of Life.

Death and Sin in the Kingdom Age

Do people die in the Kingdom Age? We just read how the righteous are given a crown of life, meaning immortality. We know from Revelation 2:11 that the righteous overcomer will never taste of the Second Death, or bodily death. Let's examine this passage in Isaiah:

> I am creating new heavens and a new earth; everything of the past will be forgotten. Celebrate and be glad forever! I am creating a Jerusalem, full of happy people. I will celebrate with Jerusalem and all of its people; there will be no more crying or sorrow in that city.

255

No child will die in infancy; everyone will live to a ripe old age. Anyone a hundred years old will be considered young, and to die younger than that will be considered a curse.

My people will live in the houses they build; they will enjoy grapes from their own vineyards. No one will take away their homes or vineyards.

My chosen people will live to be as old as trees, and they will enjoy what they have earned. Their work won't be wasted, and their children won't die of dreadful diseases.

I will bless their children and their grandchildren. I will answer their prayers before they finish praying (Isa. 65:17–24 CEV).

When I first read this passage, I immediately thought of it as a description of a distant future event when YHWY creates a new Heaven and Earth after the final White Throne Judgment. (See Revelation 21). After this event (the White Throne Judgment), the New Jerusalem descends, and YHWY lives among His people. However, according to the book of Revelation, death ceases to exist when YHWY creates the New Heaven and Earth (Rev. 21:4). Plus, the promise in Isaiah 65 mentions that YHWY creates a Jerusalem "full of happy people," not a New Jerusalem where YHWY lives. So we must conclude that the passage we just read in Isaiah 65 refers to the Kingdom Age.

According to the passage in Isaiah 65, people live to a "ripe old age," and "anyone a hundred years old will be considered young." The Amplified Bible translation for this verse provides additional context:

> There shall no more be in it an infant who lives but a few days, or an old man who dies prematurely; for the child shall die a hundred years old, and the sinner who dies when only a hundred years old shall be [thought only a child, cut off because he is] accursed (Isa. 65:20 AMPC).

According to the passage, sinners are cutoff from the Tree of Life in the Kingdom Age and do die. However, the righteous continue to access the Tree of Life! The prophet Enoch also describes access to the Tree of Life in the Kingdom Age:

> And as for this **fragrant tree** no mortal is permitted to touch it till the great judgement, when He shall take vengeance on all and bring (everything) to its consummation for ever. **It shall then be given to the righteous and holy**.
>
> Then shall they rejoice with joy and be glad, And into the holy place shall they enter; And its fragrance shall be in their bones, And they shall live a long life on earth, Such as thy fathers lived: And in their days shall no sorrow or plague or torment or calamity touch them (1 Enoch 25:4-6, emphasis added).

Enoch confirms that only the righteous and holy access the Tree of Life. There are sinners in the Kingdom Age, but they don't live as long as the righteous.

I believe the Kingdom Age of the Saints lasts approximately 1,000 years.[69] Billions of saints live the full time and never taste the Second Death. Recall that in the Old Testament, Adam, Methuselah and others lived to be over 900 years old, establishing precedent for long life for the righteous.

Every unrepentant person perishes in the Fire Judgment. When we return from our encounter with Yeshua, the entirety of the world population comprises either a) servants of YHWY, or b) innocent children too young to choose YHWY. In the latter category, the vast majority recently resurrected from the dead! As we raise these children, they all come to the point of the First Death, when they must choose whether or not to receive Yeshua as their Lord and Savior. Satan, the great tempter, remains loose during this time and will try to mislead each of these children. We must be vigilant caretakers of these children, teaching them YHWY's ways so they make the right choice.

While I believe that most choose YHWY—many won't. Satan remains unbound during the Kingdom Age of the Saints as do Unclean Spirits. Satan attempts to derail these tender children when they reach the age when they need to select YHWY. We must stand on YHWY's promise, "My hands shall cover thee, so that thy children shall not see hell" (2 Esd. 2:29 NRSV). We still act upon our faith in the Kingdom Age!

---

[69] Thomas, *Blast of Fire*, 181-183.

Timing of Yeshua's Appearance

The tribulation under the Fourth Beast continued from the time of Yeshua's ministry on Earth to the present. YHWY showed many prophets the tyranny and rule of the Fourth Beast, and how he would die in the Stone Judgment. The acceleration of famine, earthquakes, disease, wars, abortions, etc. are all signs that Yeshua spoke about as birth pangs in Matthew 24:8 and in other places. These birth pangs intensify until the end of the old age before we move into the Kingdom Age.

The Stone Judgment, the final battle of the old age, started already. We already discussed how the Stone Judgment includes three parts:

1) Shaking of Nations
2) End Times Harvest
3) Fire Judgment, during which Yeshua appears

The Shaking of Nations began back in 2017, and likely ends in 2024 with the defeat of the Fourth Beast, as discussed in Chapter 9. Also, the End Times Harvest already began. Reports surface from many evangelists that unusual miracles occur and humanity receives Yeshua at record rates in countries like Iran, China, and other "hard to reach" places. After the Shaking of Nations completes, the End Times Harvest intensifies, for humanity recognizes the goodness and mercy of YHWY. However, the End Times Harvest ends abruptly with the Fire Judgment, when our Lord appears in the clouds. When does this happen?

Yeshua's appearance in the clouds of Glory marks the end of the old age, and the beginning of the Kingdom Age. Yeshua Himself says, "Concerning that day and exact hour, no one knows when it will arrive, not even the angels of heaven—only the Father knows" (Matt. 24:36). However, Yeshua provides three important clues regarding timing:

Sign #1: The Fig Tree

> Now learn the lesson from the parable of the fig tree. When spring arrives and it sends out its tender branches and sprouts leaves, you know that ripe fruit is soon to appear. So it will be with you, for when you observe all these things taking place, you will know that he is near, even at the door (Matt. 24:32-33 TPT)!

Most scholars properly attribute the fig tree as a symbol of Israel. However, many mistook the State of Israel's formation in 1948 as the fulfillment of End Times prophecy. Believing 1948 significant, quite a few wrote books and derived forecasts based on a parallel verse in Luke 21:32 which says, "This generation shall not pass away, till all be fulfilled" (KJV). Authors interpreted a "generation" to mean 40 years after 1948, or 1988. Clearly, all these estimates proved false. Either Yeshua misguided us, or the formation of the modern State of Israel represented the wrong fig tree! As I stated in Chapter 3, the modern State of Israel represents an imposter fig tree, explaining why almost 80 years later, Yeshua yet appears.

Alternate translations to the King James Version of Luke 21:32 provide more context about the people living when the fig tree, *true* Israel, produces new shoots:

- Truly I tell you, **this generation (those living at that definite period of time) will not perish and pass away** until all has taken place (from AMPC).
- I tell you the truth, all these things will happen **while the people of this time are still living** (from NCV).
- I assure you, **the end of this age will not come** until all I have spoken comes to pass (from TPT).

As emphasized in bold, other translations indicate Yeshua appears quite rapidly after true Israel forms. The Passion Translation states that the *age won't end* until true Israel shoots forth. As stated in Chapter 9, according to the prophet Daniel, the old age ends by 2027. As of this writing, the corrupt government of the State of Israel begins to implode. Soon, Jerusalem falls into the hands of the seed of Jacob, its rightful heirs. Saints, when this happens, Yeshua stands at the door!

Sign #2: Times of Peace (Days of Noah)

You surely know that the Lord's return will be as a thief coming at night. People will think they are safe and secure. But destruction will suddenly strike them like

> *the pains of a woman about to give birth. And they*
> *won't escape (1 Thess. 5:2-3 CEV).*

Unless one understands the Stone Judgment, this verse makes no sense. During the Shaking of Nations, the military alliance executes YHWY's judgment and eliminates the worst-of-the-worst leaders currently in charge of the deep-state-led New World Order. However, they won't prosecute everyone involved. Many dodge justice and believe they are safe. The Bible describes these mistaken people in the verse we just read.

Recall from Daniel 7, that "The *fourth* beast was killed, and its body was thrown into the blazing fire." (v. 11b TPT). The military kills the Fourth Beast during the Shaking of Nations, but YHWY burns the entirety of its carcass in the Fire Judgment—with no survivors.

Many are lulled into a false sense of security after the fall of the Fourth Beast. Peace on Earth causes many to go on with life, not recognizing the times. Yeshua compares this time to the days of Noah:

> For it will be exactly like it was in the days of
> Noah when the Son of Man appears. Before the
> flood, people lived their lives eating, drinking,
> marrying, and having children. They didn't realize
> the end was near until Noah entered the ark, and
> then suddenly, the flood came and took them all
> away in judgment (Matt. 24:37–39).

During the End Times Harvest, the world experiences unprecedented peace. The Fourth Beast, now dead, no longer terrorizes humanity. The wicked decide it's a great time to party, get married, and have children. The alert and awake righteous understand the urgency—the Fire Judgment occurs next. Like Noah, we warn the world of what's coming. Once the Fire Judgment begins, no second chances exist for humanity.

Sign #3: Gospel Preached to Whole World

Yet through it all, this joyful assurance of the realm of heaven's kingdom will be proclaimed all over the world, providing every nation with a demonstration of the reality of God. And after this the end of this age will arrive (Matt. 24:14 TPT).

We know the preaching of the Gospel to the entire world remains an unrealized sign. Note again that the worldwide preaching of the Gospel occurs before the *end of the age.*

On our own strength, we can bring the Gospel to the world by AD 2033. Bible translators believe they will produce a Bible in every language by 2033.[70] However, experts in AI-assisted language translation believe the process rapidly accelerates. I recently spoke to Jim Schmidt, the Senior International Client Advisor for Tongues Translation Services, a leading AI language, voice, and broadcast service. Jim's organization helps many churches and Bible translators translate text into other languages. Jim told me

---

[70]"Why Audio?" *Faith Comes by Hearing*, accessed June 23, 2023, https://www.faithcomesbyhearing.com.

that, "The 2033 initiative began before AI really hit the scene. Using AI tools, I estimate we will translate the Bible in every language by 2029, probably earlier."

While AI translation acceleration helps spread the Gospel faster, it's worth mentioning another potent force— word of mouth. As evil empires are smashed and millennia of oppression ends worldwide, people want to know, "Who did it!" When news gets out that YHWY in His divine mercy averted the destruction of humanity by raising up anointed Soldier Saints to execute His judgment, word travels fast over the Internet.

The Gospel message rings truer to the rescued prisoner. When Yeshua set people free from disease and other bondage during His earthly ministry, many immediately followed Him. A modern-day miracle of interrupting and destroying Satan's sinister agenda for humanity will awake multitudes to the goodness of YHWY. Could the Gospel be preached to the entire world by 2027 after YHWY sets the world free from the Fourth Beast? You bet! Recall the scripture we read from the book of Enoch:

> On the day of affliction on which evil shall have been treasured up against the sinners. And the righteous shall be victorious in the name of the Lord of Spirits: and He will cause the others to witness (this), that they may repent and forgo the works of their hands (1 Enoch 50:2).

Every person with a heart of righteousness should receive Yeshua. We must work hard as laborers during this time to bring many to the Lord.

Varying Degrees of Glory

The Bible indicates the robes of Glory we wear shine at different shades of brilliance. In other words, some shine brighter than others. In the book of Daniel, we are provided with clues regarding the varying shades of Glory:

> And the teachers and those who are wise shall shine like the brightness of the firmament, and those who turn many to righteousness (to uprightness and right standing with God) [shall give forth light] like the stars forever and ever (Dan. 12:3 AMPC).

In the passage, YHWY rewards soul-winners with a brighter level of Glory than the teachers and wise alone. This should motivate us even more to bring in the lost during the End Times Harvest!

An old friend of mine preaches the Gospel to everyone in his path. The cab driver, the bellman, the waiter at the restaurant. He now goes into prisons and preaches the Gospel to felons. His business never took off, and he always seems short on cash. However, he won many to Yeshua in his lifetime. Many times, I envied his courage in winning people to Yeshua. I picture this man shining brightly in the Kingdom Age, proudly introducing people that he won to Yeshua to others on the street.

We don't know the precise date that Yeshua appears during the Fire Judgment, concluding the End Times Harvest. However, based upon my analysis in Chapter 9, the End Times Harvest lasts between two and eight years. The old age ends by 2027. Make the most of this precious time by choosing to evangelize the lost with your testimony. You won't lack resources during this time. Use your time to win the lost. YHWY rewards you in the Kingdom Age as you shine as bright as the stars forever!

A Hungry Prayer

I long to drink of you, O God,
drinking deeply from the streams of pleasure
flowing from your presence.
My longings overwhelm me for more of you!
My soul thirsts, pants, and longs for the living God.
I want to come and see the face of God.
Day and night my tears keep falling
and my heart keeps crying for your help
while my enemies mock me over and over, saying,
"Where is this God of yours? *Why doesn't he help you?*"

— Ps. 42:1-3 TPT

12. Prepare to Shine

*It seemed like a dream when the LORD brought us
back to the city of Zion. We celebrated with laughter
and joyful songs. In foreign nations it was said, "The
LORD has worked miracles for his people." And so we
celebrated because the LORD had indeed worked
miracles for us.*

— Ps. 126:1-3 CEV

YHWY's divine plan for humanity thrills the heart and
expands the mind. We soon embark on an electrifying
journey back to the Garden of Eden, clothed in Glory.
Presently, we encounter our Lord Yeshua in the clouds for a
divine appointment. When we return to Earth after our
divine encounter we embrace our "lost" children and other
loved ones. Parents with autistic or disfigured children then
witness them made completely whole. Parents who lost

righteous children in wars see them again. We will also enjoy the fellowship of the saints gone before us.

The earth to which we return after our encounter brims with joy and expectation. Even the animals celebrate as YHWY shows them who His children are (Rom. 8:19)! The earth, now completely refreshed, rebounds in beauty and emanates the sweet aroma of Glory. Gone from Earth are creatures or plants reflecting the genetic deviation from YHWY's original purpose.

As I meditate on the future of the Ekklesia, I feel a release inside, an awakening and kindling of something I never felt before. My inner man begins to transform already in anticipation. The events described in this book are not hundreds of years out—not decades out—they are only a few months away. In fact, they transpire as I write!

So how does one prepare for what's next? How can we enlarge our hearts to receive what YHWY prepares for us? Christians who died in car accidents or other tragedies weren't afforded the luxury we possess—death unexpectedly thrust them into an encounter with Yeshua in Heaven. Yet, we now understand that we will meet Yeshua in a matter of months or years for a divine encounter, and *can* prepare! So what do we do to prepare for our encounter?

Shed Captive-Breeding

The first step in preparation for our encounter involves shedding our "captive-bred" mentality. The more I study the next age and dream of YHWY's wonders, the closer I draw to Him. Almost unfathomable, YHWY's immaculate plan for the future boggles the mind while also untethering the shackles of bondage the Fourth Beast so desperately imposed on us for centuries.

Envision a caged lion in a zoo gets released in the wild. For a few hours, he might wander around and not know what to do. The cage that confined him for his whole life eventually stood for comfort, security, and meal-times. At some point, however, the lion realizes no meal gets dumped into his enclosure—he now lives in a new world. Hunger begins to ignite the long-forgotten wild instinct of hunting. Studies indicate only about 30% of such animals survive. Believers all survive, in that we make it to the Kingdom Age. However, we can prepare for our encounter with Yeshua by allowing YHWY to reignite our Garden of Eden instincts. We need to picture ourselves with the crown of Glory now.

Imagine the emotions the lion faces after experiencing freedom for the first time. He saunters around, puzzled. If he allows himself, the instincts however faint eventually return. Our instincts from the time of our earthly father, Adam, are still there. YHWY designed us to rule and reign over the earth and to enjoy unfettered fellowship with Him. That's how He made us. Let that instinct come back to life. Begin to see Satan and his minions as usurpers, unlawful rats that need to be killed with a stick and swept out of your kitchen. Start telling Satan what to do, instead of allowing him to order you around. Banish Demon-gods and Evil Spirits from Earth, as we discussed prior. We need to see ourselves the way YHWY sees us: righteous, holy, and victorious.

After I understood YHWY's immaculate plan for His people, I began to understand better the behavior of the early Ekklesia. They feared nothing. They knew if Rome killed their bodies, they simply returned during the next age. Any unfinished business in the old age they planned to complete in the next age! They focused every day on spreading the Good News, healing the sick, and raising the dead. They knew they were strange fellows, aliens of the old age. Their "full salvation" would come in the next age. If physical death cut their assignment short, no worries. Any regrets were confined to failure to accomplish all YHWY intended in the short time they lived on the "alien planet"—Earth under Satanic control. Many probably only realized their ignorance of authority over Satan after they moved to Heaven.

Envisage how depressed Satan soon becomes. Every saint he martyred, every baby he aborted, every righteous person he killed with disease—comes back from the dead in the Kingdom Age. Thousands of years of work to carefully contrive control structures, enslavement systems, and clever deceptions burn in a single day. Satan accomplishes absolutely nothing. Yes, he manages to deceive many and make things uncomfortable for YHWY's elect, but even suffering accomplishes YHWY's purposes. Struggle simply makes a righteous person draw closer to YHWY.

Let the YHWY-instinct placed in man 6,000 years ago begin to ignite your inner man. See yourself as heirs of YHWY, and co-heirs with Yeshua of His Glory. "And since we are his children, we are his heirs. In fact, together with Christ

270

we are heirs of God's glory. But if we are to share his glory, we must also share his suffering" (Rom. 8:17 NLT).

Like billions of saints before us, we shared in the sufferings under the evil empires of the world. Our predecessors saw YHWY's immaculate plan for them. "They were glad just to see these things from far away, and they agreed that they were only strangers and foreigners on this earth" (Heb. 11:13b CEV). What our patriarchs saw from "far away," we possess the honor and absolute privilege of seeing nearby—literally in just a few years.

The days of suffering under satanic rule are almost over. You passed the test! Make the most of it and recognize the immense blessing of living in our time and belonging to a remnant that won't taste the Second Death.

Don't Fear the Matrix

Admittedly, for several years I feared the deep state. After much research, I discovered the immense and murderous infrastructure they put in place to persecute and confine the righteous. I also witnessed how they canceled or killed detractors to their agenda.

At one point, I became a deep state target. In the Summer of 2019, Black Lives Matter (BLM) and Antifa protesters showed up in Lincoln Park in Washington DC to protest and recruit new people. They put up vulgar signs full of messages, like "F$@& the Police" and "Kill the Cops." My small children began to ask me what the signs meant. When these "peaceful protesters" began to scope and measure the statue of President Lincoln in the park, I knew they planned to tear it down. After repeated calls to the DC Metropolitan police, they finally admitted, "Look, Mayor Bowser wants Lincoln gone. There is nothing we can do about it!" Nothing made sense. Freed slaves purchased the bronze statue of President Lincoln in the park holding his name. *This* was the statue the "Black Lives Matter" thugs wanted to tear down? If the statue of Lincoln came down, inevitably some demonic edifice would take his place.

After getting no help from the police, I decided to take matters into my own hands. I told the protesters to leave Lincoln alone, because if they attempted to take down the Lincoln statue my friends and I would shoot them with air rifles. (FYI, air rifles are legal in DC). As a youngster growing up on Texas ranches, my friends and I would have BB-gun fights—it stung but no one got hurt. We later moved onto paintball fights. The incident was caught on tape, and the Fourth Beast media machinery went to work. After a local paper doxxed my identity, 200 Antifa protesters showed up at my house and plastered hideous graffiti all over my yard—terrorizing my family. A few days after the protesters trashed my yard, a frantic detective showed up and told me to leave my home, because "a mob is heading here from Lafayette Square and we can't stop them—we think they are coming to your house!" In the meantime, the Washington Post and other media outlets hounded my family for a story. DC then issued a misdemeanor arrest warrant on me for "terroristic threats," even though I kept my cool as a BLM agitator screamed in my face in front of my young children, hurling expletives.

After the incident, I began to approach the problem in the spirit-realm. I anointed the corners of the park with oil. I spoke the biblical promises of protection over my neighborhood. When I saw witches conducting seances in the park, I immediately ran over, broke curses, and drove them off. President Lincoln's monument still stands in Lincoln Park, although the replica statue got torn down in Boston. We are not "wrestling with blood and flesh, but with the principalities, with the authorities, with the world-rulers of the darkness of this age, with the spiritual things of the evil in the heavenly places" (Eph. 6:12 YLT). Praise YHWY the rulers of the darkness of this age soon face judgment!

My story by no means compares to the many others. Many J6-ers rot in jail for simply expressing their first amendment rights. Jack Phillips suffered numerous court battles after refusing to bake a cake for a homosexual couple, based upon his Christian convictions, paying millions in legal fees. The livelihood of DC Attorney Jeffrey Clark continues to be threatened for simply providing legal advice to President Trump on the stolen election in 2020 in an unsigned draft letter. All these persecutions represent desperate moves of the Fourth Beast system to shut down strong men and women who are willing to act *with conviction.*

Battle the enemy in the spirit-realm. Remember, praying friends of Peter moved Heaven to provide an angel to break him out of prison in Acts 12:

> Peter, therefore, indeed, was kept in the prison, and fervent prayer was being made by the assembly unto God for him...

> And lo, a messenger of the Lord stood by, and a light shone in the buildings, and having smitten Peter on the side, he raised him up, saying, 'Rise in haste,' and his chains fell from off his hands (Acts 12:5, 7 YLT).

Miracles still happen today. Intercede. Command the prison doors to open for the J6-ers and other political prisoners. We possess more authority in the spirit-realm than we know.

Neo, the main character in *The Matrix* movie, figured out how the Matrix worked and stopped fearing it.[71] In a famous scene, the agents emptied their entire magazines on Neo, and he simply put his hand up to stop the bullets from harming him. From then on, the Matrix held no power over him. True Soldier Saints must wake up to the declining power of the Fourth Beast. The Fourth Beast matrix represents a near-extinct race, the last of a dying breed. We have *nothing* to fear. YHWY provides supernatural protection, especially during times of judgment.

I discovered several promises specific to *these times*, promising protection for the righteous in time of YHWY's judgment. *If* we access and stand on these promises, the Fourth Beast remains completely powerless over us:

> My people will live in safety, quietly at home. They will be at rest. Even if the forest should be destroyed and the city torn down (Isa. 32:18-19 NLT).

---

71   *The Matrix*, dir. The Wachowskis, prod. Joel Silver, 1999.

For the LORD is our judge, our lawgiver, and our king. He will care for us and save us. The enemies' sails hang loose on broken masts with useless tackle. Their treasure will be divided by the people of God. Even the lame will take their share (Isa. 33:22-23)!

And the earth shall be wholly rent in sunder, And all that is upon the earth shall perish, And there shall be a judgement upon all (men). But with the righteous He will make peace, and will protect the elect, and mercy shall be upon them. And they shall all belong to God (1 Enoch 1:7-8a).

Though a thousand fall at your side, though ten thousand are dying around you, these evils will not touch you. Just open your eyes, and see how the wicked are punished (Ps. 91:7-8 NLT).

Once I understood the special promises available for me during the Stone Judgment, I chose not to fear. YHWY proffers special protection for His people, but we must trust Him. The judgment disembowels the old world system—it's not for us. I no longer look over my shoulder, sensing YHWY's cocoon of total protection.

We still need to rely on the leading of the Holy Spirit. For instance, I would hesitate to travel to Israel right now. Notwithstanding, YHWY speaks to His servants in Israel concerning how to stay safe! We must remain exactly where YHWY wants us to enjoy His full protection. Lately, He wants me at home, resting in Him.

Anticipate Blessings

The more I meditate on YHWY's glorious plan for His people, the more blessings come. A lady began to read my books and internalize YHWY's amazing plan. Over weeks and months, she meditated on YHWY's breathtaking plan for her future, raising her expectation and also praising YHWY in advance for the fulfillment of His plan.

Remarkable miracles began to happen in her life. Recently, nearly $50,000 dropped into her bank account from the Social Security Administration, accompanied by a letter that said, in effect, "We realized we owed you money." The same woman accepted a buyout on an oil well for over $100,000 *after* she was told the same well worthless just a few years prior. Early recipients of YHWY's blessings related to the Kingdom Age raise their level of expectation in their hearts. We must *believe* His plan.

If you believe YHWY's prophecies concerning our future, then take a step of faith. That step involves crafting a strategy to bless humanity with the wealth you receive in the wealth transfer. Plans need to be clear and even list the people you expect to work with. Your giving plan maybe as simple as buying groceries for people in your neighborhood. In my plan, I include buying certain companies Satan currently uses for evil and transforming them into forces for good. I happen to possess unique turnaround management experience, which I believe uniquely prepares me to serve as a Soldier Saint in YHWY's turnaround plan for the world. Once you complete your plan, get a notary to acknowledge it.

This simple act of faith prepares you to receive YHWY's blessing and favor.

Remember the Commands

YHWY gives us His commands for us in the Kingdom Age. They are summarized in the book of 2 Esdras 2:10-23:

- Lead the lost to your light (Yeshua).
- Raise our children in the fear of the Lord.
- Honor and do no harm to YHWY's prophets.
- Do right by the widows.
- Defend the orphans.
- Clothe the naked.
- Heal the broken and weak.
- Defend the maimed.
- Take care of your old and young in your home.
- Bury the dead, if you discover them unburied.

The Kingdom Age commands are basic. However, we must purposely act them out. These commands are summarized in Yeshua's supreme command, encapsulating YHWY's law:

> And you must love the LORD your God with all your heart, all your soul, all your mind, and all your strength. The second is equally important: Love your neighbor as yourself. No other commandment is greater than these (Mark 12:30-31 NLT).

The other day I went on a run. While running, I began to meditate on YHWY's Kingdom commands and also on the

277

upcoming prophetic events. I spotted a very old couple in the park where I routinely run laps. The Lord impressed upon me to speak to the couple about Yeshua. The Lord reminded me of His forthcoming Fire Judgment, and let me know that their blood would be on my head if I did not speak to them. He further shared with me that they did not know Him.

I stopped running and spoke to them. They claimed they were Jewish and no one ever spoke to them about Jesus. After a brief dialog, I shared with them a short message—exactly how God instructed me to speak with them. While they did not choose to receive Him then, I knew I did the right thing. I began to pray for them afterwards to receive the Lord. I also committed to the Lord to obey in the future. I am now in a "running ministry!" Wherever you go, pray that the Lord shows you who to share your faith with—the time is short!

The wealth transfer happens before the Fire Judgment. But don't let wealth and sustenance distract you from the mission of sharing your faith. We must share our testimony and bring as many into YHWY's Kingdom as possible before the Fire Judgment—for then it's too late. Many billions soon recognize YHWY's goodness, and are already ripe to receive Yeshua. Start gathering now—He will show you whom to speak with.

Yesterday's Manna Stinks

While Israel remained in the wilderness, YHWY fed them with manna, a flaky white "bread" that tasted like honey. YHWY commanded the Israelites to gather only enough for that given day. Anything left over, unless gathered ahead of time for the Sabbath, spoiled. Yesterday's manna "bred worms and became foul" (Ex. 16:20b NRSV).

There are many books and Bible commentaries out there that represent old, foul manna. When YHWY showed me His divine strategy for the future, He instructed me to study His Word and avoid reading any commentary, other than for language study. I literally discarded hundreds of DVDs and books I had amassed on the topic, picked up my Bible, and asked the Holy Spirit to show me YHWY's glorious plan for humanity in His Word.

YHWY indicated to Daniel that many of His prophecies are sealed until closer to when they would occur. "But you, Daniel, keep the words secret and the book sealed until the time of the end" (Dan. 12:4a). Now that we near the end of the age, YHWY unseals not only the book of Daniel, but many other apocalyptic books, such as Enoch. The sudden popularity of these books represents a work of the Holy Spirit—open up your heart to receive fresh manna. Because apocalyptic books remained hidden, many older interpretations or attempts to unseal End Times prophecies missed the mark. One simply cannot understand YHWY's amazing blueprint for the future without reading the "extra-biblical" books the early Ekklesia studied.

Bible commentary helps us understand Hebrew, Greek, or Aramaic meanings of words in the Bible. However, much Bible commentary teaches old interpretations of End Times. I found myself striking out bracketed comments, for instance in the Amplified Bible, which many times "taught" old

279

doctrines related to End Times by imparting incorrect interpretations. The Scofield Bible uses commentary extensively, which also seeks to impart incorrect End Times ideology and ridicules the gifts of the Spirit.

I found that The Passion Translation provided a superior translation of the book of Isaiah and the New Testament compared to most other translations. The book of Isaiah literally came alive for me when reading from The Passion Translation, a more recent translation. In some ways, even the existence of more vibrant Bible translations fulfills Daniel's prophecy of keeping "the book sealed until the time of the end!"

The Holy Spirit remains our teacher on concepts in the Bible. Begin to trust the Holy Spirit inside of you for confirmation on YHWY's Word. In this book, I reference hundreds of scriptures. I encourage you to dive into these scriptures for yourself and receive "fresh manna."

Youth Lead the Way

The Bible indicates that our young leaders receive special anointings in the coming days. The prophet Joel describes the Stone Judgment in vivid detail in Joel 2:1-27. He then says, "Then, after doing all those things, I will pour out my Spirit upon all people. Your sons and daughters will prophesy. Your old men will dream dreams, and your young men will see visions" (Joel 2:28 NLT). The prophetic anointing coming over young people astounds the older generation of Believers. Our sons and daughters hear from the Lord! Embrace and encourage that anointing. We will soon be surrounded by kids—all the aborted and miscarried children destroyed by the Fourth Beast and Demon-gods come back in the resurrection. What a great opportunity to train our children up in the ways of YHWY, including the supernatural.

During the Kingdom Age, the seven mountains of cultural influence transform to bless our children. Today, the Fourth Beast controls education, arts, media, entertainment, etc. and uses these to influence our children negatively. The prophet Ezra promises in the Kingdom Age, "seven mighty mountains on which roses and lilies grow; by these I will fill your children with joy" (2 Esd. 2:19b NRSV). We should expect our children to grow up as powerhouses for Yeshua! They will be afforded opportunities that our generation failed to experience.

The prophet Enoch indicates the younger generation produces mighty explorers of yet undiscovered regions of Earth:

> And in the day of the tribulation of the sinners,
> Your children shall mount and rise as eagles, and
> higher than the vultures will be your nest, and ye
> shall ascend and enter the crevices of the earth,
> And the clefts of the rock forever as coneys before
> the unrighteous (1 Enoch 96:2).

I immediately thought of regions beyond Antarctica, an area presently banned by governments for exploration. Our children will lead the exploration teams. The mention of nests higher than vultures also speaks to new technologies, such as anti-gravitational technology, capable of sustaining sky-cities.

Focus on the Mission

Believers soon come into extraordinary blessing. Use this blessing as a testimony to fulfill the mission—gathering many into the Kingdom of YHWY before the Fire Judgment. Invite people to dinner and share your faith. Be a soul-winner. "But a life lived loving God bears lasting fruit, for the one who is truly wise wins souls" (Prov. 11:30 TPT).

Right now, it's tempting to be distracted by the news. Many check their *Telegram* and favorite news websites several times a day, looking for the latest bit of "intel." So much information comes out it's difficult to process. The underground war against the deep state begins to bubble to the surface and it's exciting to watch!

Over the past few years, I found myself addicted to news updates. I began to see quite a bit of repetition in articles, and frankly learned nothing new most of the time. If you really want to know the future, get in YHWY's Word— it's all in there! At one point, after spending over an hour on *Telegram*, the Lord spoke to me and said, "Son, quit trying to figure out *how* I set humanity free—focus on my assignment for you." Our assignment from the Lord represents our mission. We need to stay on mission and avoid any distraction.

Soldier Saints serve as obedient warriors for YHWY as they fearlessly move out in their high calling, regardless of the cost to their reputation or safety. Soldier Saints call out tyranny, right wrongs, and know how to fight for the truth. Qualities of Soldier Saints include:

#1. **Obedient:** We know our mission. We execute YHWY's assignments promptly. We draw others into YHWY's family at every opportunity.

#2. **Courageous:** We know who we are—we won't back down in the face of opposition or persecution. We skillfully wield our sword, YHWY's Word, over any and all situations with boldness. We don't compromise.

#3. **Wise:** We spot Satan's infiltrators and snuff them out. We *never* take off the armor of YHWY, especially our breastplate of righteousness.

#4. **Sensitive:** We know YHWY's voice because of daily fellowship with Him. We are sensitive to what YHWY is doing in others' lives. We recognize and honor YHWY's anointing on others.

#5. **Hungry:** We possess an insatiable appetite for YHWY's word. We know YHWY's promises regarding every situation. We hunger and thirst for our "full salvation."

#6. **Loving:** We walk in YHWY's love with all interactions, including at home. We forgive immediately. We are loyal.

#7. **Generous:** We give time and resources to help others. We don't ignore the needy around us.

YHWY's Word describes all of these attributes for Believers. Soldier Saints remain on mission all the time. YHWY soon puts Soldier Saints in charge of the nations of Earth. It remains a high honor to serve as one of YHWY's Soldier Saints. Strive to exude the attributes of a Soldier Saint in all facets of your own life. With YHWY, age, educational background, or experience don't matter—He values obedience. YHWY promises, "Every valley should be raised up, and every mountain and hill should be made flat. The rough ground should be made level, and the rugged ground should be made smooth" (Isa. 40:4 NCV). Right now, the wicked stand on mountains of influence and the righteous remain hidden in the valley. This soon changes. YHWY raises up His finest Soldier Saints to lead mountains of influence—are you ready to lead?

YHWY called King David out of the shepherd's field. He called King Josiah to lead as King of Israel at eight years old. He called the prophet Jeremiah to speak to nations as a youngster. He called Gideon, a fearful prepper, to deliver Israel. He called out a rag-tag bunch of fisherman and vagabonds to be Yeshua's disciples. He called out Moses, a stutterer, to deliver Israel from Egypt. None of these servants possessed any particular skill set. However, they all answered the call of YHWY.

A few months ago, I found myself grumbling about something when I stumbled on, the "Warrior's Creed: I Am a Soldier." While the author of the Warrior's Creed remains unknown, his or her words powerfully inspire. I shrank the page down and pasted it in my prayer journal. Anytime I am weary or something goes wrong, I consult the creed and repeat it out loud. I included the full Warrior's Creed in the

Appendix. I highly recommend reading it out loud regularly. From the Warriors Creed:

> I am a soldier. I am not a wimp. I am in place, saluting my King, obeying His orders, praising His name, and building His kingdom! No one has to send me flowers, gifts, food, cards, candy, or give me handouts. I do not need to be cuddled, cradled, cared for, or catered to.

Remember Israels' deliverance as a "wake up call." They faced the most amazing redemption in human history. Before they even left Egypt, they began to complain. I saw a meme online that said, "No one said taking out a 6,000-year-old death-cult would be easy." An epic level of deliverance persists underground for YHWY's people—be patient. Use this time to get yourself ready for the Kingdom Age. Start bringing others into YHWY's Kingdom. Maintain an attitude of humble gratefulness—do not complain!

Recognize that we live in the most blessed generation in human history, and decide to be thankful for YHWY's deliverance! We don't want to commit the same sins of Israel after their deliverance from Egypt. Their stubbornness kept an entire generation out of the promised land.

Know Who You Are

When we encounter Yeshua in the sky during our glorious one-on-one appointment, we change forever. First John explains the mystery:

> Beloved, we are God's children right now; however, it is not yet apparent what we will become. But we do know that when it is finally made visible, we will be just like him, for we will see him as he truly is. And all who focus their hope on him will always be purifying themselves, just as Jesus is pure (1 John 3:2-3 TPT).

When we see Yeshua, "we will be just like him." How will we be just like Yeshua? The verse continues, "for we will see him as he truly is." After our encounter with Yeshua, we proudly wear our new Glory suit—not before. When we understand our destiny—our purpose—to reign as a co-heir with Yeshua, we *then* qualify for our Glory suit. Our encounter with Yeshua shatters all defeatism, all pessimism, and all useless doctrines of man. John G. Lake, a powerful healing evangelist who lived around the turn of the 20th century, wrote extensively on the topic of seeing Yeshua as He is:

> If we stop to think that one-half of the great Christian world is still carrying a little crucifix representing a dead Christ, we realize how the mind of man is yet chained to the cross of Calvary, to a dead Christ, to a tomb not empty, but the tomb that contains the One they love...
>
> While we revere the cross of Calvary, while the soul of man will ever love to think of Him who gave His life for us, yet I believe the triumph of the Christ began at the cross and ends only when the race, like Himself, has received from God the

Father, through Him, the grace, power, and glory of God that makes them sons of God like Himself...

Beloved, the secret of Christianity is the secret of the Christ possessing the heart of man; man being yielded to Him so that His victory, His consciousness, and His power possess your spirit and mind. Then bless God, we are kings. Not because we say we are kings, but because we know we are kings and because we feel we are kings by the grace of God and His inworking power.[72]

Seeing Yeshua face-to-face causes us to recognize that powerful instinct from the day YHWY created man in the Garden of Eden, our original purpose. It's an "aha" moment when the lies Satan pounded into us our whole life strip off, and we realize that we are *already* citizens of Heaven— *already* joint-heirs with Yeshua. While the breaking off of the curse of death on our lives remains supernatural, the realization of who we are in Yeshua can happen now as we internalize YHWY's promises and see Yeshua "as He is"—the mighty resurrected Savior who conquered death, hell, and the grave. Begin to ascend in your hearts today as you meditate on YHWY's Word and let it change you. Like the lion that escaped from the cage in the zoo, the instincts are still there—nurture them.

I would rather Yeshua not need to exhort me during the encounter. He should find us following His plan for our life

---

[72] Liardon, Roberts. *John G. Lake; The Complete Collection of His Life Teachings.* (Tulsa, Albury Publishing: 1999), 208-210.

before our encounter! If Yeshua needs to correct us, He will do it with complete love and patience. But wouldn't you rather hear, "Well done, thou good and faithful servant!"

One Summer during my college years, I read another story by John G. Lake that touched me. Lake had a vision whereby an angel flew with him over many towns and dropped off three wreaths; one white, one pink, and one black. The angel dropped the white wreath on a minister that accomplished all with excellence. The angel dropped off the pink wreath on a minister that accomplished some of his calling, but got distracted. The black one he dropped on a person that knew YHWY and turned his back on Him. After reading Lake's vision, I prayed on a local junior high football field at night, and cried out, "God, I want the white wreath!"

My hunger and thirst for truth on End Times came after several years of fearful doomsday prepping left me spiritually bankrupt. I feared the Fourth Beast then. I cried out to YHWY for months to show me His plan—He honored my request. Several months ago, I asked the Lord why He gifted me with unsealing the Bible on End Times, when so many others failed to see His immaculate plan. He reminded me of that incident, now over 30 years ago, on the football field. You see, great rewards follow those who hunger and thirst after YHWY. Our Fathers' rewards in our life invariable bless others because when the favor of the LORD is upon the king, it is for those around the king.

Spiritual Hunger

John G. Lake wrote a sermon in 1924 relevant to our time today. Lake taught on the scripture, "Blessed are they which do hunger and thirst after righteousness: for they shall be filled" (Matt. 5:6 KJV). The following is an excerpt from Lake's sermon:

> Many look forward to the second coming of Jesus —His coming again—as though mechanical, on a certain date, when certain events come to pass, Jesus is going to arrive. I do not see it that way. I see on the other hand that there must be a tremendous hunger, an overwhelming hunger, for the Lord's coming in the hearts of men, so that a prayer such as was never prayed in the world before for Christ to come will rise to heaven. And, bless God, when it rises to heaven on the part of sufficient souls, it will take Jesus Christ himself off the throne and bring Him down to earth.
>
> Daniel says that he was convinced by the study of the books of prophecy, especially that of Jeremiah, that the time had come when they ought to be delivered from captivity in Babylon. The seventy years was fulfilled but there was no deliverance. So he diligently set his face to pray it into being (Daniel 9).
>
> Here is what I want you to get. If it was going to come to pass mechanically, by a certain date, there would not have been any necessity for Daniel to get that hunger in his soul, so that he

fasted and prayed in sackcloth and ashes that deliverance might come.

No sir, God's purposes come to pass when your heart and mine gets the real God cry, and the real God prayer comes into our spirit and, the real God yearning gets our nature. Something is going to happen then.

No difference what it may be your soul is coveting or desiring, if it becomes in your life the supreme cry—not a secondary matter, or the third, or the fourth, or the fifth or tenth, but the first thing; the supreme desire of your soul, the paramount issue—all the powers and energies of your spirit, of your soul, and of your body are reaching out and crying to God for the answers. It is going to come, it is going to come, it is going to come.[73]

The Holy Spirit moves in the hearts of men to pray and intercede for prophetic promises until they come to pass. Now that we know the prophetic events and dates concerning the Stone Judgment, the Ekklesia needs to pray. We need to use our authority, in Yeshua's name, to expose the Fourth Beast. We must speak the Word to stop desperate final moves of the Fourth Beast minions. Now we must expel Demon-gods and Evil Spirits from Earth.

---

[73]   Roberts, *John G. Lake,* 453-454.

Time to Pray

I shared with you my knowledge on YHWY's immaculate plan for humanity. Years of fasting and prayer led to a personal explosion of revelation on the topic of End Times. What you read in this book, combined with my prior books, reflects YHWY's future plan for humanity with great clarity.

By completing the Revelation Riddle trilogy, you have the knowledge you need to thrive during the next biblical event for humanity, the Stone Judgment. In *Blast of Fire*, I taught how we can discover ourselves in the Bible, yielding insight into our high calling. I also taught how President Trump fulfills prophecy related to the Stone Judgment *right now*. In *KAS*, I taught how to discern the times and recognize evil. I also uncovered a riddle in the book of Revelation describing the Kingdom Age of the Saints. This book provides the complete timeline and sequence for YHWY's immaculate plan for humanity, and how to prepare for our encounter with Yeshua.

It might be tempting to sit back, relax, and wait for things to happen. However, based on what we just read in Lakc's sermon, I am convinced that we must hunger and thirst for our encounter with Yeshua and His complete redemption of humanity. Yeshua appears for a hungry Ekklesia.

The example Lake provided concerning the prophet Daniel perfectly matches our situation today. We know that the old age ends by 2027. We know the third millennia after Yeshua's resurrection begins in either 2027, 2030, or 2033.

However, we also know Yeshua told us no one knows the exact day or hour of His coming—not even Him.

The prophet Daniel knew the timeline in his day better than anyone. However, the target date came and went with no deliverance—until Daniel prayed and fasted. Daniel's hunger and thirst for the Lord ushered in Israel's deliverance from Ancient Babylon. Yet, Daniel's hunger also unlocked revelation from YHWY regarding the "target date" for our deliverance from modern Babylon—the Fourth Beast system! The reward of spiritual hunger invariably blesses others. Now it's our turn to get hungry for YHWY.

Hunger and thirst for Yeshua's coming and the completion of the Stone Judgment. Fast at least one day a week (water only) and spend time praying for Yeshua to appear. Pray daily for the safety of our soldiers, fighting for the survival of humanity. Pray for President Trump. Banish Demon-gods and Evil Spirits from Earth. Tamp down pride in your life. The Ekklesia must pray and hunger to once again wear the Glory of YHWY like fine clothing. Desire YHWY's presence more than food or water.

The hunger of YHWY's remnant ushers in the most glorious adventure in human history. See you in the Garden of Eden!

For more information or to access regular podcasts by the author, please visit revelationriddle.com

Appendix

Don't Wait, Receive Yeshua Today!

So you will be saved, if you honestly say, "Jesus is Lord," and if you believe with all your heart that God raised him from death. God will accept you and save you, if you truly believe this and tell it to others.
— Rom. 10:9-10 CEV

In this book, I talk about the judgment of YHWY falling on Earth at the end of the current age. This judgment is not for YHWY's people, but for the world and people that reject Him. Now is an especially important time to know YHWY and be close to Him. Don't wait, receive Yeshua today! It's the most important decision you will make in your entire life.

YHWY wants a relationship with you. Not only that, He has a plan and destiny for your life. To have a relationship with YHWY we must accept His Son Yeshua as our Savior and Lord. You see, sin separates us from YHWY, and we must accept Yeshua as Savior to allow His blood to wash away our sins and make our spirits white and pure. This is the first step on our adventure with YHWY.

Receiving Yeshua as Lord starts with a prayer that acknowledges our sin and asks Him to wash us clean as we accept His sacrifice on the cross for us. Nothing you have done in your past is too big for YHWY's forgiveness. Yeshua paid the ultimate price so that we would not have to. But we must, by faith, believe in our hearts and say out loud a prayer of Salvation. Ready? Say this:

"Dear Lord Yeshua, I need you. Come into my life, and wash me clean. Set me free from all bondage. Heal my body, mind and spirit. Wash me with your blood and protect me with your blood going forward. Fill me with your Holy Spirit. You are my Lord and Savior. Give me the strength to serve you all my days."

Find a local church that believes in the miracles of YHWY. Get a Bible and ask Him to give you the Holy Spirit to show you how to read it. Tell others what happened to you. After your decision to serve the Lord, pressure may arise that causes you to doubt. Don't worry about this, it's normal. Satan tries to steal YHWY's Word out of your heart. (See Mark 4). Stay close to YHWY through prayer. Talk to YWHY the same way you would talk to a close friend; you will soon recognize His voice. He loves you so much, and wants only the best for you.

Prayer of Protection

YHWY, you are my protector. I fear no evil. You promised special protection during your judgment of evil. Now You are judging the evil age and I access Your protection based on Your promises. I live in safety, quietly at home. I am at rest. You are my Judge, Lawgiver and King. You care for me and save me. You made peace with me, and promised to protect me and have mercy on me, for I belong to You. Though a thousand fall at my side, and ten thousand die around me, no evil touches me.

I plead the Blood of Yeshua on my home, my family and my property. I plead the Blood of Yeshua on my extended family. I ask You to draw them into your Kingdom if they don't know You. You promised my household would be saved, so I claim that promise over insert name(s) today.

I pray for supernatural cloaking angels to make me invisible to any enemy seeking to harm me. I send forth angelic hosts to protect my neighborhood and city from any harm the enemy plans. I declare Satan's plans against me, my neighborhood, my state and my country are powerless and ineffective.

I declare the Soldier Saints on the front lines fighting the Fourth Beast and Little Horn are supernaturally protected with the Blood of Yeshua. I send out the warrior-hosts to fight alongside them and protect them. I declare all the enemy's plans are exposed, revealed, and stopped. I pray a special protection over all members of the military alliance You put together for this time of judgment, in Yeshua's name.

Banishment of Principalities

*** *Start in your local community, then your city, then your state.* ***

Demon-gods and Evil Spirits, you must leave Earth. According to the Word of God, it is time for your imprisonment in the outer heavens until your final judgment. Leave now in Yeshua's Name.

You were judged by the Most High in the Court of Heaven. Yeshua pronounced the judgment on you. Therefore, you no longer possess authority on Earth. Leave now.

I break the power of principalities causing war, mischief, deception, and chaos. All your plans are useless vanity because you are here unlawfully. Leave now. I banish you from Earth in Yeshua's name.

Satan, I declare your age of authority ended. You can no longer harm, maim, poison, afflict, or persecute humanity. Your authority is broken. You are powerless. YHWY's Kingdom now rules on Earth.

Demon-god of false religion, your rule expired—Go. Demon-god of the arts, your rule expired—Go. Demon-gods of governments worldwide, your rule expired—Go. Demon-god of corrupt media, your rule expired —Go. Demon-god of family corruption, your rule expired—Go. Demon-god of perverse education, your rule expired—Go. Demon-god of corrupt business, your rule expired-Go.

I declare all things done in darkness come to light. Every government, business or organization aligned with the Fourth Beast falls apart. Every wicked leader falls from power. YHWY's Kingdom now rules on Earth, in Yeshua's name.

Warrior's Creed: I Am a Soldier

I am a soldier in the army of God. The Lord Jesus Christ is my Commanding Officer. The Holy Bible is my code of conduct.

Faith, Prayer, and the Word are my weapons of Warfare. I have been taught by the Holy Spirit, trained by experience, tried by adversity, and tested by fire.

I am a volunteer in this army, and I am enlisted for eternity. I will either retire in this Army or die in this Army; but, I will not get out, sell out, be talked out, or pushed out.

I am faithful, reliable, capable, and dependable. If my God needs me, I am there.

I am a soldier. I am not a baby. I do not need to be pampered, petted, primed up, pumped up, picked up, or pepped up.

I am a soldier. No one has to call me, remind me, write me, visit me, entice me, or lure me.

I am a soldier. I am not a wimp. I am in place, saluting my King, obeying His orders, praising His name, and building His kingdom! No one has to send me flowers, gifts, food, cards, candy, or give me handouts. I do not need to be cuddled, cradled, cared for, or catered to.

I am committed. I cannot have my feelings hurt bad enough to turn me around. I cannot be discouraged enough to turn me aside. I cannot lose enough to cause me to quit. When Jesus called me into this Army, I had nothing. If I end up with nothing, I will still come out even. I will win.

My God will supply all my needs. I am more than a conqueror. I will always triumph. I can do all things through Christ. Devils cannot defeat me. People cannot disillusion me. Weather cannot weary me. Sickness cannot stop me. Battles cannot beat me. Money cannot buy me. Governments cannot silence me, and hell cannot handle me!

I am a soldier. Even death cannot destroy me. For when my Commander calls me from this battlefield, He will promote me to a captain. I am a soldier, in the Army, I'm marching, claiming victory. I will not give up. I will not turn around. I am a soldier, marching Heaven bound.

FOR GOD AND COUNTRY THAT OUR CHILDREN WILL ALWAYS BE FREE WWG1WGA *(Author unknown)*

Pride Self-Assessment

Symptoms of pride (check all that apply):

- ☐ Jealous when others are blessed
- ☐ Angry when you don't get your way
- ☐ Insist on "being heard"
- ☐ Find faults in everyone around you
- ☐ Refuse to praise others
- ☐ Think you are special, and more deserving than others
- ☐ Refuse to associate with those less fortunate
- ☐ Are impatient with others, but expect others to be patients with you
- ☐ Never show you are impressed
- ☐ Bothered when others don't notice you
- ☐ Refuse to acknowledge others' gifts or anointing
- ☐ Refuse to admit you are wrong without an excuse
- ☐ Enjoy stirring up strife
- ☐ Are a poor listener
- ☐ Always talking about yourself
- ☐ Are prideful about your false humility
- ☐ Keep a running tab of suffered wrongs
- ☐ Are fixated on what others think of you (insecurity)
- ☐ Are angry when you don't get the credit you believe you deserve

If you checked one or more boxes above, you need to deal with pride. Consider these scriptures:

> Pride goes before destruction, and haughtiness before a fall (Prov. 16:18 NLT).

> All who fear the Lord will hate evil. Therefore, I hate pride and arrogance, corruption and perverse speech (Prov. 8:13).

> God opposes the proud but gives grace to the humble. So humble yourselves before God. Resist the devil, and he will flee from you (Jam. 4:6b-7).

Prayer: "Father, please forgive me for a prideful heart. I know that pride fails to please you. Lord, deliver me from pride. Show me the people my pride has hurt, so I may ask them to forgive me. I speak to the prideful spirit contaminating my soul and say, 'Go from me!' You, pride are of Satan, and I no longer yield to you. Thank you, Father that your love is in my heart, and melts away any pridefulness. Teach me to walk in your ways, Father, in perfect humility—in Yeshua's name."

Glossary of Terms

anti-Christ – The "fifth beast," a leader who rules the world after the Kingdom Age of the Saints. Is possessed by Satan, the Dragon. Has two horns. Resurrects the image of the Fourth Beast. Destroys 33% of Earth.

Blood Wars – An ancient battle between Christians, the tribes of Jacob, and Satanic forces intent upon destroying both—the real reason for war.

Court of Heaven – A courtroom in Heaven where important legal matters are resolved.

Demon-gods – Spirits of Sons of God that rebelled against YHWY in the time of Noah by sleeping with women, producing Giants as offspring (the Nephilim). Also called Unclean Beasts and Watchers. Able to cast deceptions over large swaths of humanity. Given authority to remain on Earth until the Stone Judgment.

Dragon – Another name for Satan, ruler of evil principalities including Demon-gods, Evil Spirits, and Unclean Spirits.

Evil Spirits– The surviving spirits of Giants (the Nephilim), offspring of Watchers and women during the days of Noah. Also referred to as unclean birds, a reference to vultures which consume flesh. In modern times, we call these spirits "demons." Given authority to remain on Earth until the Stone Judgment.

Fire Judgment – The final phase of the Stone Judgment. Occurs over a one-week timeframe and judges all evil men and remaining remnants of the Demon-gods and Evil Spirits. During the Fire Judgment, Yeshua appears and the righteous dead are raised. Ushers in the Kingdom Age.

First Death – The time when a child loses their innocence and must choose whether or not to serve YHWY.

First Beast – Ancient Babylon. Ruled from 605 to 539 BC. Destroyed the first Judean Temple.

Fourth Beast – A pagan empire that began with Ancient Rome and continued to rule to the present day, as Revived and Divided Rome. Recognized by YHWY as beginning in 133 BC, with the assassination of Tiberias Gracchus. The final empire prior to the Stone Judgment. Is guided by a Demon-god named Leviathan. Has ten horns and seven heads. Destroys 25% of Earth.

Khazarian Mafia (KM) – Turkic-Ugrians race which adopted false Judaism in around 800 BC and proceeded to take over the modern banking and finance system. Originated from modern-day Ukraine.

Little Horn – An "insignificant race" (not the seed of Jacob) that rises to power and subdues three powerful heads of the Fourth Beast. Represented by modern-day false Jews (see Khazarian Mafia).

New Earth – A new Earth YWHY creates after the White Throne Judgment.

New Heaven – A new Heaven YHWY creates after the White Throne Judgment.

Second Beast – Medo-Persia. Ruled from 539 to 331 BC.

Second Death – Physical death.

Shaking of Nations – A type of God's judgment limited to evil empires. The first shaking was against Ancient Egypt. The second shaking focuses on the Fourth Beast, the Whore of Babylon, and the Little Horn.

Third Beast – Ancient Greece. Ruled from 331 to approximately 146 BC.

Unclean Spirits – Fallen angels that rebelled alongside Satan. Given authority to remain on Earth until the Battle of Armageddon.

White Throne Judgment – The final judgment, when the dead are judged and all evil principalities are thrown in the Lake of Fire.

Whore of Babylon – A false religion adopted by the Fourth Beast, represented chiefly by the Catholic Church.

www.ingramcontent.com/pod-product-compliance
Lightning Source LLC
Chambersburg PA
CBHW071142130626
46553CB00004B/1482